Written by Teresa Fisher
Where to sections by Tim Jepson

Copy edited by Rebecca Snelling
Americanization by Margaret Cavanaugh
Verified by Paola Ursino, Colin Follett
Indexed by Marie Lorimer

Edited, designed and produced by AA Publishing
© Automobile Association Developments Limited 2001
Maps © Automobile Association Developments Limited 2001
Reprinted 2003

Published in the United States by AAA Publishing,
1000 AAA Drive, Heathrow, Florida 32746
Published in the United Kingdom by AA Publishing

ISBN 1-56251-416-4

Cover design and binding style by permission of AA Publishing

Color separation by Leo Reprographics
Printed and bound in China by Leo Paper Products

10 9 8 7 6 5 4 3 2

A01486

the magazine

Did You Know?...

Florence's celebrated Bar Vivoli Gelateria (▶ 73) claims to make "the best ice cream in the world." Try it and judge for yourself!

Florentines and Tuscans are known throughout Italy as the *mangiafagioli* (the "bean-eaters") because pulses form a part of so many local dishes.

Michelangelo – the great Florentine artist and creator of such masterpieces as *David* (▶ 98–99) and *Bacchus* (▶ 63) – claimed that his talent as a sculptor was due to the marble dust in the milk of his wet-nurse. She came from Carrara, a town to the northwest of Florence famous since Roman times for its precious white marble, quarried in the surrounding Alpi Apuane.

Florence Nightingale was born in Florence in 1820. In 1837, she returned to the city of her birth to study the language and art, but actually spent much of her time nursing a sick Englishwoman back to health – marking the start of an illustrious career. There is a memorial to her in the first cloister of Santa Croce.

Florentines claim to have invented French cuisine, following the marriage of 14-year-old Catherine de' Medici to Henri II of France in 1535. She took with her a full complement of chefs and an

According to tradition, you can ensure your return to Florence by rubbing the shiny, polished snout of Il Porcellino, the bronze "Little Pig" in Florence's Mercato Nuovo, and then throwing a coin into the fountain.

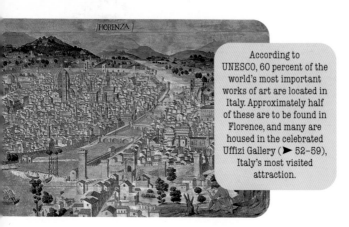

According to UNESCO, 60 percent of the world's most important works of art are located in Italy. Approximately half of these are to be found in Florence, and many are housed in the celebrated Uffizi Gallery (➤ 52–59), Italy's most visited attraction.

encyclopedia of Tuscan recipes, allegedly giving rise to such Gallic dishes as duck with orange (Tuscan *papero alla melarancia*), *dolce forte* (Tuscan *lepre dolce e forte*) and even vol au vents (Tuscan *turbanate di sfoglia*). She apparently also introduced the French to the fork! Before long the Medici became renowned for their elaborate recipes and showy banquets – birds flying out of pies, children leaping naked from desserts – and Catherine de' Medici was dubbed the "mother of French cuisine."

In his Italian Journal, 19th-century French novelist Stendhal (Henri Marie Beyle) tells how, after an intensive day of sightseeing, he was struck by a strange illness on visiting the Church of Santa Croce in Florence, where he had gone to admire Giotto's frescoes. The doctors diagnosed what we would now probably describe as an "overdose" of culture. As a consequence, a department at the hospital of Santa Maria Novella now devotes serious study to the "Stendhal Syndrome," a strange malaise that affects over-sensitive visitors.

The following movies were all filmed in Florence: Anthony Minghella's "The English Patient," James Ivory's "A Room With a View," Kenneth Branagh's "Much Ado About Nothing" (left), Jane Campion's "Portrait of a Lady," Bernardo Bertolluci's "Stealing Beauty" and, most recently, Franco Zeffirelli's "Tea With Mussolini."

FLORENCE'S FOUNDATIONS

They say, "the present glory of Florence is its past," but few people think back beyond its great Renaissance heyday to the city's ancient dawning as a Roman settlement from which its latter-day classical flowering stemmed.

Above: The Roman theater in Fiesole Below: The Florentine flag

By 3000 BC, Italic tribes had settled in the area, but the true ancestors of Florence came from the hilltop settlement of Fiesole (► 179–181), an important Etruscan city settled around 800 BC. Following a dispute, some of its inhabitants came down the hillside and set up a small village on the northern bank of the Arno river. In *The Divine Comedy*, Dante Alighieri recalls them as "that ungrateful and malignant race/which descended from the Fiesole of old/and still have rock and mountain in their blood" (Inferno XV, 61–63).

During the first century BC, the Etruscans were defeated by the Romans in their gradual conquest of Italy. They seized control of Fiesole's territories and used the very "rock and mountain" of the hilltown and

surrounding countryside (two different sandstones called *pietra serena* and *pietra forte*) to build the city of *Florentia* and its defensive walls. The line of these walls is still recognizable in the quadrangle formed by Piazza del Duomo, Piazza San Firenze, Piazza Santa Trinita and the extreme western end of the Via dei Cerretani, while the *cardo* (north–south axis) and the *decumanus* (east–west axis) crossed in today's Piazza della Repubblica (➤ 127), site of the Forum.

The Roman settlers farmed the surrounding countryside and introduced vineyards and olives. They also developed one of Florence's main industries, wool-dyeing. From the very start, the city set itself apart from other Roman colonies in style and attitude. Instead of the usual militaristic settlements of the Roman Empire, here they favored the Virgilian idea of *rus in urbe* (the "country in the town"), constructing instead theaters, thermal baths, villas and gardens.

With the fall of the Roman Empire and a succession of hostile barbarian tribes invading Tuscany, the following centuries saw the demise of *Florentia*. Only with the "refounding" of Florence by Charlemagne in the early

ninth century did the city again begin to thrive, gathering momentum throughout the Middle Ages to become a world leader in the arts, culture and commerce. Ironically, to achieve this they rewound the clocks to the city's classical origins, thereby creating the great Florentine "Renaissance."

Roman Farmers Appraise Their Horses and Cattle (etching by M van der Gucht, 1709)

The Marzocco lion, an emblem of Florence, symbolizing its power

What's In a Name?

Theories about the name Firenze (Florence) abound. It probably originates from one of the following: *Fiori* after the bountiful wild "flowers" of the surrounding countryside – even the city's emblem is a flower (*Iris florentia*, shaped like a fleur-de-lis) and the Duomo is dedicated to Santa Maria del Fiore (St. Mary of the Flowers); the Roman *Ludi Floreales* (Floral Games), which took place in springtime to honor the goddess Flora; *Fluentia*, because of its location on the banks of the "flowing" Arno river or *Florentia*, the name of the original Roman settlement, meaning "destined to flourish."

A WHO'S WHO OF THE MEDICI

Few cities are as closely linked to one family as Florence is to the Medici, the powerful dynasty of bankers who ruled the city almost continuously for more than three centuries and whose generous patronage of the arts contributed to the city's Renaissance revival.

Museums, galleries, piazzas, palazzi...everywhere you go in Florence, the Medici name crops up. Here's a "who's who" of the key players to see you through.

Giovanni di Bicci – The Banker

The prosperity of the Medici was largely due to Giovanni di Bicci (1360–1429), the founder of the family. He established the Medici Bank in Florence and, thanks to his shrewd business acumen, it soon became the most profitable bank in Europe. Once he'd landed the Pope's bank account, the family's fortune was secured.

Cosimo il Vecchio (the Elder) – Patron of the Arts

It was with Giovanni's son, Cosimo (1389–1464), that the Medici rule really began. Pope Pius II called him "king in everything but name" and the city's governing body, the *Signoria*, bestowed upon him the title Pater Patriae

Cosimo the Elder, popular governor of Florence

(Father of the Country). Even so, he kept a low profile, rejecting Filippo Brunelleschi's designs for the family palace (► 104–105) as too ostentatious, and settling for a more discreet symbol of Medici power from which to govern the city.

Cosimo inherited his father's financial acumen, and increased the family fortune tenfold, but he is best remembered for his ardent support of the arts and humanism during the flowering of the Renaissance in Florence. Keen to build churches, palazzi and libraries that would last a thousand years like the buildings of ancient Rome, Cosimo commissioned the city's finest architects to construct scores of

buildings (including the churches of San Marco and San Lorenzo) and appointed some of the greatest artists of the day to adorn them.

He died leaving a peaceful, prosperous city – "the new Rome." He was succeeded by his sickly son, Piero the Gouty (1416–69), who died soon afterward, leaving Cosimo's grandson, Lorenzo, to assume power.

Lorenzo il Magnifico – Poet and Humanist
Lorenzo (1449–92), a humanist and great poet, preferred literary pursuits to affairs of state and devoted much of his time to promoting the study of Dante, Boccaccio and Petrarch.

His rule was not uneventful: Pope Sixtus IV withdrew the papal bank account from the Medici Bank, causing near bankruptcy; then there was the Pazzi conspiracy of 1478 – an attempt by the rival Pazzi family to assassinate Lorenzo and bring about the downfall of the Medici. Following Sixtus's death, Lorenzo befriended the new Pope Innocent VIII, and his son, Giovanni de' Medici, was made cardinal. Three weeks after Giovanni's consecration, Lorenzo died, leaving the Pope to declare, "The peace of Italy is now at an end."

The Pazzi family tried to murder Lorenzo during Mass in the Duomo. They failed, killing his brother instead

He was right. Two years later, in 1494, Charles VIII of France invaded Italy and Lorenzo's eldest son, Piero, surrendered the city. The citizens instantly drove him out for not having resisted the French king effectively, and, swayed by the persuasive oratory of Dominican monk Girolamo Savonarola (► 70), they formed a republic. (Savonarola was later condemned to death for heresy and burned at the stake in Piazza della Signoria, ► 60–61.)

Keeping it in the family – the first Medici Pope, Leo X, with Cardinals Luigi Rosso and Guilio de' Medici

Giovanni de' Medici – The First Medici Pope
In 1512, the Medici forced their way back into the city, led by

The Medici Coat of Arms

Throughout the city you'll notice the ubiquitous Medici coat of arms: a cluster of red balls on a gold background. Some say it signifies the shield of the legendary knight Averado, a descendant of the family; others claim they are medicinal pills, recalling the family's possible origins as doctors (medici); or perhaps pawnbroker's coins, a symbol of their financial background.

Below right:
Equestrian
statue of
Cosimo I in
Piazza della
Signoria

Alessandro's coat of arms

Cardinal Giovanni (1475–1521), and the disillusioned Florentines welcomed them back. From then on, the Medici were determined to maintain power, using force if necessary to do so. In 1513, Giovanni was crowned Pope Leo X. He continued to rule Florence from Rome.

Alessandro – A Dissolute and Tyrannical Leader

On Leo X's death, his son Alessandro (1510–37) took control of the city's government, guided by Pope Clement VII (Giulio de' Medici, son of Lorenzo the Magnificent) in Rome. Under him the Florentine state became a duchy, but Alessandro proved a corrupt, despotic duke. He was murdered by his cousin, Lorenzaccio.

Cosimo I – A Forceful Ruler

Cosimo I (1519–74) succeeded Alessandro and immediately set about destroying all opposition: he publicly executed the leaders of exiled republican armies in Piazza della Signoria and asserted Florentine authority with brute force by attacking the other major cities of Tuscany. Siena lost half its population during one such stampede and, to this day, many Sienese still refuse to set foot in Florence.

Unlike his predecessors, Cosimo I didn't patronize the arts for art's sake, but rather for self-glorification. He did, however, commission Vasari to build magnificent new offices to house his administration (uffizi), and he established a highly effective government machine. His descendants, however, who nominally ruled Florence for another six generations, preferred the high life to state affairs. Yet nobody ever challenged them. After all, they were the Medici – the all-powerful, invincible dynasty of Florence. When Anna Maria Ludovica, the last in the line, died in 1743, the entire city grieved.

So Many firsts

Think Florence, think Renaissance, the Uffizi, Michelangelo's David, the Arno, the Ponte Vecchio...But how many people think street paving, opera and eyeglasses – all Florentine innovations?

Even the origins and history of the Italian language are rooted in medieval Florence – in the poems of the academic group, Dolce Sil Novo, who mostly came from Florence. Later, the high-brow language of Dante Alighieri's *The Divine Comedy* was so admired that it fell into common usage and became the basis of modern Italian. At the same time

Florence was the cradle of Italian literature, with Tuscan-born Francesco Petrarca (Petrarch) and Giovanni Boccaccio paving the way for **modern poetry and modern prose** respectively.

In 1252, Florence became the first city to mint its own **gold coins**. Before long they were widely used and became the only coins generally accepted throughout Europe. Some countries still refer to coins in their modern currencies as florins (so called after the city). In 1235, records show that **street paving** began in the city and that by 1339 Florence had paved all its streets, making it the first city ever to do so. Another first is recorded on a stone tablet in the Church of Santa Maria Maggiore: "Here Lies Salvino d'Amato degli Armata of Florence, the Inventor of **eyeglasses**. May God Forgive his Sins, Year 1317."

The 15th century gave rise to the Renaissance, a period of immense artistic, social and intellectual fervor during which the financiers of Florence taught Europe banking; the city became the world's leading center of mathematics and astronomy; her alchemists turned science into the separate disciplines of **chemistry, physics** and **biology**. Such sculptors as Leonardo and Michelangelo benefited hugely from their studies of anatomy and, in 1430, Donatello's sculpture of *David* (▶ 62–65) was billed as the first free-standing nude statue of the Renaissance. He also created the first free-standing equestrian statue.

The Renaissance also heralded the age of humanism, with key Florentine figures stamping their personalities on the cultural,

The great poet Petrarch sought inspiration from the Tuscan countryside

Left: The foremost artists, writers and scientists of the day met with Galileo, among them English poet John Milton

Galileo Galilei
Pisa-born Galileo (1564–1642) was one of a handful of brilliant scientists who benefited from Medici patronage during the 17th century, making Tuscany a leading center of astronomical and scientific innovation. The **Museo di Storia della Scienza** (▶ 70) contains his telescopes and the lens he used to discover the satellites of Jupiter. His experiments laid the foundation for modern empirical science and, in his memory, Florence founded the world's first ever scientific institution, the Accademia del Cimento (Academy for Experimentation) in 1657.

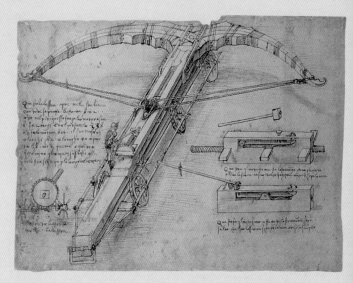

Vinci, Leonardo's Town

The small hilltop town of Vinci, just 50 km (31 miles) northeast of Florence, is the birthplace of Leonardo da Vinci (1452–1519). In his honor, in the center of the town, the Museo Leonardiano (Castello di Conti Guidi, tel: 0571 56055) contains models of many of his brilliant creations. The models are based on the drawings from his notebooks, which are shown alongside the exhibits. They are extraordinary, ingenious contraptions, way ahead of their time, and include skis designed for walking on water, a machine-gun, a paddlewheel boat, a bicycle, a primitive car and an aircraft, proving Leonardo to be one of the greatest inventors of all time.

The Florentine navigator, Amerigo Vespucci

artistic and literary world: Leon Battista Alberti initiated **art criticism**; Giorgio Vasari, with Michelangelo and Andrea del Sarto as his teachers, conceived **art history**; and Niccolò Machiavelli, through his treatise *The Prince* (outlining the single-minded skills required to be a successful politician), is acknowledged as the originator of **modern political science**.

Europe's first **orphanage** (Spedale degli Innocenti, ► 107) was founded here in 1445. Mothers could leave unwanted babies on a rotating stone cylinder and ring the bell. The stone would then be turned around and the anonymous child taken into care.

In 1235, records show that street paving began in the city

Also in the 15th century, one of the members of a Florentine merchant family – **Amerigo Vespucci** – gave his name to the New World. The contemporary art world's rules of perspective put Florentine navigators and cartographers one step ahead of

Pavement art – people and pigeons in Piazza del Duomo

the rest. So, when Columbus set out from Spain on his great transatlantic voyage in 1492, he carried with him charts drawn by Florentines. On his return, King Ferdinand of Spain recruited Vespucci, already renowned for his navigational skills, to check whether Columbus really had discovered a New World. Vespucci confirmed that there was a new continent, subsequently called "Amerigo" in his honor, and Florentine **mapmakers** were the first to produce maps of it, based on detailed accounts of his voyage.

At the beginning of the 16th century, the first **public lottery** to pay out prizes of money was started – *La Lotto de Firenze*. It was so popular that it took little time to spread to other Italian cities and beyond. In 1597, the world's first **opera** – *Dafne* by Jacopo Peri – was staged at the Palazzo Cori in Florence to celebrate the marriage of Maria de' Medici to Henri IV of France.

Further claims to fame (some lacking substantial evidence) are that Florence is the home of modern **soccer** and that ice cream and **minestrone soup** were first made and eaten here. Florentines even claim to have invented **French cuisine** (► 6) and in 1711, the **pianoforte**. The list goes on....

A Tuscan Menu

Florentine restaurants serve some of the finest cuisine in Italy – la cucina Toscana – combining the most popular Italian culinary traditions with robust, country-style cooking and bold, sun-drenched flavors such as olive oil, tomatoes, garlic, salamis, hams and beans. A typically Tuscan menu focuses on fresh, top-quality ingredients, prepared with the minimum of fuss – thick soups, juicy steaks, bean stews in terra-cotta pots, plenty of vegetables and hearty wines. Even the most sophisticated restaurants seek to produce homey dishes a la nonna ("just like grandma used to cook").

the most popular are *zuppa di ceci* (chickpea soup) or *ribollita* (a vegetable soup with beans and Tuscan black cabbage, thickened with yesterday's bread). If you'd prefer pasta, one uniquely Tuscan dish is *pappardelle con la lepre* (wide noodles with a bolognese-style sauce made with hare).

Secondi Piatti

For *secondi* (the main course), no trip to Tuscany would be complete without the celebrated *bistecca alla fiorentina* – an enormous steak from Italy's finest beef cattle, the Tuscan Chianina breed. Although considered a typical local dish, it was originally cooked by the Florentines for the 18th-century English tourists: the name *bistecca* comes from beefsteak. The best *bistecca* in Florence is said to be served at Buca Lapi. Unless you're feeling particularly ravenous, consider ordering one portion between two.

Other popular meat dishes include *arista al fiorentina* (porkloin with rosemary), named after the Greek *aristos*, meaning "very good," and game – especially *cinghiale* (wild boar) – in season. Many genuinely Tuscan meat dishes are based on or around offal, a tradition dating back to ancient times when the rich people ate the meat and the poor people

Olives are sold in a variety of marinades

Below: Al fresco – the ultimate dining experience

Antipasti

A typical Tuscan meal will begin with antipasti of *bruschetta* (small pieces of toast drizzled with oil or spread with olive, anchovy, tomato or chicken liver paste). For *primi piatti* (starters), thick soups often take the place of pasta. Among

got the leftovers. Specialties include *trippa alla fiorentina* (tripe in a rich tomato sauce), *lampredotto* (pork intestines) and *fegatelli* (pork liver sautéed in wine). Fish lovers should try *baccalà* (dried salt cod served with garlic, parsley and tomatoes) – delicious!

To accompany your main meal, the most Tuscan of *contorni* (vegetables) are, without a doubt, small white cannellini beans cooked in a variety of ways: *fagioli all'uccelletto* (with tomato and sage) is the most popular, but look out for more unusual preparations too, like *fagioli cotti al fiasco* (slow-cooked in ashes in a Chianti bottle).

Dolce

Dolce (desserts) are, less enthralling. Apart from the ubiquitous *tiramisù* and *panna cotta* (cooked cream), most restaurants round off the meal with fruit, cheese (usually made with sheep's milk, such as pecorino) or *cantucci* (sweet biscuits) with a glass of *vin santo* (see box, below). Many Florentines skip the dessert course and buy an ice cream from a local *gelateria* instead, as part of an after dinner stroll.

> *Many Florentines skip the dessert course and buy an ice cream from a local gelateria instead*

Tuscan wines provide a perfect complement to the region's cuisine

---

Chianti Country

Tuscany is one of Italy's main wine-producing regions. The predominantly red wines complement the wholesome regional cuisine perfectly. Just outside Florence, the wine producers of Chianti Country, who make Italy's best-known red wines, have been enjoying something of a renaissance – a move away from quantity toward quality. No longer is the name Chianti synonymous with inexpensive red wine, but rather the district now produces some of the country's most sought-after wines. For the best reds, look for the labels Chianti Rufina, Brunello di Montalcino and Vino Nobile di Montepulciano; for the best white try Vernaccia di San Gimignano, and be sure to taste *vin santo*, a sweet Tuscan wine made from grapes left to dry for up to four months.

Celebrity Viewpoints

The Good...

"I have seldom seen a city so lovely at first sight as Florence," wrote the poet Percy Bysshe Shelley in a letter to his wife in 1818. "It is the most beautiful city I have ever yet seen." Shelley was one of the first to visit Florence as part of a Grand Tour (the cultural odyssey which completed every wealthy, well-educated gentleman's education), but not the first to have admired it. In the 14th century, Italian writer Dino Compagni described it as "well populated, its good air a healthy tonic; its citizens are well dressed, its women are lovely and fashionable, and its buildings are very beautiful." In the Middle Ages, the Italian writer Giovanni Boccaccio reckoned "its great beauty excels all others in Italy," and four centuries later Mozart agreed, writing to his mother, "If only you could see this place! One should live and die here."

> *I have seldom seen a city so lovely at first sight as Florence*
> *Percy Bysshe Shelley*

The Bad...

Not all first impressions of the city were so favorable. English author W.S. Landor described mid-19th century Florence as "the filthiest capital in Europe... overrun with tame pigs, rotten grapes, smelly goats' cheese, children covered with vermin," while Johann Wolfgang von Goethe, the father of the Italian Grand Tour, wrote in his *Italian Journey*, "I took a quick walk through the city to see the Duomo and the Battistero...but I did not wish to stay long. I hurried out of the city as quickly as I entered it." Like most young men on the Grand Tour, he hadn't come to appreciate Renaissance art, but rather to see such classical treasures as the *Medici Venus* (▶ 57), later condemned by the influential 19th-century writer and critic, John Ruskin as an "uninteresting little person."

It was Ruskin's enthusiasm for Renaissance art and architecture in the early 19th century that encouraged a new type of visitor. Charles Dickens remarked: "What light is shed upon the world from amidst these rugged Palaces of Florence! Here the ancient Sculptors are immortal, side by side with Michelangelo, Canova, Titian, Rembrandt, Raphael, poets, historians, philosophers – the illustrious men of history..." (*Pictures from Italy*, 1844).

Ruskin may have raved about Florentine art, but he was less enthusiastic about its citizens... "Everybody here is idle, and therefore they are always in the way. The square is full of listless, chattering, smoking vagabonds...and the noise, dirt, tobacco smoke and spitting are so intolerable in all the great thoroughfares that I have quite given up." His sentiments were echoed by Mark Twain, who took aversion to the "dark and bloody Florentines" (*The Innocents Abroad*, 1869).

And the Uncertain...

Even in the 20th century, reactions to Florence and its

citizens remained mixed: D.H. Lawrence found that the "servants were rude, cabmen insulted one and demanded treble fare" in the 1920s; Dylan Thomas, when he visited in the 1940s, complained of "the rasher-frying Florentine sun"; and Aldous Huxley noted, "The spectacle of that second-rate provincial town with its repulsive Gothic architecture and its acres of Christmas card primitives made me almost sick. The only good points about Florence are the country outside it, the Michelangelo tombs, Brunelleschi's dome, and a few rare pictures. The rest is simply dung when compared to Rome."

Thankfully, most modern visitors generally leave with a more favorable impression of Florence, more akin to those of E.M. Forster's heroine Lucy Honeychurch in his novel *A Room with a View* (1908). She loved "to lean out into the sunshine with beautiful hills and trees and marble churches opposite, and close below, the Arno, gurgling against the embankment of the road." And those visiting the surrounding area would do well to heed Charles Dickens's advice and "look back on Florence while we may, and when its shining dome is seen no more, go travelling through cheerful Tuscany, with a bright remembrance of it; for Italy will be the fairer for the recollection."

18th-century Florence: the Arno with the Ponte Vecchio by Bernardo Bellotto

Everybody here is idle, and therefore they are always in the way   John Ruskin

Florentines are extremely fashion-conscious. The average citizen spends 1 million lire ($450) a year on clothes, and with such a rich legacy of craftsmanship it's hardly surprising that Florence was once the headquarters of Italy's fashion industry. "Only we Florentines," they claimed, "love and understand the female body. How can we not, surrounded from birth by paintings of glorious nudes!"

Florentine Fashion

Though Florence relinquished its status as Italy's fashion capital to Milan in the 1970s (a change prompted by the city's lack of an international airport as much as anything else), nearly 10 percent of the city's income still comes from the fashion industry. Its shop windows read like an A–Z of top couturiers: Armani, Prada, Trussardi, Versace...not forgetting Gucci, Pucci and Ferragamo, whose very names evoke the essence of style, artistry and craftsmanship so typical of Florence.

Gucci – Florentine Fashion Icon

Gucci is still based at 7 Via della Vigna Nuova (together with Via Tornabuoni, the city's most elegant shopping street) where the firm was founded three generations ago by Guccio Gucci (1881–1953). Guccio had developed his taste for beauty and elegance while working as an elevator attendant in London's opulent Savoy Hotel at the beginning of the 20th century. In 1921, he opened a small workshop selling luggage and saddlery – hence the trademark bit and stirrups, derived from the company's humble origins – which soon came to represent Gucci's success.

Around the 1950s and '60s, such Gucci classics as the bag with the bamboo handle, the moccasin with the metal bit and the flowered Flora silk scarf were created. The company also adopted the GG logo, taken from the initials of its founder, as an ornamental motif for handbags, accessories and luggage made in Gucci's

Far left: The unlikely looking fashion guru – Gucci and his wife
Left: Distinctive Gucci designs

distinctive, tan-colored canvas and honey-cured leather.

More recently, Gucci went through a tricky period of family in-fighting and had to weather the financial repercussions resulting from the glut of fake Gucci products that flooded the market. Today, under the new ownership of Pinault-Printemps-Redoute and steered by the talented New York designer Tom Ford, Gucci has been relaunched as one of the fashion world's most powerful global brands.

> *There was a time when a Pucci print dress cost more than its equivalent weight in gold*

politician, began by chance. In 1948, a fashion designer captured him on film on the ski slopes of St. Moritz wearing a stylish, sleek-fitting outfit that he'd designed himself. From that day on, ski clothing changed forever and a new fashion empire was born.

Pucci was best known for his opulent colors, supple fabrics and extravagant prints. He dyed silks (using age-old techniques) in rich hues and designed unmistakable patterns using combinations of bright and pastel colors and geometric shapes on silk jersey. There was a time when a Pucci print dress cost more than its equivalent weight in gold, and no fashionable celebrity or jet-setter boarded a plane without at least one packed in her suitcase. Soon Pucci prints were everywhere – on shoes, purses, luggage, pajamas, lingerie. He also designed the stylish blue uniforms of the Florentine *vigili urbani* (traffic police); bookings increased on Braniff International Airways when he created their unique flight attendant uniforms with their bubble-shaped space helmet headwear; and the Apollo 15 crew carried a Pucci-designed flag to the moon!

Until his death, Pucci lived in the Palazzo Pucci, the Florentine ancestral home at 6 Via de' Pucci. His designs remain every bit as popular today, and his empire is now directed by his daughter. The shop is at 97–99r Via della Vigna Nuova.

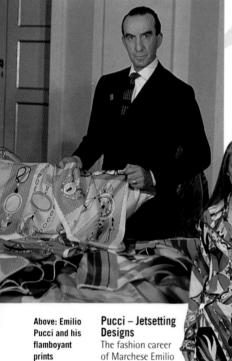

Above: Emilio Pucci and his flamboyant prints
Right: Pucci's trademark silk jersey dress

Pucci – Jetsetting Designs

The fashion career of Marchese Emilio Pucci (1914–92), the aristocratic Florentine fighter-pilot and war hero turned designer turned

Ferragamo – Shoemaker of Dreams

The life of Salvatore Ferragamo (1899-1960) is one of Florence's greatest success stories. He went from rags to riches almost overnight. Ferragamo learned his trade as a young boy, making shoes for the inhabitants of his village in southern Italy. When he was just 15, he emigrated to America and opened a custom-made shoe store in Hollywood. His maxim – "There is no limit to beauty, no saturation point in design, no end to the materials a shoemaker may use to decorate his creations so that every woman may be shod like a princess and a princess may be shod like a fairy queen" – earned him the title "shoemaker of dreams." Before long he was making his fortune crafting shoes for the greatest movie stars of the era, including Greta Garbo, Vivien Leigh, Marilyn Monroe and Audrey Hepburn.

On returning to Italy in 1927, Ferragamo chose to settle in Florence – a city already renowned for its artistic masterpieces and artisan traditions. From here, Ferragamo played a pivotal role not only in the history of shoemaking, but also in international fashion. His studies of the foot's anatomy and lasts (the wooden forms used to mold the leather of the shoes) led to the invention of the Ferragamo method, a revolutionary technique in the art of shoemaking. In his quest for the perfect fit in the absence of quality leather during the war years, he experimented with new materials ranging from the legendary cork wedge (patented in 1936 and immediately imitated throughout the world) to uppers in raffia, rope or candy wrapper cellophane.

His family still administers his fashion empire from the original flagship store at 2 Via Tornabuoni, and also produces accessories and clothing to accompany the trademark shoes. In 1995, they opened a small museum (tel: 055 3360456, open Mon., Wed., Fri. 9–1 by appointment only), with photographs, patents, sketches, lasts of famous feet, and more than 10,000 shoe models designed by Ferragamo – a testament to the life and work of one of Florence's best-known fashion icons.

Above: Not only shoes...but Ferragamo fashions too

Left: elaborate footwear can be found in Florence's many shoe shops

RESTORING A CITY

Restoration is a never-ending task in Florence. As the cradle of the Renaissance, the city now shoulders a huge responsibility – to preserve its artistic heritage for the rest of the world. Consequently, it has become one of the leading centers for art restoration. Throughout the city, especially in the streets around Santo Spirito and Santa Croce, you'll find tiny workshops where craftsmen lovingly repair their treasures.

You'll find tiny workshops where craftsmen lovingly repair their treasures

On every visit to Florence, you'll see churches, palazzi, sculptures and paintings hidden behind scaffolding. Restoration work has always been big business here, but it has increased in importance significantly following the devastating flood of 1966 when

thousands of paintings, manuscripts and other works of art were damaged, some beyond repair.

Restoration experts at the time estimated that it would take approximately 20 years for all the damaged treasures to be restored, but over 30 years later about a third are still under-going repair.

The institution hardest hit by the flood was the low-lying National Library, with a million and a half volumes damaged. Until this time, not a great deal was known about paper restoration. But as a direct consequence of the disaster, the world's top experts hurriedly pooled their know-how and devised new drying methods, chemical treatments and rebinding techniques.

The most celebrated work to be wrecked was Giovanni Cimabué's 13th-century wood-and-canvas Crucifix in Santa Croce. The flood had submerged the church beneath nearly 20 feet of mud and the crucifix had lost most of its paint. Its restoration proved highly

David – A Checkered Past

The life of Michelangelo's *David* has not always been easy. The world-renowned sculpture has undergone repeated restoration work. In 1527, someone threw a bench out of the window of the Palazzo Vecchio, breaking the sculpture's left arm in three places. In 1544, the left shoulder fell off, killing a poor peasant who happened to be passing. When moved to the Accademia in 1873, *David* was kept wrapped up for nine years while a room was specially built to house him. When eventually revealed, he was covered in mold. The final straw came in 1992, when his left foot was smashed with a hammer.

Fresco Restoration

Fresco means the art of painting onto a layer of thin, freshly laid plaster. The paint is absorbed by the wet plaster and the color sets as it dries. During the process, the pigments react with the lime in the plaster, resulting in strong, bold colors. As the paint doesn't lie on the surface (as in a canvas painting), restorers can clean off the superficial dirt from frescoes without affecting the original colors. It is a slow and painstaking process, involving a variety of equipment from computer-aided pigment analyzers to simple rags.

controversial. The work was entrusted to Professor Umberto Baldini, who removed all the peeling and damaged paint, painstakingly restored the rest and cleaned off the varnish that had previously given the painting a green tinge. Then, contrary to normal practice, rather than recreating the missing sections, he replaced them with areas of neutral color to blend in with the overall tone of the original sections. The moving end-result (on show in Santa Croce's refectory,
➤ 66–69) is today considered a symbol of the city's "wounds."

Restoration of the city's most precious treasures is undertaken by two main organizations, the Istituto per l'Arte e il Restauro and the Opificio delle Pietre Dure. The original function of the Opificio, founded in 1588, was to restore hard-stone mosaics. Later it added picture restoration to its specialties, and since 1975 it has restored bronze, glass, marble, textiles, furniture...just about anything. Both organizations incorporate thriving teaching departments and are considered world leaders in restoration.

MODERN-DAY FLORENCE

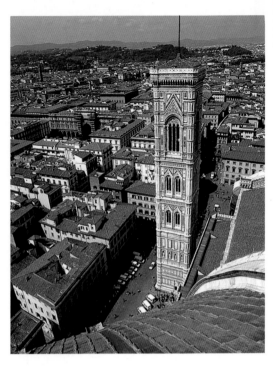

The pride of Florence lies in its past. At first glimpse it would appear that the city lacks a sense of modernity. As Stendhal once remarked: "Ask the Florentines what they are, and they will respond by telling you what they were." It's true. Look closer, though, and you'll find that the city is lively, thriving and full of innovation. Police dress in designer uniforms. There are electric minibuses and striking modern architecture alongside Renaissance palazzi – signs of a city anxious to survive.

The Florentines are the first to appreciate their vast artistic wealth and they care passionately what happens to it. The devastating flood of 1966 (► 124) and more recently the 1993 car bomb that exploded in an alleyway behind the Uffizi forced them to take stock of the city's future and to tackle some of the problems.

Politics and Corruption

In the early to mid-1990s, Florence was not without its fair share of the political corruption and bribery that wrecked successive Italian governments. But those MPs caught with their hands dirty (including then Prime Minister Andreotti) were jailed as a result of the *Mani Puliti* (Clean Hands) campaign, which sought governmental reform.

Traffic

Over the years, there has been a growing problem in the city with *il traffico*. In addition to the noise and congestion it creates, there are mounting concerns that the increasing high levels of pollution are irreparably corroding the city's ancient statuary and stonework. Florence has a staggering number of outdoor works of art, and, like *David*, many have had to be moved indoors to prevent further deterioration.

> *The Florentines are the first to appreciate their vast artistic wealth and they care passionately what happens to it*

In 1988, measures to combat the pollution and congestion were finally introduced. Originally set up as an experiment to reduce the amount of traffic in the city center between 7:30 a.m. and 6:30 p.m., the scheme proved so popular that the restrictions (areas called Zona Blu) are still in place today. Since then, environmentally friendly electric minibuses and Free Bike points where you can pick up and deposit a bicycle have been introduced. Even a subway system has been approved, although it is hard to imagine how it will ever be built – considering all the precious Etruscan and Roman remains lying beneath the city.

Tourism

Another problem facing Florence is the sheer number of visitors. Florence is relatively small compared to other popular European cities, but its already sizable population of 400,000 is increased by more than 7 million a year. Thankfully, tour buses are now no longer allowed in the center, and there is a 15-minute parking limit at Piazzale Michelangelo, while passengers rush to take snapshots of the

city. There is even talk of limiting the number of visitors allowed into Florence each day, or the possibility of levying a daily "art charge" on tourists – putting the onus on visitors to preserve the treasures of the city. But it seems unlikely that either plan will be instigated, as the city is heavily dependent on the income generated by tourism.

For centuries foreign residents have been attracted to Florence and the surrounding countryside. Initially the city drew artists, writers and wealthy visitors from other parts of Europe intent on broadening their horizons. In 1737 Englishman Sir Horace Mann declared: "If I could afford it, I would take a villa near Florence but I am afraid of it becoming a cheesecake house for all the English."

Architecture

As urban expansion escalates, a popular trend to emerge is "memory architecture" – new buildings inspired by Florence's glorious past. Santa Maria Novella railroad station, designed in 1935 by Giovanni Michelucci, Florence's greatest modern architect, was hailed as the first functionalist building in

The modern face of the city: Michelucci's church of San Giovanni Battista (left) and Santa Maria Novella railroad station (below)

Sunset at the Ponte Vecchio
Inset: The Uffizi buildings, designed by Vasari in 1560

Left: The Duomo – a timeless architectural masterpiece

plan devised by Fiat and the insurance group La Fondiaria. It will contain homes, shops, hotels, leisure facilities, law courts, office space and a huge Fiat factory. The first foundation stone of this 15-year building plan was laid in 1999.

The Future?

So with the project for new Florence underway, what will become of the old city? The future is hazy. Of course it will always have its art treasures. Anna Maria Ludovica, the last of the Medici, made sure of that by bequeathing the entire family fortune to the city on condition that none of it should ever be moved from Florence.
But whether the city remains a vital and living metropolis, maintaining the thriving commercial activities that made the region the wealthiest and most innovative in Europe eight centuries ago, or becomes trapped in its past remains to be seen.

Italy. Another great landmark of modern architecture just outside the city is Michelucci's magnificent church of San Giovanni Battista (1964), near Amerigo Vespucci Airport.

The future of Florentine architecture is somewhat controversial. A new city, Firenze Nuova, is being created to the north of Florence, following a

THE BEST OF FLORENCE

Best Viewpoints

San Miniato (► 150–151)
Piazzale Michelangelo (► 178)
Forte di Belvedere (► 176)
Duomo's dome (► 94)
Giotto's Campanile (► 92)

Best *Last Suppers*

Santa Croce: *Last Supper* (1333) by
Taddeo Gaddi (► 66–69)
Santo Spirito: *Last Supper* (1370) by
Andrea Orcagna (► 153)
Ognissanti: *Last Supper* (1408) by
Domenico Ghirlandaio (► 126)
Sant'Apollonia: *Last
Supper* (1444)
by Andrea del
Castagno
San Marco:
Last Supper
(1482) by
Domenico
Ghirlandaio
(► 100)
San Salvi:
Last Supper (1526–27) by Andrea del
Sarto, pictured above

Opening ceremony to the Calcio in
Costume in Piazza della Signoria

Best Buys

• **Wine,** especially red
Chianti and sweet *vin santo*.
Try Zanobini (► 109) or
Casa del Vino (► 108)
• Italian **designer fashions**
and quality **leather goods**
from the city's exclusive designer shops
(► 133) or San Lorenzo market (► 45).
• **Stationery,** particularly hand-
marbled **paper.** Try Pineider (► 81)
• Fresh **pasta** and **olive oils**
• **Handmade toiletries** from the
Farmaceutica di Santa Maria Novella
(► 126).

If You Only Go to One

Museum: The Uffizi (► 52–59), for some
of the finest paintings in the world.
Shop: Gucci (► 133), the ultimate
Florentine shopping experience.
Excursion: Siena (► 160–165)

Best Festivals

Carnevale – Carnival festivities in the
days leading up to Lent
Scoppio del Carro – The Explosion of
the Carriage (Easter Sunday)
Festa degli Aquiloni – Kite Festival
(Sunday after Easter)
Maggio Musicale – The main arts
festival (May/early June)
Festa del Grillo – Cricket Festival
celebrating springtime. (Sunday after
Ascension)
Calcio in Costume – Soccer in
Costume ► 46.

Finding Your Feet

First Two Hours

Don't be daunted by the prospect of getting to Florence or finding your way around once you're there. The public transportation systems are easy to use and there is an excellent road and rail network.

Arriving by Air

Galileo Galilei Airport, Pisa
The main airport for Florence and Tuscany is located at **Pisa** (80 km, 50 miles west of Florence). In addition to scheduled services (including Alitalia, British Airways and Lufthansa), it also handles a number of charter companies.
■ For further **airport information** (tel: 050 500 707; www.pisa-airport.com).

There are two principal ways to reach Florence from here:
By train A **direct service** links Pisa Airport with Florence and takes just over 1 hour. Trains run approximately once an hour from 8:49 a.m. to 00:49 a.m. Depending on the time of your arrival, it is sometimes quicker to take a taxi to Pisa Centrale railroad station in the center of Pisa (a 10-minute drive from the airport), where there are additional trains to Florence. There is an extremely helpful information/ticket office inside Arrivals at the airport, which will be able to advise you on your best option.
   On your **return journey**, the AirTerminal (tel: 055 216 073) inside Florence Santa Maria Novella railroad station provides check-in facilities for passengers leaving by train for Pisa Airport (except for Ryanair passengers).
By car It costs less to rent a car for the day and leave it in Florence than it does to take a taxi. There are several **rental car desks** at the airport including Hertz Italian (tel: 050 43220), Avis (tel: 050 42028) and Europcar (tel: 050 41017). Pisa Airport is located beside the main A11 Florence–Pisa *autostrada* (highway). The journey takes about 1 hour. See Driving, ➤ 37.

Amerigo Vespucci Airport, Florence
Sometimes referred to by its old name of **Peretola,** this small airport is located just 4 km (2.5 miles) northwest of Florence on the plain between Florence and Sesto Fiorentino. It serves business travelers and tourists traveling on Meridiana and the occasional charter flight.
■ For further **airport information** contact SAF (Società Aeroporto Fiorentino, tel: 055 30615; www.safnet.it).

By car All the **major rental car companies** have offices here, including Hertz (tel: 055 307 370), Sixt (tel: 055 309 790) and Italy by Car (tel: 055 300 413) but, considering the short distance involved, you may want to take public transportation into the center.
By public bus This is the cheapest but least convenient way to get into town. To catch **orange ATAF bus No. 62,** go out of the main entrance of the airport and the bus leaves from a stand on the right side. The journey takes about 30 minutes. Buy a ticket before you get on. They are available from the airport bar inside the Departures terminal (upper level) or from the ticket machine in the Arrivals terminal. Tickets are valid for 1 hour.
By "Fly by Bus" SITA bus company organizes a **regular shuttle service** to and from central Florence with departures roughly once an hour. Look for the light

blue SITA buses immediately outside Arrivals. Tickets are sold on board and the journey takes approximately 20 minutes. For further information, contact SITA (tel: 055 478 2231).

By taxi This is the most expensive option. A taxi to the city center takes about 15 minutes. Expect to pay about €62, plus possible surcharges for baggage, traveling on Sundays, etc. The rate will be indicated on the meter. There is a **taxi stand outside Arrivals.** For further information, contact Radio Taxi Firenze (tel: 055 4242 4390).

Guglielmo Marconi Airport, Bologna

This sizable airport 105 km (65 miles) northeast of Florence caters to both **scheduled services** (including Alitalia, Air France, BA, SAS, Lufthansa) and **charter airlines.** For further **airport information** (tel: 051 647.96:15; www.bologna-airport.it).

There are two main ways to reach Florence from Bologna:

By train Frequent, fast trains (two or three an hour) run from **Bologna Centrale railroad station** straight to Florence and the journey takes just over 1 hour. (An "aerobus" shuttle service ferries passengers from the airport to the station every 15 minutes from 5:20 a.m. to midnight.)

By car You'll find all the usual rental-car booths inside **Terminal A** (Arrivals) including Hertz (tel: 051 647 2111), Avis (tel: 051 647 2032) and Maggiore (tel: 051 647 2007). Shop around for the best deal. The highway journey takes about 1½ hours.

Arriving by Train

Santa Maria Novella Railroad Station

Florence is one of the **main arrival points** for trains from Europe, with direct rail links with Paris, Frankfurt and Ostend. The station lies right at the heart of the city (tel: 055 212 245).

Rail Travel
When using the Italian rail network, always remember to validate your train ticket by stamping it in one of the yellow-colored machines located at the entrance to most platforms. Otherwise the ticket controller on the train may charge you a heavy fine.

Getting Around

Florence is a very compact city, centered around its majestic Duomo (▶ 88–94) in Piazza del Duomo. The best way to see the sights is on foot. A large part of the city center, from the Duomo south to the Uffizi (▶ 52–59), is pedestrianized.

Driving

Driving in Florence is not easy. Much of the center is **closed to traffic** and there is a complex one-way system. **Parking** is also extremely difficult in the city center.

Public Transportation

Florence's bus service is relatively foolproof and you can pick up **timetables and maps** for the local bus services from the tourist information offices (▶ 39) or any ATAF ticket office (there is one in Piazza di San Marco and one outside Santa Maria Novella rail station).

■ Environmentally friendly **electric minibuses** called A, B, C and D ply the main tourist routes. For further information, contact ATAF (Terminal Piazza Stazione, tel: 055 5650222, www.comune.firenze.it/ataf, Mon.–Sat. 7:15 a.m.–1:15 p.m.; also open Tue. and Thu. 2:45–5:45).

Electric minibuses

Bus A Starts at Santa Maria Novella station and heads south into the old center (past Palazzo Strozzi, Orsanmichele, Piazza della Repubblica), then out to the northeast quarters of town to Beccaria.

Bus B Runs a circular route more or less along the north bank of the Arno from Vittorio Veneto to Piave and back.

Bus C Runs from Piazza San Marco through the eastern quarters of the city, past Santa Croce, across the river and ends at Santa Maria Sopararno near the Ponte Vecchio.

Bus D Starts at Santa Maria Novella station and heads south of the river past Carmine, Santo Spirito and Palazzo Pitti continuing eastward to Ferruci.

■ Tickets can be bought from newsstands, tobacco shops and bars displaying the bus company sign, or at the bus termini. Remember to **stamp tickets** in the small orange machines on board the bus when you start your journey. It is not valid unless you do so.

■ A **single ticket** (valid for 60 minutes) costs €0.77; one valid for 3 hours costs €1.3 (no matter how many different buses you travel on within the time limit).

■ A *multiplo* gives you four 60-minute tickets for around €3; a *multiplo notturno* gives you four 60-minute tickets usable only between 8:30 p.m. and 1:30 a.m., and costs around €2.6.

■ A *Carta Arancio* (Orange Card) costs €20.65 and gives you seven days of unlimited use on all buses and trains in the Florence district.

■ If you're staying any length of time in the city, it would be worth considering a **monthly pass** for €27.37 (€15.5 for students, €13 for seniors). You will need ID and a passport photograph. A special **ecological monthly pass** (for buses A, B, C and D only) costs €12.91.

Taxis

■ **Official taxis** are usually white and can be rented from **official stands** at the station, Piazza di Santa Maria Novella, Piazza di San Marco, Piazza della Repubblica and Via Pellicceria.

■ Taxis are not an inexpensive option. You must be prepared to pay extra for baggage placed in the trunk, for journeys between 10 p.m. and 7 a.m., for travel on Sundays and public holidays and for journeys to and from the airport. Generally speaking, when you get into a taxi the meter will be set at €2.3 (plus extra charges mentioned above), then the cost of your journey will be around €0.75 per kilometer traveled, with a minimum charge for each journey of €3.61.

■ Also beware…if you **phone for a taxi** the meter starts to run from the moment you book it, *not* when it picks you up. For radio taxis tel: 4390 or 4798.

■ Taxi drivers are generally **honest** and all taxis should have a meter. If the driver pleads that it's broken, agree on a price before you start.

Useful Websites
- For **general information** try the following:
www.firenze.turismo.toscana.it
www.enit.it
www.informacitta.net
www.fionline.it
www.firenze.net/welcome.html
www.mega.it

- For travel information, try the Ferrovie dello Stato at www.fs-on-line.com
- For information on museums, art and history try
www.arca.net/tourism/florence/arthisto.htm
www.enit.it/musei
www.uffizi.firenze.it

City Center Tourist Information Offices
A visit to one of Florence's four tourist information offices is a good first stop for maps and information. Ask for an up-to-date list of opening hours for all main museums and galleries and for a copy of their annual *Avvenimenti* (Events) booklet for details of temporary exhibitions and festivals.

Main Office
✉ Via Cavour 1r
☎ 055 290 832
🕐 Mon.–Sat. 8:15–7:15, Sun. 8:30–6:30

West City Center
✉ Piazza Stazione 4
☎ 055 212 245
🕐 Mon.–Sat. 8:30–5:30, Sun. 8:30–1:30

Airport Office (Peretola)
✉ Aeroporto Amerigo Vespucci
(Arrivals) ☎ 055 315 874
🕐 Daily 7:30 a.m.–11:30 p.m.

East City Center
✉ Borgo Santa Croce 29r
☎ 055 234 0444
🕐 Daily 9–2 (9–7 in summer)

Street Addresses
- Don't be put off by Florence's **dual address system.** Each street has a double set of numbers: a black or blue number indicates a hotel or private residence, while a red number denotes a shop, restaurant or business.
- Throughout *Spiral Florence* you'll notice that some addresses have the **letter 'r'** after the street number. This stands for *rosso* (red) and distinguishes it from a residential address.

City Tours
What better way to get to know a city than to join in an organized sightseeing tour? The best include:
- **Associazione Guide Turistiche Fiorentine** (Via Ugo Corsi 25, tel: 055 4220901; www.florenceguides.it): **academic tours** of Florence and the surrounding countryside.
- **Walking Tours of Florence** (Piazza Santo Stefano 2, tel: 055 2645033; www.artviva.com); **fun itineraries** with such themes as "Beautiful Views of Florence" and "Highlights of the Uffizi."
- **Florence by Bike** (Via Zanobi 120r, tel: 055 488992; www.florencebybike.it): see the city at a **sedate pace.**
- **The Accidental Tourist** (Piazza Demidoff, tel: 055 699376; www.accidentaltourist.com): **cycling and walking** in the Tuscan countryside.

Admission Charges
The cost of admission for places of interest is indicated by price categories:

Inexpensive under €3.09   **Moderate** €3.09–€5.16   **Expensive** over €5.16

Accommodations

Florence has a wide range of accommodations, but it suffers from a shortage of good hotels in the mid-range price bracket. Prices are usually higher than elsewhere in Italy, and you'll need to reserve well in advance for much of the year. Where you stay is not a vital factor, although the city's least expensive hotels are mostly in the least appealing or least convenient locations.

Rating

You'll find a range of accommodations in Florence, from the budget to the expensive. The old *pensione* classification, which referred to a simple hotel or set of rooms, no longer exists, but you may still see budget hotels calling themselves a *pensione*.

Rating criteria are complicated. Generally budget hotels have shared bathrooms or a handful of rooms with private bathrooms. An en suite bathroom, telephone and TV are standard in most mid- to high-end properties. The luxury hotels are a class apart.

Always ask to see a selection of rooms, as you may be shown the worst first. Air-conditioning is rare in all but the most upscale hotels.

Location

In Florence, the main concentrations of budget hotels are in the streets east of the railroad station – Via Faenza, Via Nazionale and Via Fiume – and the far less convenient streets around Piazza della Libertà on the northeast edge of the city center. You'll need to take a bus or taxi if you're staying in the latter. The former are far more convenient, but – as in most cities – the area around the station is relatively unappealing (but rarely dangerous).

Noise can be a problem anywhere in Florence, even in the best hotels. It may be worth asking for a room at the back of a hotel or looking onto a central courtyard or garden. On hot summer nights – unless there's air-conditioning – you'll probably need to open windows.

Prices

■ Prices for every room in a hotel are set by law and must be displayed in the reception area and in each room. Prices can vary within a hotel, so ask to see a variety of rooms if you're not happy with the first room you're shown.

■ Prices should include all taxes, but **watch out for surcharges,** especially over-priced breakfasts *(prima colazione)*, which may or may not be included in the room rate. Where it's optional, it's invariably less expensive and more fun to have breakfast in a bar. Good buffet-style breakfasts are becoming more widespread, but a Florentine hotel "breakfast" generally means little more than a roll, jam and coffee.

■ Hotels may also have surcharges for air-conditioning and garage facilities, if appropriate. Laundry, drinks from minibars and phone calls from rooms invariably incur high tariffs.

Reservations

■ Reserve all hotels in advance year-round. Florence doesn't have an off-season to speak of. The quietest months are November, January and February. Easter and June through September are always busy.

■ Reservations should be made by phone and followed by a fax or e-mail confirmation. It is also a good idea to reconfirm reservations a couple of days before arrival. A double with twin beds is *una doppia*, and if there's a double bed, *una matrimoniale*. A single is *una singola*.

■ Hoteliers are obligated to register guests, so when checking in you have to hand over your passport. It's returned within a few hours or on the day of departure. Check-out times range from 10 a.m. to noon, but you should be able to leave luggage at the front desk to pick up later in the day.

Prices are for a double room with private bathroom
$ under €129
$$ €129–€258
$$$ over €258

Alessandria $
Noise is unlikely to be a problem at this mid-range hotel on a peaceful back street running from Santa Trìnita (➤ 129) toward the Ponte Vecchio. Rooms are spacious and some have nice touches such as wooden floors, but only around half have private bathrooms (those with shared bathrooms are less expensive). About the same number have TVs and air-conditioning.

🞧 203 E5 ✉ Borgo SS Apostoli 17 ☎ 055 283 438; fax: 055 210 619; www.hotelalessandria.com

Bellettini $
Like the similarly priced Casci (see below), the Bellettini stands out in its class. The 27 rooms are plain but clean, though half have TVs, and all have telephones and air-conditioning. Better still, the atmosphere is welcoming, the breakfasts more generous than in many hotels, and the location – in a small street west of the Cappelle Medicee (➤ 95) – central and convenient.

🞧 199 E2 ✉ Via dei Conti 7 ☎ 055 213 561; fax: 055 283 551; www.firenze.net/hotelbellettini

Brunelleschi $$$
The upscale, 87-room Brunelleschi has an excellent central location in a quiet back street between the Duomo and Piazza della Signoria. A wonderful conversion of an historic site, it was designed by leading Italian architect Italo Gamberini, and is built around a Byzantine chapel and the fifth-century Torre della Pagliazza, one of the city's oldest known structures. It even contains a small in-hotel museum devoted to some of the Roman and other archeological treasures unearthed during construction. Rooms and communal areas combine a modern and pared-down look with features – notably the fine exposed brickwork – that have been retained or copied from the original buildings.

🞧 199 F1 ✉ Via dei Calzaiuoli-Piazza Santa Elisabetta 3 ☎ 055 27370; fax: 055 219 653; www.hotelbrunelleschi.it; e-mail: info@hotelbrunelleschi.it

Casci $
The Casci is one of the best mid-range hotels in Florence, thanks to its location (just north of Piazza del Duomo), the warm welcome of its multilingual family owners, a good buffet breakfast, fair prices and range of clean rooms, all of which are decorated in a pleasant, modern style. All 25 rooms have TVs and only a handful face the busy Via Cavour (but these have efficient double-glazed windows). The frescoed main salon is a delightful place for breakfast.

🞧 199 F3 ✉ Via Cavour 13 ☎ 055 211 686; fax: 055 239 6461; www.hotelcasci.com

Firenze $
The Firenze has 57 rooms, so there's a good chance of finding space here when other places are full. The rooms are plain – but well-kept – and almost all have private bathrooms and TVs. Rooms on upper floors are brighter. The central location is first-rate – on a small square almost midway between the Duomo and Piazza della Signoria.

🞧 199 F1 ✉ Via del Corso-Piazza dei Donati 4 ☎ 055 214 203; fax: 055 212 370

Helvetia & Bristol $$$

The 18th-century Helvetia & Bristol may have rivals for the title of "best hotel in Florence," but none can really compete with the historic pedigree and panache of this elegant luxury retreat. It is located between Via de' Tornabuoni and Piazza Strozzi in the west of the city center, and its past guests have included Pirandello, Stravinsky, Gary Cooper, De Chirico and Bertrand Russell. The decor of the communal areas, 34 rooms and 18 suites is mostly old-world and elegant – antiques, rich fabrics and period paintings – but the facilities and standards of service are modern and efficient. A first choice if money is no object.

➕ 199 D1 ✉ Via de' Pescioni 2
☎ 055 287 814; fax: 055 288 353;
e-mail: ppanelli@charminghotels.it

Hermitage $$

You need to book early to have any chance of securing one of the intimate rooms at this charming mid-range hotel. It owes its popularity to the amiable service, the good facilities (several bathrooms have Jacuzzis) and a superb position almost overlooking the Ponte Vecchio. Not all rooms have river or bridge views, however, and those that do can be relatively noisy, despite double-glazed windows: if this is a concern, request courtyard rooms. In summer, you can enjoy breakfast on the delightful roof terrace.

➕ 203 E5 ✉ Vicolo Marzio 1-Piazza del Pesce ☎ 055 287 216; fax: 055 212 208; www.hermitagehotel.com

Loggiata dei Serviti $$

Being well to the north of Piazza del Duomo, this hotel isn't the best-located of Florence's hotels – you'll have a longish walk to most sights – but there are few complaints about its tremendous sense of style and good taste. The 25 rooms and four suites vary in size and individual decoration, but all have a largely serene and minimal look – a nod to the building's original 16th-century role as a Servite monastery – that is

lightened by fine fabrics and the occasional painting and antique. Choose between rooms that look over Brunelleschi's piazza or the unexpected treat of the gardens of the Accademia delle Belle Arti to the rear.

➕ 200 C3 ✉ Piazza SS Annunziata 3
☎ 055 289 592; fax: 055 289 595;
www.venere.it/firenze/loggiato_serviti
e-mail: loggiato_serviti@italyhotel.com

Maxim $

The friendly and well-run Maxim is a budget hotel, so don't expect too much in the way of frills, but its location – on Via dei Calzaiuoli about 30 seconds from the Duomo – could hardly be better. There is a choice of plain but clean rooms with and without private bathrooms. If possible, ask for the quieter rooms looking over the central courtyard rather than those overlooking Via de' Medici.

➕ 199 E1 ✉ Entrances at Via dei Calzaiuoli 11 (with elevator) and Via de' Medici 4 (stairs) ☎ 055 217 474; fax: 055 283 729; www.firenzealbergo.it/home/hotelmaxim

Morandi alla Crocetta $$

This mid-range hotel is a real gem. It bears the cultivated stamp of its owner, Kathleen Doyle, who has lived in Florence since she was 12. Her charm and good taste pervade the hotel's 10 rooms, all of which – while individually decorated – boast antiques, attractive fabrics, period prints and paintings, and colorful rugs laid over polished wooden floors. The nicest room features fragments of fresco from a converted chapel from the monastery that once occupied the site. Via Laura lies east of Piazza Santissima Annunziata, so the hotel doesn't have a particularly convenient location, but such is its popularity that you'll still have to book well in advance to secure one of its rooms.

➕ 201 D3 ✉ Via Laura 50
☎ 055 234 4747;
fax: 055 248 0954;
www.hotelmoranid.it

Food and Drink

Eating and drinking in Florence can be every bit as memorable as the city's museums and galleries. Restaurants run the gamut, from gastronomic temples to one-room trattorias with home-cooked meals and rudimentary decor. There's also a broad range of cafés and bars, good for anything from a creamy cappuccino or light meal to a snack lunch or hunk of bread and cheese washed down with a glass of wine.

Places to Eat

The difference between types of restaurant in Florence is becoming increasingly blurred. Once, a restaurant *(una ristorante)* was chic and expensive, a trattoria was simple and less expensive, an *osteria* even simpler and budget priced, and a pizzeria a no-frills place to fill up on pizza and little more. These days, the old-style trattoria is fast disappearing and being replaced by a more modern, informal type of place (often called an *osteria*) with young owners and younger attitudes to style and cuisine. The term *ristorante* can now be applied to most eating places, and pizzerias now often serve a range of pastas, salads and other main courses. The chief thing to remember is that price and appearance are no guarantee of quality; you can eat excellent food in humble-looking places at fair prices.

Other terms you may come across are *enoteca*, which means wine bar and usually indicates a place to buy wine by the glass or bottle and the chance to eat a limited selection of light meals or snacks. A *fiaschetteria* or *vinaio* is similar, but often much simpler; these were once found all over Florence – today, they're a dying breed. The same cannot be said of the *gelateria*, or ice cream parlor, a mainstay of just about every Italian town or city.

Eating Hours

- Bars open at 7 a.m. or earlier to serve **breakfast** *(la colazione* or *la prima colazione)* which generally consists of coffee (cappuccino or caffè latte) and a plain or filled sweet croissant *(una brioche)*.
- **Lunch** *(il pranzo)* starts around 12:30 and finishes at about 2, although most restaurants stay open a little later.
- **Dinner** *(la cena)* begins at about 8, although many restaurants open before this to cater to tourists used to dining earlier.
- Bars that are busy in the day usually close at around 8 or 9 p.m., but there are plenty of **late bars** such as Rex (➤ 82), which are aimed more at the nocturnal visitor. An *enoteca* (wine shop, with a bar) usually follows bar opening times, but some may close in the afternoon.

Meals

- Italian meals start with antipasti and are followed by a first course, or *il primo*, of pasta, soup or rice. The main or second course *(il secondo)* is the meat *(carne)* or fish course, and is accompanied by vegetables *(contorni)* or salad *(insalata)* which are usually served separately. Fruit *(frutta)* or cheese *(formaggio)* are often served as an alternative to *dolce* (pudding). For more information on Tuscan specialties ➤ 20–21.
- Most meals are accompanied by bread *(pane)* and mineral water *(acqua minerale)*, for which you pay extra. Ask for mineral water fizzy *(gassata)* or still *(non gassata)*.
- Meals are followed by grappa, a bitter digestif such as *amaro*, an espresso coffee *(un caffè)*, or an infusion such as camomile – note that Italians never drink cappuccino after dinner.

- You are not obliged to wade through every course. At lunch or in less expensive restaurants it is perfectly acceptable to have a pasta and salad and little more. More expensive and popular restaurants, however, may take a dim view of such an approach, especially at dinner.

Cafés and Snacks

- In cafés and bars it always **costs less to stand at the bar** – prices for bar service and for sitting down (*terrazza* and *tavola*) should be listed by law somewhere in the bar. If you choose to order at the bar, the procedure is to pay for what you want first at the separate cash desk (*la cassa*) and then take your chit *(lo scontrino)* to the bar and repeat your order. You cannot pay at the bar. If service seems slow, a coin placed on the bar as a tip with your *scontrino* often works wonders.
- If you sit down, then a waiter will take your order. It's very bad form to pay at *la cassa* and then try to sit down – the owner or waiter will soon appear to move you on if you try. If you do pay to sit down, however, you can sit for almost as long as you wish having made a single purchase.
- Cafés and bars are excellent sources of sandwiches *(tramezzini)*, filled rolls *(panini)* and sometimes light meals. Also look out for small shops or bakeries selling pizza by the slice *(pizza al taglio)*.

Set Menus

- Try to avoid restaurants that seem full of foreigners – they'll invariably be overpriced and substandard – or places that offer *un menù turistico* (a tourist menu). Such menus may appear to offer a good deal but portions are often small, wine (if offered) poor, the food quality third-rate, and the dishes unimaginative (usually a pasta with simple tomato sauce and plain grilled meat with a salad or single side dish).
- In better restaurants, *un menù degustazione* or *menù gastronomico* offers several samples of the restaurant's signature dishes and can be a good way of approaching a meal if you can't decide what to eat from the à la carte menu.

Paying

- The **check** in Italian is *il conto* – at the end of meal ask, *'Il conto, per favore'* (the check, please). This should come as a formal itemized receipt – if it appears on a scrawled piece of paper, the restaurateur is breaking the law and you are within you rights to demand a proper check *(una ricevuta)*.
- Until recently, virtually all eating places included a **cover charge** known as *pane e coperto* (bread and cover), something the authorities are trying to discourage. If included, it is not optional.
- A service charge *(servizio)* may sometimes be included on the check. If it isn't, **tip at your discretion**. Round up to the nearest €2–€5 in pizzerias, *enotecas* and other less expensive places; otherwise tip 10 to 15 percent of the total amount.

Etiquette and Smoking

- Your fellow visitors may not dress up, but Florentines generally make a sartorial effort when dining out. Neat but casual is good enough for most places, although you should be more elegant in top restaurants such as the Enoteca Pinchiorri (➤ 77) or Alle Murate (➤ 76).
- Smoking is far more acceptable in public places in Italy than in other countries, so few restaurants are non-smoking or have non-smoking sections *(non fumatori)*. You're also unlikely to get far asking diners at adjoining tables to stop smoking.

Shopping

Florence is excellent for shopping. Across the city you'll find a wide variety of shops selling mouthwatering food and wine, exquisite designer clothes, wonderful shoes and leather goods, fine jewelry, sumptuous fabrics, artisan items such as marbled paper, and a host of paintings, prints and antiques.

Specialist Shops

- Florence is relatively affluent, and its chief strengths for shoppers are **luxury goods**, especially leather and high-quality shoes and clothes. The main **designer stores** are west of the city on Via de' Tornabuoni and its surrounding streets, notably Via della Vigna Nuova. Shops selling **leather** are widespread, but workshops and mid-market stores center on the Santa Croce district. **Jewelers** are found primarily on and around the Ponte Vecchio, their home since the 16th century, although you'll find jewelers on most busy streets. The same goes for **artisans' workshops** and craft shops, although there are concentrations in the Oltrarno, especially on and just off Via Maggio, as well as streets like Via della Porcellana in the west of the city. Here you can buy everything from furniture to marble paper, a Florentine specialty.
- Via Maggio and its adjacent streets are also home to many of Florence's **antique shops** and commercial **art galleries**. Such shops can also be found elsewhere across the city center.
- The center is also where you'll find most of the **bookshops**, **kitchen** and **household goods** shops – another area in which Italy excels – and **department stores**, of which Coin and Rinascente are the best (▶ 80 and 133).
- **Food** and **wine** are good buys, but check import restrictions on meat and other products if you wish to take purchases home: safe items include pasta, wine, olive oils, most cheeses and specialties such as the spicy Panforte cake of Siena. You can buy good produce in most neighborhood food stores (known as *alimentari*), but for the best array of gourmet and other provisions, head for the superlative **Mercato Centrale** near San Lorenzo (▶ 111).

Markets

- Outside the Mercato, the streets around **San Lorenzo** are filled with a general market, a good place for inexpensive clothes, bags and souvenirs.
- Other less well-known markets include **Sant'Ambrogio** (▶ 81), a food market northeast of Santa Croce, and the small flea market, **Mercato delle Pulci** (▶ 81), nearby in Piazza dei Ciompi.
- Florence's biggest weekly market is held in the **Parco delle Casine** near the Arno to the west of the city center every Tuesday (8–1): few visitors come here, and prices for goods of all descriptions are highly competitive.

Opening Times

Opening times for most stores are traditionally Tuesday to Saturday from 8 or 9 a.m. to 1 p.m. and 3:30 or 4 to 8 p.m. Most are closed on Monday morning or one other half-day a week, but increasingly Florence's shops are open all day (known as *orario continuato*), which means Tuesday to Saturday from 9 or 10 to 7:30 or 8. Department stores are also open on Sunday.

Credit Cards

Credit cards are accepted in most large shops, but cash is still preferred in small stores: check before making purchases. Visitors from the U.S. and Canada can take advantage of tax-free shopping on some goods: many shops are members of the Tax-Free Shopping System and will guide you through the procedures.

Entertainment

Florence offers a broad spectrum of entertainment, from world-class orchestras and music festivals to funky bars and huge dance clubs. Most of the cultural entertainment is easily accessible to visitors, except for theater and movies, where most presentations and productions are in Italian. The city also hosts several major festivals, most notably the Maggio Musicale, one of Italy's leading classical music festivals.

Information

- The best sources of information are the city's various visitor centers (► 39), which generally have full lists, pamphlets and posters of upcoming concerts and other cultural events.
- Alternatively, consult the listings section of Florence and Tuscany's main daily newspaper, *La Nazione*, or the monthly *Firenze Spettacolo*, a detailed and dedicated listings magazine. It contains a section in English, but the layout is such that you should be able to understand the listings even if you don't speak Italian. The magazine is available from many newsstands and bookshops such as Feltrinelli (► 110).
- The *Guida Gay Italia* and the national monthly gay magazine, *Babilonia* (available from newsagents), provide helpful information for gay travelers. A useful website for information on gay venues and events in and around the city is www.gay.it/pinklily

Tickets

Tickets for events can be obtained from individual box offices or through **Box Office,** the city's central ticket agency, which has outlets at 39 Via Alamanni (tel: 055 210 804) and 8r Chiasso dei Soldanieri off Via Porta Rossa on the corner with Via de' Tornabuoni (tel: 055 219 402).

Festivals

The key festivals in Florence are detailed below, but there are also many more events, and you can obtain information about these from visitor centers.

The year opens with the **Sfilata dei Canottieri,** a regatta of traditional boats on the Arno river on New Year's Day (January 1). From mid-March through early April is **Diladdarno**, three weeks of music and events celebrating the traditions of the Oltrarno district. Holy Week (preceding Easter) sees special services and processions held in churches across Florence. The **Scoppio del Carro,** or "Explosion of the Cart," concludes the Easter Sunday ceremonies, when a cart of flowers and fireworks is ignited at noon by a mechanical dove that flies from the altar of the Duomo to the piazza outside. May and June see the **Maggio Musicale** arts and music festival, while on June 24 Florence celebrates **St. John's Day,** the feast of St. John the Baptist, one of Florence's patron saints, with a parade and fireworks display around Piazza le Michelangelo.

The **Festa del Grillo,** or "Festival of the Cricket," is held on Candlemas, the first Sunday after Ascension Day (usually in June). It involves a large market, but traditionally revolved around the sale of crickets in small cages, released for good luck. The most vivid of the city's festivals is the **Calcio Storico (Calcio in Costume)**, three fast, violent soccer games played in medieval dress on the day after the Feast of St. John (see above): other dates are picked from a hat on Easter Sunday. Games take place in Piazza Santa Croce or Piazza della Signoria. The Virgin Mary's birthday is marked by the **Festa delle Rificolone** (September 7) with street parties, floats and a procession of children bearing colored lanterns to Piazza Santissima Annunziata.

Eastern
Florence

Getting Your Bearings

This district represents the very heart of Florence. Here you will find some of the city's finest buildings. Its main square and the showcase of its power and might is Piazza della Signoria. The masterpieces of some of the world's greatest painters reside in the internationally renowned Uffizi Gallery.

Farther east, you'll find Santa Croce, Florence's pantheon and one of its most remarkable churches. The surrounding neighborhood provides a rare glimpse of workday Florence – an area few tourists penetrate. It has lively local markets, tiny workshops and simple homes.

This eastern area also embraces the city's medieval kernel, from the maze of tiny alleyways and hidden lanes of Dante's neighborhood north of Piazza della Signoria to such imposing civic buildings as the Palazzo Vecchio and the Bargello – once the prison, but now one of Italy's leading sculpture museums. All around are grand buildings, reminders of Florence's prime, when it was among the richest and most celebrated cities in Christendom.

You'll also find the largest selection of shops, bars and restaurants here. By night, this is the liveliest part of town and, with most of its streets pedestrianized and many of the buildings illuminated, the perfect venue for an after-dinner stroll.

At Your Leisure

LU ACCIA
Po Vecc
Corridoio Vasariano
Torre Mannelli
VIA DE' GUICCIARDINI
Santa Felicità
PIAZZA DE' PITTI
Palazzo Pitti

Previous page: The Uffizi's sculpture collection is on show in the main corridors

⭐ **Don't Miss**

Above: Via dei Calzaiuoli – one of
the main shopping thoroughfares
Left: The Classical facade of the
Uffizi, designed by Vasari

PIAZZA SAN

stero
GIOVANNI
Campanile

PIAZZA

Duomo

DEL   DUOMO

VIA D CALZAIUOLI

VIA DEL PROCONSOLO

VIA   DEL   CORSO

BLICA

6 Orsanmichele

VIA   MARIA

DELLA CONDOTTA

7 Casa di
   Dante

Badia
Fiorentina **8**

9 Museo
   Nazionale
   del Bargello

VIA G GHIBELLINA

VERDI

11 Casa
   Buonarroti

5 Piazza
   della
   Signoria

PIAZZA
SAN
FIRENZE

10 Bar Vivoli
   Gelateria

BORGO ALLEGRI

4 Loggia
   Lanzi

3 Palazzo
   Vecchio

BORGO DE' GRECI

PIAZZA
DI SANTA
CROCE

Santa Croce **12**

VIA DI SAN GIUSEPPE

2 eria
   egli
   ffizi

VIA DEI CASTELLANI

VIA DE' BENCI

Cappella
dei Pazzi

1

eo di Storia
ella Scienza

LUNGARNO GEN DIAZ

PIAZZA
MENTANA

VIA DE' GRAZIE

14 Museo
   Horne

13 Museo dell'
   Opera di
   Santa Croce

VIA DE' BARDI

LUNGARNO TORRIGIANI

Arno

PONTE ALLE GRAZIE

LUNGARNO DELLE GRAZIE

LUNG D ZECCA
VECCHIA

0   200 metres
0   200 yards

These two itineraries are a must for art lovers, photographers and everyone who wishes to visit several of the greatest sights that Florence has to offer.

Eastern Florence in Two Days

Day One

Morning
The world-famous **Galleria degli Uffizi** (Uffizi Gallery, ➤ 52–59) is on every visitor's must-see list. Make sure you arrive really early (preferably well before the doors open at 8:30) to avoid the worst lines (left).

Lunch
Enjoy a light lunch at the tiny Fiaschetteria Gia Vecchio Casentino (➤ 58) or at Caffè Italiano (➤ 79), just off **Piazza della Signoria** (➤ 60–61). Complete your lunch break with a coffee on one of the café terraces in the piazza and marvel at the mass of statuary in front of you and in the **Loggia dei Lanzi** (left, ➤ 71–72).

Afternoon
It's easy to while away a couple of hours inside the **Palazzo Vecchio** (➤ 70–71) – the imposing former town hall and home of the Medici family – in Piazza della Signoria. Remember to reserve in advance if you want to visit the secret passageways.

Evening
Join the immaculately preened locals on their evening ritual *passeggiata* (stroll), window-shopping and people-watching in boutique-lined Via dei Calzaiuoli and Via Roma. Then round off the evening with dinner at Cibreo (➤ 77).

Day Two

Morning

Spend a couple of hours admiring the dazzling collection of Renaissance statuary and bronzes (left) at the **Museo Nazionale del Bargello** (➤ 62–65), one of Italy's most important museums.

Treat yourself to a mid-morning ice cream at **Bar Vivoli** (➤ 73), reputedly the finest *gelateria* in Italy. The various chocolate flavors, including bitter, white and chocolate orange, are particularly delicious.

Stay with the sculptural theme at **Casa Buonarroti** (➤ 74). Here you can see Michelangelo's sketches and his earliest known work.

Lunch

Have lunch at Pizzaiuolo (➤ 78). The owner is a genuine Neapolitan and the pizzas are superb.

Afternoon

Make your way to Piazza di Santa Croce (below). Visit the impressive Gothic church of **Santa Croce** (➤ 66–69) to see the tombs of many famous Florentines, including Michelangelo, Machiavelli and Galileo. Be sure to visit the **Museo dell'Opera di Santa Croce** and the **Cappella dei Pazzi** (➤ 74) in the two cloisters alongside the church (separate entrance). Afterward, spend some time in the cloisters, one of the most tranquil spots in Florence.

Stroll back to the city center along the banks of the Arno, stopping en route at the **Museo di Storia della Scienza** (➤ 70), a shrine to Galileo housed in one of the city's oldest buildings.

Evening

Stop at one of the riverside cafés beyond the Ponte Vecchio (➤ 122) for an early evening aperitif. Then try out some of the regional specialties at the tiny Buca dell'Orafo (➤ 125).

Galleria degli Uffizi

The Uffizi is a gallery of superlatives: it is one of the greatest art galleries in the world; one of the oldest (inaugurated by Francesco I de' Medici in 1581); and the most visited museum in Italy. Other galleries may have more works of art, but what makes the Uffizi's 1,800-strong collection so remarkable is that every single painting is noteworthy.

The gallery was originally designed to house the administrative offices (*uffizi*) of the Grand Duchy of Tuscany, and the matching pair of handsome arcaded buildings is considered Giorgio Vasari's finest architectural work. The lower floors incorporated a secretariat, the city archives, a church, a theater and the mint, while the fourth-floor corridors, lit by huge glass windows, were lined with antique sculptures and paintings from the Medici villas, along with scientific instruments, arms and other *objets d'art*. In 1737, Anna Maria Ludovica, sister of Gian Gastone, the last Medici Grand Duke, bequeathed the Uffizi and the entire art collection to the city.

Early Days

Many people think of the Uffizi primarily as a gallery of paintings, but for a long time after its opening visitors came mainly to see the splendid collection of Hellenistic and Roman sculptures. In the 19th century these ancient statues were a must for most visitors to Florence. Edward Gibbon made 12 tours of the gallery before looking at a single painting, and Percy Bysshe Shelley ignored them altogether. The enthusiasm of the English writer and critic John Ruskin for the Renaissance paintings here, however, encouraged a new breed of visitor to the Uffizi – artists who copied the Renaissance style, giving birth to the Pre-Raphaelite movement. The statuary is still on display – in the vestibule at the top of the stairs, in room 1 (often closed) and in the main corridors.

✚ 203 E5
✉ Piazzale degli Uffizi
☎ 055 294 883; web: www.musa.uffizi.firenze.it
🕐 Tue.–Fri. 8:30–6:30, Sat. 8:30 a.m.–10 p.m., Sun. 8:30–8, May.–Oct.; Tue.–Sat. 8:30–6:50, Sun. and public holidays 8:30–7, Nov.–Apr. Closed Jan. 1, May 1 and Dec. 25. Note: times are subject to change. Last tickets sold 45 min. before closing
🚌 23 and B
💶 Expensive

Getting In

Rule one: be patient! The Uffizi greets more than 1.5 million visitors a year and, for security reasons, only 660 people are allowed in at any one time. There are three clearly marked entrances – one for individuals, one for groups and one for pre-booked visitors (► Inside Info, page 59). Each usually has long lines, so make sure you're standing in the right one.

To minimize your time standing in line, arrive very early (at about 7 a.m.) or in the late afternoon. The busiest times are weekends, Tuesdays and the lunch hour (11–3). November to March is marginally quieter than the summer season. Allow at least half a day for your visit. Be prepared to stand in line for a couple of hours and plan on spending at least three hours inside the gallery.

Finding Your Way Around

The gallery is located on the fourth floor and has 45 rooms spanning European art from the 13th to the 18th century. The glittering collection of Florentine Renaissance paintings attracts the most attention, but there are many other fine works from elsewhere in Italy (Siena and Venice in particular), the Netherlands, Germany and Spain. Paintings that have been restored are marked with a round red label.

The museum is very well laid out, with all the rooms arranged by school and in chronological order. Florentine and Tuscan Gothic and early Renaissance paintings take up most of the East Corridor (rooms 1–15). A short South Corridor (with diverting views of the Arno) connects to the West Corridor, which is devoted to 16th-century Italian paintings (High Renaissance and Mannerism) and works by non-Italian artists, among them Dürer, Rubens, Van Dyck, Rembrandt and Goya. The entrance to the Corridoio Vasariano (see panel, below) is located here, as is a small café-bar.

Above: The galleries of the Uffizi and the Corridoio Vasariano fringe the Arno

Room 2

This is one of the most fascinating rooms of the entire collection. Here you will find three Gothic altarpieces depicting the **Maestà** (the Madonna enthroned) by Giovanni Cimabué (c.1285), Duccio di Buoninsegna (c.1285) and Giotto di Bondone (c.1310). The paintings illustrate the progressive strides within this period away from the stylized tradition of Byzantine art toward naturalism and control of perspective. This is particularly apparent in Giotto's depiction of Mary, whom he portrays as a real woman. Her breasts and knees show through

Right: Giotto uses perspective to create depth and realism in his *Madonna Enthroned*

Corridoio Vasariano

In 1565, Francesco I commissioned Giorgio Vasari to build an elevated walkway linking the Uffizi with the Palazzo Pitti on the other side of the river, so the Medici and their entourage could walk from one to the other without mixing with the hoi polloi on the streets below. The resulting "corridor" is a remarkable achievement: half a mile in length and supported on brackets, it crosses the Ponte Vecchio, skirting the Mannelli Tower and the church of San Felicità en route to the Palazzo Pitti. It is lined with a collection of artists' self-portraits and is well worth the guided tour, if you're lucky enough to find it open.

her clothes, her hair can be seen under her veil and her cheeks and lips are pink. By contrast, Cimabué's solemn Madonna does not have such realistic features. Duccio's Madonna shows the development of the Sienese School, with its great attention to decorative detail and to the alternating use of color. However, Duccio's Madonna is even less realistic than Cimabué's. The throne in Giotto's work is firmly on the ground, while angels and saints gather round – even *behind* the throne. This marks the beginning of a major artistic revolution – the use of perspective to provide depth and realism, which was to develop in Florence over the next 200 years.

Rooms 3–4

Simone Martini's lyrical **Annunciation** (1333) and Ambrogio Lorenzetti's **Presentation of Jesus in the Temple** (1342) demonstrate the flowering of 14th-century Sienese painting. The Lorenzetti painting is another example of early experimentation with techniques of perspective.

Rooms 6–7

Gentile da Fabriano's Gothic **Adoration of the Magi** (1423) in room 6 and Domenico Veneziano's early Renaissance **altar panel with Santa Lucia dei Màgnoli** (1445) in room 7 are striking examples of the development of perspective. Veneziano followed the rules of linear perspective (newly formulated by Filippo Brunelleschi) in his work to create architectural space. Note also the halos, which appear as transparent circles of gold, painted with depth and perspective. Up until then, the convention had been to paint them as flat gold discs.

The **diptych of The Duke and Duchess of Urbino** (c.1465) by Piero della Francesca (in room 7) is among the best-known portraits in the Uffizi. The Duke wanted to be portrayed faith-

fully, warts, wrinkles and all, but he insisted on being depicted in profile to show off his war wound – a hooked nose caused by a sword blow. The town in the Duchess' portrait is Gubbio in Umbria, where she died giving birth to her ninth child and first son. The portrait was painted posthumously.

Room 8

The **Madonna and Child with Two Angels** (c.1465) in room 8 is a masterpiece of warmth and humanity. It was painted by the monk Filippo Lippi, who ran away with a nun – the model for this painting.

Piero della Francesca's diptych portraying the Duke and Duchess of Urbino

Rooms 10–14

These four small rooms, containing Botticelli's most celebrated works, are the museum's most popular. His paintings have an innocent, idealistic quality about them, unlike the work of his contemporaries, who were focusing on perspective, proportion and anatomy. In **Primavera** (c.1478), he depicts a perfect forest

Botticelli's *Birth of Venus*, one of the artist's greatest works

La Tribuna

The Medici kept their finest treasures in the Tribune (room 18), a small octagonal room designed to represent the cosmos: the red walls symbolized fire; the weathervane air; the mosaic floor of *pietre dure* earth; and the cupola, with its mother-of-pearl lining, was the heavenly vault. Today the Tribune's star attraction is the *Medici Venus* – a masterpiece of classical sculpture from the third century BC, considered antiquity's most erotic statue.

in springtime – where all the fruit is ripe and all the flowers are in full bloom. Venus and her assistant Cupid are in the center; on the right is Zephyr, the west wind who joins Flora to give life to Spring (in the floral dress). On the left are the three Graces and Mercury, who's working hard to keep the clouds away from the forest.

Botticelli's *Birth of Venus* (1485) was the last of his mythological paintings and the first "pagan" nude of the Renaissance. By painting Venus instead of the Virgin Mary, Botticelli expressed his fascination with classical mythology, in common with many Renaissance artists. It is probably the most celebrated painting in the gallery, yet, like so many of the famous works of art here, it still has the power to overwhelm despite its overexposure on calendars and greetings cards.

Room 15

It is often said that Botticelli brings the 15th century to a close, while the genius of Leonardo da Vinci introduces the 16th, and this room certainly demonstrates the passage from "antique" to "modern." Look for the *Baptism of Christ* (c.1470) by Andrea del Verrocchio, Leonardo's teacher. Leonardo helped out by painting the angel in blue. When Verrocchio saw his work outclassed by his young protégé, he vowed he would never paint again. Alongside is Leonardo's unfinished *Adoration of the Magi* (1481).

The *Doni Tondo* – a veritable masterpiece by Michelangelo

Room 25

The *Doni Tondo* (c.1504), a circular portrayal of the Holy Family commissioned by Angelo Doni on the occasion of his marriage to Maddalena Strozzi, is the earliest confirmed painting by Michelangelo. It is striking for its vibrant colors, the unusual, twisted pose of the Virgin and its anatomical detail. A sculptor at heart, Michelangelo was so interested in studying the human body that he attended dissections in order to understand its structure better.

Room 28

Venus of Urbino (1538) by Titian (Tiziano Vecellio) is considered one of the most beautiful nudes ever painted, described by poet Lord Byron as "the definitive Venus." The model was possibly Eleanora Gonzaga, wife of Francesco Maria della Rovere, who is portrayed with her clothes on in the painting alongside, together with the same dog.

Rooms 41–45

The final rooms of the Uffizi contain important 17th- and 18th-century **European artworks** including works by Rubens, Canaletto and Van Dyck, Caravaggio's **Bacchus** (room 43) and two Rembrandt **self-portraits** (room 44).

TAKING A BREAK

The tiny wine bar **Fiaschetteria Gia Vecchio Casentino** (Via dei Neri 17r, tel: 055 217 411) serves toasted sandwiches, *crostini*, simple pasta dishes and other snacks.

This sensual nude by Titian was purchased by the Duke of Urbino – hence its name *The Venus of Urbino*

Parmigianino's Mannerist *Virgin of the Long Neck* (1534–36) in room 29

GALLERIA DEGLI UFFIZI: INSIDE INFO

Top tips If you are able to plan your visit, book a ticket in advance by credit card (tel: 055 294 883). Pre-booked tickets specify an entrance time, but you can stay inside the gallery as long as you like and this will dramatically

cut down on time spent in line. You pay a small fee and pick up the tickets at the gallery at the time of your visit. Book at least five days in advance.
• If you have come especially to see a **favorite painting,** check at the information desk to ensure it is on display *before* paying the entry fee, as rooms are subject to periodic closure.
• The small **café-bar and rooftop terrace** in the West Corridor (beyond room 45) is a good place to escape the crowded galleries.

In more depth Art **aficionados** will probably want to visit the Uffizi at least twice. Concentrate your first visit on the **Florentine Renaissance** (rooms 1–15) and save the **High Renaissance** and **Mannerism** in Florence (rooms 16–29) for a second visit.

Hidden gems The *Madonna of the Magnificat* (rooms 10–14), notable as one of Botticelli's earliest religious paintings, is every bit as beautiful as the more famous *Primavera* and *The Birth of Venus* but is often overlooked in the clamor to see the more celebrated paintings.
• In room 26, look for Raphael's *Madonna of the Goldfinch* (c.1506), an exceptionally tender painting portraying the Virgin Mary with babies Jesus and John the Baptist caressing a small bird.

Piazza della Signoria

Piazza della Signoria is Florence's most famous square. With its daily hubbub of visitors and locals, handsome palazzi, sophisticated café terraces and dazzling collection of buildings and statuary, it is also where the city's heart beats loudest.

For centuries the square has been at the center of Florentine affairs and it was here that Roman *Florentia* was founded. In the Middle Ages, the land was owned by the Ghibellines (a group of feudal lords who claimed to represent imperial power) but they were eventually defeated by the Guelphs (a rival feudal faction who supported the autonomy of *Comunes* or consular magistracy). The Guelphs destroyed all the Ghibelline houses, decreed that nothing was to be built where the traitors' buildings had once stood, and consequently created the magnificent square as a symbol of their power.

The piazza is dominated by the **Palazzo Vecchio** (➤ 70–71), built at the end of the 13th century. The bell in its campanile is rung to summon citizens to the square for *parlamenti* (public meetings). In front of the palace, a series of patriotic sculptures graces the *arringhiera* (oration terrace), where orators once stood to "harangue" the citizens. The works include **Marzocco**

(a lion with its paw on the coat of arms of the city), named after Mars, god of war and ancient protector of Florence (the original is in the Bargello, ➤ 62–65); a bronze **Judith and Holofernes** by Donatello, symbolizing liberty; and a copy of Michelangelo's **David**, a work regarded as the embodiment of Republican triumph and placed here, rather than in its planned location near the Duomo. Nearby is

Soaking up the view from the terrace of the Café Rivoire

the **Loggia dei Lanzi** (➤ 71–72), which shelters copies of some of Florence's finest sculptures.

Among the other statues in the square is the awkward fountain of **Neptune** by Bartolommeo Ammannati, which symbolizes Cosimo I's naval victories. Nicknamed *Il Biancone* (the Big White One), the work was much criticized by contemporaries, provoking the harsh exclamation (attributed to Michelangelo) "Ammannati, Ammannati, what lovely marble you have ruined!" Cosimo himself is depicted on horseback in the center of the square (➤ 13).

✚ 203 F5   ✉ Piazza della Signoria   🚌 23 and B

TAKING A BREAK

An especially pleasant way to admire the square is to sit on the terrace of the classy **Café Rivoire** (➤ 79), sipping a cup of its celebrated hot chocolate.

Crowding the square – people in marble, bronze, stone and flesh

PIAZZA DELLA SIGNORIA: INSIDE INFO

Top tip Allow at least **half an hour to admire** the unique collection of buildings and statuary here. Then take time to **people-watch** and to soak up the atmosphere of the busy square.

One to miss Baccio Bandinelli's ungainly statue *Hercules and Cacus* (alongside the copy of Michelangelo's *David*) was described by Benvenuto Cellini as an "old sack full of melons."

Hidden gem Look out for the ravishing **bronze water nymphs** adorning the Neptune Fountain (beside the Palazzo Vecchio).

Museo Nazionale del Bargello

The Bargello houses one of Italy's most important collections of sculpture, with celebrated works by Michelangelo, Giambologna and Donatello among others. It is also the oldest surviving civic building in Florence.

The mighty Bargello fortifications

The fortress-like structure has had many incarnations. It was originally constructed in 1255 as the head-quarters of the Capitano del Popolo (a post holding supreme authority in the government), then briefly became the home of the *Podestà* (chief magistrate). From the 16th century until 1859, the Medici turned it into the residence of the Bargello (head of police), a torture chamber and the city jail. Finally, in 1865, after extensive renovation, it became one of the first National Museums of Italy. The building's design, with its mighty battlemented facade and skinny 12th-century tower (which possibly predates the original structure), was so popular that it was used as a model for the grand Palazzo Vecchio.

The Courtyard

The museum occupies three floors, centered around a porticoed courtyard with a well and an elegant external stair-way decorated with ancient terra-cotta plaques and coats of arms. Until 1786 this was the scene of executions, and those sentenced to death would spend their last night in the chapel on the second floor. Following execution, their bodies were hung from the windows. It was also customary to paint effigies of condemned men on the wall facing Via della Vigna Vecchia. Evidently, Andrea del Castagno became so good at this that he earned himself the unfortunate nickname "Andrea of the Hanged Men."

➕ 200 B1
✉ Via del Proconsolo 4
☎ 055 238 8606
🕐 Daily 8:30–1:50; closed first, third and fifth Sun. and second and fourth Mon. of the month, Jan. 1, May 1 and Dec. 25
🚌 14, 23 and A 💶 Moderate

Sculptural Highlights

The first room of the museum, dedicated to Michelangelo and his contemporaries, is one of the finest. Michelangelo's best-known sculpture here is **Bacchus** (1496–97), a witty interpretation of the god of wine and enjoyment, portrayed in an unsteady, drunken pose. Alongside is a more conventional *Bacchus* by Sansovino (Andrea Contucci).

Other works by Michelangelo include the highly innovative **Pitti Tondo** (c.1503), in which the Madonna's head comes out of the circular frame, adding life and movement to the figures. Michelangelo also used the technique of *non-finito*, whereby some of the marble is smoothed to reflect the light, whereas other parts are left rough and "unfinished," lending depth. He used this technique again in **Brutus** (1540), the only bust he ever sculpted, to give the face a strong, masculine expression. It is thought that the bust was inspired by an event that occurred three years previously: Lorenzo de' Medici killed Duke Alessandro, his unpopular cousin and a tyrannical ruler of Florence, just as Brutus had killed Julius Caesar.

When the Bargello was a jail, these arches were walled up and filled with cages containing prisoners

Michelangelo's tipsy *Bacchus*

Other noteworthy sculptures in the room include a large bronze bust of *Cosimo I* (1548) by Benvenuto Cellini and Giambologna's famous bronze **Mercury** (1564). You'll find further Giambologna sculptures, including **The Turkey** and an aviary of other bronze birds (made for the animal grotto at the Medicis' Villa di Castello), on the second-floor loggia.

Adjoining the loggia, the Salone del Consiglio Generale (General Council Hall) contains a host of works by Donatello. In the center of the room is the **Marzocco lion** (► 9), the symbol of Florence that once sat in Piazza della Signoria. To its left stands Donatello's early marble sculpture, **David** (1408–12), remarkable for its attention to detail – originally there was even a strip of leather running from David's right hand to the body of the sling resting on the giant's head. Here too you'll find Donatello's later sculpture of **St. George** (1416–20) and his most celebrated bronze – yet another **David** (1440), the first free-standing nude statue by a Western artist since antiquity. If you compare the bronze *David* with the earlier marble sculpture, it is hard to believe that they are the work of the same artist. The bronze, inspired by the sculptures of classical Rome, was designed to be viewed from all sides. This was a novel concept in the 15th century, because until then sculptures had been used solely to decorate architecture and the figures' backs were usually against a wall or in a niche.

Finally, look out for Brunelleschi's and Lorenzo Ghiberti's trial bronze panels depicting Abraham about to sacrifice Isaac, their entries to the competition held in 1401 for the commission to create Florence's Battistero doors (► 92–93).

If you are short of time, skip the remaining rooms on the second floor and make your way instead to the colorful, enameled **terra-cottas of the della Robbia family** on the third floor. You'll notice similar terra-cottas adorning many public buildings throughout the city. Also on this floor is the most important collection of small **Renaissance bronzes** in Italy, comprising animals, statuettes and bells, among other objects, with pieces by Giambologna and Cellini (► Inside Info panel, opposite).

Donatello's *David* (1440) marked a turning point in Renaissance sculpture

TAKING A BREAK

Da Penello (Via Dante Alighieri 4r, tel: 055 294 848), a traditional *osteria* renowned for its superb antipasti buffet, is an excellent place to stop for a meal.

Bernardo Baroncelli

Bernardo Baroncelli was one of the Bargello's most notorious prisoners. He was executed here in 1478 for his part in the Pazzi conspiracy – the failed attempt to assassinate Lorenzo the Magnificent in the Duomo – and his body was hung from a window as a warning to other anti-Medici conspirators.

The lavish interior of the Bargello is as impressive as its handsome exterior

MUSEO NAZIONALE DEL BARGELLO: INSIDE INFO

Top tips You may have to **stand in line** to get into the museum. Note that **last admission** is at 1 p.m. and the staff start asking visitors to leave at 1:20.
• Ideally, allow yourself **a couple of hours** once inside the museum.

Must-sees *Bacchus* by Michelangelo (first floor).
• *Mercury* by Giambologna (first floor).
• Donatello's bronze, free-standing *David* (second floor).

One to miss Don't spend time in the small second-floor exhibition rooms or the Arms and Armour Collection (third floor), unless this is your particular interest.

Hidden gems Look for the medieval **Madonna sculptures** in the Sala del Trecento on the first floor.
• Make time to see Giambologna's delightful bronze birds on the second-floor loggia – they are easily neglected en route to Donatello's more famous statues in the General Council Hall.
• On the third floor, look for *Lady with a Posy*. Attributed to Andrea del Verrocchio, it is possibly the work of Leonardo da Vinci.

Bronze birds grace the loggia

Santa Croce

Together with the Duomo (▶ 88) and Santa Maria Novella
(▶ 118), the mighty Gothic Franciscan church of Santa Croce
is one of three churches funded by the *comune* (the city
government) as symbols of civic pride. At the time of its
construction (c.1294), it was one of the largest churches in
the Christian world, reflecting the then immense popularity
of Franciscan preaching. The white-, green- and pink-striped
marble neo-Gothic facade was added between 1853 and 1863,
and the campanile was added in 1847.

Florentine Pantheon

On first impression, Santa Croce's architectural austerity, open
timber roof (typical of all Franciscan churches), gloomy lighting
and huge proportions give it the feel of a large barn. On closer
inspection – with its numerous tombs, funerary monuments
and nearly 300 tombstones – it resembles a cemetery or a
museum of religious sculpture. For
this is the city pantheon, where the
most illustrious Florentines are buried
or remembered, together with wealthy
local dignitaries, who paid vast sums of
money to be buried alongside them.

The first monument along the right
aisle is the **tomb of Michelangelo**, a
cumbersome work by Giorgio Vasari
incorporating a bust of the great artist
and allegorical figures representing
painting (left), sculpture (center) and
architecture (right). Michelangelo died
in Rome in 1564 and was buried here a
few days later. He had previously
chosen the spot but never finished the
Pietà (▶ 67) he'd intended for his
tomb. It would have been a more
moving memorial.

Other monuments and tombs worth
viewing (all in the right aisle beyond
Michelangelo's tomb) include those of
the philosopher Niccolò Machiavelli

Santa Croce's
imposing facade
pierces the
Florentine
skyline

✚ 204 C5
✉ Piazza di Santa Croce
☎ 055 244 619
🕐 Church: Mon.–Sat. 8–5:45, Sun. 8–1 for worship only, 3–5:45 for tourist
visits, Easter–Oct.; Mon.–Sat. 8–12:30, 3–5:45, Oct.–Easter. Masses weekdays 8 and 9 a.m. and 6 p.m., Sat 6 p.m., Sun and holidays 8, 9:30 and 11
a.m., noon, and 6 p.m.
🚌 23 and C
♿ Free

Michelangelo's colossal tomb

(d.1527); composer Gioacchino Antonio Rossini (d.1868); scholar and humanist Leonardo Bruni (d.1444), whose effigy holds a copy of his masterpiece, *History of Florence*; and Dante, perhaps the greatest poet of all time, who died in exile in Ravenna, where he was buried.

For centuries, Florentines tried to get Dante's body back and in the 16th century Michelangelo promised to sculpt a magnificent tomb for him. When his tomb in Ravenna was eventually opened, it was empty except for a casket containing a parchment scroll written by two monks. It explained how they'd removed his remains for safekeeping lest he be taken back to the city that had once so cruelly banished him.

Floor-to-ceiling treasures – even the pavements are adorned with tombstones

Treasured Art

At one time the walls of Santa Croce were completely decorated with frescoes by Giotto and his pupils. But in the 16th century, Cosimo I instructed Vasari to plaster them over while "rearranging" the church. Nevertheless, some magnificent Trecento frescoes have been preserved in the transept. They provide a fascinating opportunity to compare the masterworks of Giotto with those of his predecessors.

Galileo Galilei

In the left aisle stands one of the most imposing monuments in the church. It is devoted to Florentine scientist Galileo Galilei (1564–1642). His actual tomb, however, is kept out of sight in a locked chapel beyond the sacristy. The reason? His popularization of the Copernican view of the universe, with the sun rather than the earth at its center, brought him into conflict with the Church; he was condemned by the Inquisition and denied burial on consecrated ground.

The **frescoes** in the Cappella Peruzzi and Cappella Bardi (to the right of the sanctuary) were painted by Giotto toward the end of his life. Unfortunately he painted them on dry plaster rather than on more durable wet plaster and, having badly deteriorated, they were covered in whitewash for many years. Eventually restored in 1959, these fragmentary, pastel-hued frescoes count among some of his finest works. The Cappella Bardi shows **scenes from the life of St. Francis** (c.1317) and the Cappella Peruzzi depicts **scenes from the life of St. John the Divine** (on the right wall) and **the life of St. John the Baptist** (on the left wall), painted between 1320 and 1325. The frescoes are notable for their sense of pictorial space, naturalism and narrative drama, especially those in the Cappella Bardi. See how Giotto conveys the feelings of **St. Francis** (above the arch) as he receives the stigmata.

The move toward realism marked a decisive break with the artistic traditions of the preceding century, and the start of the modern era in painting. You can see just how revolutionary Giotto's work was if you compare his frescoes with the 13th-century altarpiece here, which also illustrates scenes from the life of St. Francis.

The frescoes in the Cappella Baroncelli portraying **scenes from the life of the Virgin Mary** (in the right transept) were once thought to be by Giotto, but they have since been attributed to his pupil Taddeo Gaddi. The scene in which the angels announce the birth of Christ to the shepherds is considered the earliest night scene ever painted in fresco (1338). The Cappella Castellani in the south transept has some later, more decorative frescoes by Taddeo's son, Agnolo, while in the left transept the second Cappella Bardi contains a wooden Crucifix by Donatello, scathingly dismissed by Filippo Brunelleschi as resembling "a peasant on a cross."

Next to the church, housed in two cloisters, you will find the Museo dell'Opera di Santa Croce and the Cappella dei Pazzi (➤ 74–75).

Santa Croce's marble facade was added in the 19th century

TAKING A BREAK

Alongside Santa Croce, **Enoteca Baldovino** (➤ 79) serves mouthwatering *panini*, quiche, salads, cheese platters and fine Tuscan wines.

Frescoes in the
Cappella
Baroncelli by
Taddeo Gaddi

SANTA CROCE: INSIDE INFO

Top tip Have some **loose change** handy to illuminate Giotto's frescoes and to listen to the polyglot phone commentary.

One to miss The sacristy contains a largely unremarkable collection of reliquaries, missals and vestments from different centuries.

Hidden gems The marble **pulpit** by **Benedetto da Maiano** is notable for the five intricately sculpted scenes from the life of St. Francis.
• Look for Donatello's relief, the ***Annunciation***, in the right aisle. This superb work in gilded *pietra serena* is one of the finest reliefs of the early Florentine Renaissance.

In more depth To see more treasures from the church, visit Museo dell'Opera di Santa Croce and the Cappella dei Pazzi (➤ 74–75).

At Your Leisure

⓵ Museo di Storia della Scienza

Housed in one of the city's oldest buildings, the Museum of the History of Science is a must for anyone interested in Tuscan-born scientist and mathematician to the Medici court, Galileo Galilei (1564–1642), or the development of science. During the 16th century, the Florentines

Scientific instruments belonging to Galileo are housed in the Museo di Storia della Scienza

strove to foster scientific knowledge, and the collection contains more than 5,000 instruments, appliances and mathematical tools, offering fascinating insights into chemistry, electricity, magnetics, surgery and gynecology.

Several rooms are devoted to Galileo; exhibits include two of his original telescopes, his middle finger (cut from his dead body), various instruments, and the broken lens with which he discovered the satellites of

Jupiter (rooms 4–5). Other highlights include the Florentine globes and the massive sphere used to illustrate the motion of planets and stars (room 7).

➕ 204 A4　✉ Piazza dei Giudici 1
☎ 055 239 8876; 055 293 493
(24-hour recorded information)
🕐 Mon., Wed.–Fri. 9:30–5, Tue. and
Sat. 9:30–1, Jun.–Sep.; Mon., Wed.–Sat.
9:30–5, Tue. 9:30–1, Oct.–May. Last
tickets 30 min. before closing　🚌 23
💲 Expensive

⓷ Palazzo Vecchio

The Old Palace, with its solid, rusticated facade, crenellated roof and 300-foot bell tower, is outstanding among monuments of Florentine civic architecture and a symbol of the Republic's authority. Constructed between 1298 and 1302 as the Palazzo della Signoria, the residence of the *Signoria* (government), it became the ducal palace of the Medici. During Florence's brief spell as the capital of Italy (1865–71), it was the seat of the National Parliament. Today it houses the city council and the Children's Museum of Florence (► panel, page 75).

Be sure to see the vast Salone dei Cinquecento (Hall of the Five Hundred), created to house the new general parliament and later decorated by Cosimo I with frescoes and

Savonarola

The martyred religious leader Girolamo Savonarola spent his last days imprisoned in the Palazzo Vecchio. In 1497, he had staged his hugely popular "Bonfire of Vanities" (the burning of books, fancy clothes and works of art) in the square. Ironically, just one year later, the tide of popular opinion had turned and he was burned at the stake for attempting to bring morality and virtue to Florence.

sculptures recalling the history of Florence and the Medicis. Don't miss Michelangelo's magnificent marble group representing *Victory*, intended for the tomb of Pope Julius II; also, the ornate, windowless study adjoining the hall, used by Cosimo's son, Francesco I, for his collections of coins, glass and semi-precious stones.

The Medici suite of rooms, each dedicated to the glorification of a different family member, corresponds to the Apartment of the Elements on the next floor, where each room is dedicated to a different god, prompting Giorgio Vasari's famous comparison: "The rooms above…are where the origins of the celestial gods dwell in painting…together with the great virtues his Majesty sets in the creatures down here who, leaving a great mark among mortals…are terrestrial gods." The rooftop views from the loggia and the luxury apartments of

The inner courtyard of the Palazzo Vecchio, decorated with frescoes to celebrate Francesco I's marriage to Joanna of Austria

Eleanor of Toledo (wife of Cosimo I de' Medici), are superb.

🔲 203 F5 ⊠ Piazza della Signoria
☎ 055 276 8224. Phone in advance to reserve a place on a secret passageway tour ⏰ Mon.–Wed., Fri.–Sat. 9–7, Sun., Thu. and holidays 9–2. Last tickets 1 hour before closing 🚌 23 and B
🎟 Expensive

🇨 Loggia dei Lanzi

The loggia was conceived in 1382 as a stage for all the most important ceremonies held in Florence – an architecturally innovative structure with round arches and Classical proportions, looking toward Renaissance ideals at a time when pointed Gothic arches were still very much in vogue. Originally called the Loggia della Signoria, it was renamed after Cosimo I's body-guards, the *Lanzi* or Lancers.

The loggia was later turned into a splendid open-air museum with ancient Greek and Roman as well as Renaissance figures. One of the finest is Giambologna's fluid *Rape of the Sabine Women* (1583), carved from a single block of flawed marble (➤ 50). The most famous is *Perseus* (1554), a lifesize bronze statue by Benvenuto Cellini depicting Perseus standing over Medusa. One of the oldest works in the loggia, *Menelaus Supporting the Body of Patroclus*, is a Roman copy of the Greek original dated 400 BC.

➕ 204 A5 ✉ Piazza della Signoria
🚌 23 and B 🎫 Free

Carvings on the exterior wall niches at Orsanmichele depict members of the guilds at work

🔆 Orsanmichele

A church with a difference, Orsanmichele was built in 1337 as a grain market. Inside you can still see grain shoots and, to the left of the main entrance, above the doorway leading up to the grain stores, a carving of an overflowing bushel. The market was built on the site of a monastic garden. Soon after its completion, it was converted into a church (financed by the city's major guilds), although grain was stored on the upper floors until 1569.

Start your visit by walking around the

Facing page: Ethereal frescoes grace the ceiling of the Badia Fiorentina

building's exterior. You'll notice 14 niches, each containing a statue of the patron saint of a guild and sculptures illustrating the guild's type of work. Even after being consecrated, Orsanmichele continued to be used as a place to negotiate business deals. The interior is most unusual – square with two parallel naves of equal importance – and contains a beautiful jewel-encrusted tabernacle (1349–59) by Andrea Orcagna.

➕ 199 E1 ✉ Via dell'Arte della Lana
☎ 055 284 944 🕐 Daily 9–noon, 4–6
🚌 A 🎫 Free

🔆 Casa di Dante

Although the medieval poet Dante Alighieri once lived near here, this house is a reconstruction dating from 1911. Despite this, the small museum successfully manages to evoke Dante's life and times.

Several rooms are devoted to 13th-century Florence, with models and plans showing the development of the city, Dante's role as a Guelph, his exile from Florence in 1309 because of his sympathies with the White Guelphs when the Black Guelphs became dominant, and his works, including *The Divine Comedy*. Just up the road is the simple, unadorned Church of Santa

Dante was exiled from Florence in 1309

Margherita, where Dante first met Beatrice Portinari, who inspired his poetry, and where he married Gemma Donati. Both Beatrice and Gemma are buried here. The church is sometimes called the Chiesa di Dante, as it was at the center of the poet's social, political and spiritual life.

➕ 199 F1 ✉ Via Santa Margherita 3
☎ 055 219 416 🕓 Mon., Wed.–Sat.
10–6, Sun. 10–2, Mar.–Oct.; Mon.,
Wed.–Sat. 10–4, Sun. 10–2, Nov.–Feb.
🚌 14, 23 and A 🎫 Inexpensive

🞇 Badia Fiorentina

The Badia Fiorentina is the oldest monastery in Florence, founded in 978 by the mother of Marquis Ugo of Tuscany. The monks here enhanced the area's reputation as an important center of book production with their papermaking, illuminating and book-binding. Ugo, nicknamed the "great baron," was a hugely popular figure in medieval Florence and would organize readings of Dante's work in the church. A Mass is still celebrated in his honor on December 21.

The monastery has been restructured several times, and over the years the church has been rotated 180 degrees. Its *pièce de résistance* is a magnificent altarpiece showing *The Virgin Appearing to St. Bernard*

(1485) by Filippino Lippi. There are also excellent views of the hexagonal campanile from the fresco-clad cloisters.

➕ 204 B5 ✉ Via del Proconsolo
☎ 055 264 402 🕓 Church open for
sightseers Mon.–Fri. 4:30–6:30, Sun. and
holidays 10:30–11:30 only 🚌 14, 23
and A 🎫 Free

🔟 Bar Vivoli Gelateria

It is generally accepted that the Florentines make some of the best ice cream in the world. This *gelateria*, in a hidden alleyway at the heart of the Santa Croce district, is reputed to produce the best in town. Be prepared to get in line for the rich and creamy concoctions, which

include all the old favorites plus such unusual flavors as fig, meringue, pear, chestnut and zabaglione.

🞣 204 C5 ⊠ Via Isola delle Stinche 7r ☎ 055 292 334 🕘 Tue.–Sat. 7:30–1, Sun. 10–1 🚌 14 and A

⑪ Casa Buonarroti

This is the former home of artist and sculptor Michelangelo Buonarroti. However, you'll be disappointed if you come expecting every room to be overflowing with his works, although two of his masterpieces have become the symbols of the museum: the serene *Madonna of the Steps*, carved when he was just 15 or 16 years old and thought to be his earliest work; and the more complex *Battle of the Centaurs*.

The museum also boasts more than 200 Michelangelo drawings, the largest collection in the world. For reasons of conservation, however, just a small selection is placed on view at any one time. According to Giorgio Vasari, in 1564, shortly before his death, Michelangelo burned "a great number of drawings, sketches, and cartoons made by his hand so that no one would see the labors he endured and the ways he tested his genius, and lest he should appear less than perfect."

Other highlights include an amusing model of *David* in a wooden cart, showing how the statue was transported from Piazza della Signoria to the Accademia (► 98–99), and a gallery of frescoes depicting Michelangelo meeting with popes and sovereigns. The rest of the museum provides a rare glimpse inside a 16th-century palazzo, complete with period furnishings.

🞣 205 D5 ⊠ Via Ghibellina 70 ☎ 055 241 752 🕘 Wed.–Mon. 9:30–1:30. Guided visits with reservations 🚌 14 and A 💲 Expensive

⑬ Museo dell'Opera di Santa Croce and Cappella dei Pazzi

Adjoining Santa Croce (► 66–69) are the old monastic buildings of the

A few moments of solitude in the tranquil inner cloister of Santa Croce

church housing the Museo dell'Opera di Santa Croce and the Cappella dei Pazzi. The refectory (part of the museum) houses such radiant frescoes as Taddeo Gaddi's *Tree of the Cross* and *Last Supper*, removed from the church to reveal earlier works and, most famous of all, Giovanni Cimabué's celebrated *Crucifix*, devastated by the 1966 flood (► 28–29).

It is the Cappella dei Pazzi, however, which is the real draw for visitors. The chapel, one of the purest works of Renaissance architecture in Florence, was commissioned by the Pazzi family, arch-rivals of the Medici, and designed by Brunelleschi between 1442–46. It is striking in its simplicity: plain gray and white stone walls, with perfectly proportioned arches, domes, scallops, arcades and one small stained-glass window. The painted terra-cotta tondi depicting the Apostles are by Luca della Robbia, while the Evangelists in the pendentives, the main altar and the frieze of cherubs, and *Agnus Dei* are by Donatello.

A doorway near the Cappella dei Pazzi leads to one of the cloisters, a wonderfully peaceful corner and an ideal place to escape the city's frenetic pace and rest awhile.

✚ 205 D4 ⊠ Piazza di Santa Croce 16 ☎ 055 244 619 ⓦ Museo dell'Opera di Santa Croce: Thu.–Tue. 10–6 (last entry 5:30). Cappella dei Pazzi: Thu.–Tue. 10–6 (last entry 5:30) 🚌 23 and C 🔘 Moderate

⑭ Museo Horne

The English art historian Herbert Percy Horne was one of a handful of foreigners living in Florence at the turn of the 20th century who left a profound and lasting impression on the cultural life of the city. Following his death in 1916, he bequeathed his Renaissance palazzo home to the city in his will, together with an eclectic collection of paintings, sculptures, ceramics, furniture, ornaments,

For Kids
• **Bar Vivoli Gelateria** (➤ 73–74) is always a treat.
• The **Children's Museum of Florence**, housed in the Palazzo Vecchio (➤ 70–71), provides hours of hands-on educational fun and games for young children. There is also a play area for children between 3 and 6 years old.
• Science-minded older children will enjoy the **Museo di Storia della Scienza** (➤ 70).

Renaissance cooking utensils and other knickknacks, all reflecting his passion for the art and history of the city.

There is nothing exceptionally precious here, except a polyptych of *St. Stephen* by Giotto. The museum's charm lies more in its hodgepodge of exhibits and the homey feel of the palace, previously owned by a wealthy cloth merchant.

✚ 204 B4 ⊠ Via de' Benci 6 ☎ 055 244 661 ⓦ Mon.–Sat. 9–1 🚌 23, B and C 🔘 Moderate

Herbert Percy Horne's home, housed in a charming Renaissance palazzo, was bequeathed to the city in 1916

Where to...
Eat and Drink

Prices

Expect to pay per person for a meal, excluding drinks and service
$** under €20.65 **$$** €20.65–€41.31 **$$$ over €41.31

The area around Santa Croce has some of Florence's finest and most expensive restaurants – Cibreo, Pinchiorri and Alle Murate – but also a variety of good mid-price options. You can eat in lively, modern surroundings – notably in Baldovino – or in the simple, old-fashioned trattoria-style restaurant typified by Benvenuto. Bars and cafés are also excellent, thanks to the fact that this part of the city has several emerging districts such as

Sant'Ambrogio that have seen the arrival of new bars, night-spots and interesting shops.

Acqua al Due $-$$

Acqua al Due has been a fixture of the Florentine culinary scene for more than 20 years, yet has managed to retain a reputation as one of the new breed of Florentine restaurants. Its ambience combines a pretty stone-walled medieval interior with a bright and lively atmosphere that owes more to a bar or pub than a restaurant. Traditional Tuscan and other Italian dishes are offered but in combinations that are modern with an innovative twist. Dishes might include *pasta alle melanzane* (pasta with eggplant), *tagliata alla arancia* (slices of beef with orange) and *penne ai quattro formaggi* (penne pasta with a four-cheese sauce). A good way to start your meal is with the *assaggi di primi*, a selection of tasters.

➕ 204 B5 ⊠ Via della Vigna Vecchia 40r ☎ 055 284170 🕐 Daily 7 p.m.–1 a.m. Closed for a week mid-Aug.

Alle Murate $$$

Alle Murate ranks among Florence's top restaurants – with Oliviero, Cibreo and the Enoteca Pinchiorri – but its cool and elegant approach can border on the aloof. The food is generally excellent, combining contemporary takes on Florentine classics with creative interpretations of other Italian and international dishes. Menus change frequently, but might include dishes such as stuffed pigeon, seafood ravioli or scampi with pancetta. You'll

probably encounter tastes here you won't have experienced before. Desserts are sublime, and the wine list – with about 150 mainly Tuscan wines – is good. The main dining area is recommended for a formal and sophisticated meal, but you can enjoy a similar if pared-down menu at around half the price in the separate Vineria, or wine bar.

➕ 205 D5 ⊠ Via Ghibellina 52–54r ☎ 055 240618 🕐 Tue.–Sun. 7.45–11.45 p.m.

Baldovino $-$$

If you're in a dilemma over where to eat lunch or dinner close to Santa Croce, look no further than Baldovino, an informal combination of the modern and traditional. Restaurateur David Gardener has combined good food, which ranges from Tuscan classics to Neapolitan pizzas, innovative salads and other novelties, with a bright, young staff, pleasant decor, and a convivial and cosmopolitan atmosphere. Dishes on the inspired menu might include fresh grilled fish, *tagliatelli agli asparagi* (pasta with asparagus) or *risotto al funghi di bosco* (risotto with wild mushrooms).

Reservations are strongly recommended, especially on Friday and Saturday.

➕ 205 D4 ☒ Via San Giuseppe 22r ☎ 055 241 773 ⌚ Daily 11:30–2:30, 7–11:30, Apr.–Oct.; Tue.–Sun. noon–2:30, 7–midnight, Nov.–Mar.

Beatrice $$–$$$

Few would dispute Beatrice's claim to have one of the city's most beautiful dining rooms (it has been used as a location in several films and Italian TV programs). If you want to dress up and enjoy a formal, romantic evening, then the restaurant's single large dining room with its superb wooden ceiling and extraordinary neo-Liberty stained glass is a good option. The menu includes such Tuscan specialties as *ravioli caserecci* (homemade filled pasta), *porcini* (cep) mushrooms and *bistecca alla fiorentina* (steak).

There is also a selection of fresh fish, and the wine list is especially good. Note that the dining room is entered through the lobby of the adjacent Hotel Cavour.

➕ 199 F1 ☒ Via del Proconsolo 31r ☎ 055 239 8123 or 055 239 8762 ⌚ Tue.–Sun. 7–11 p.m. Closed for a period in Aug.

Benvenuto $–$$

This is a basic trattoria with no-nonsense food – and decoration to match – that has been serving dependable Tuscan staples, such as *ribollita* (a thick vegetable soup) and *bistecca alla fiorentina* (Tuscan beef), on this street corner not far from Piazza della Signoria for as long as anyone can remember.

➕ 204 B4 ☒ Via della Mosca 16r, corner Via de' Neri ☎ 055 214 833 ⌚ Mon.–Sat. noon–2:30, 7:30–10:30

Cibreo $$$

If you don't want to pay Pinchiorri's prices (▶ 77) and don't want the formality of Alle Murate, then

Cibreo provides a happy medium. Many Tuscan gastronomes rate it Florence's best restaurant, thanks to its imaginative and constantly changing interpretations of traditional "peasant" Florentine food. Dishes include delicious soups of fish or mushrooms, *polenta alle erbe* (polenta with herbs), *baccalà* (salt cod) or a superb *ricotta e patate con sugo di carni bianche* (ricotta cheese and potatoes with a sauce of white meat juices). The dining area is simple – rustic tables and plain painted walls – and the service and atmosphere are informal. Prices are set for each course (and include service), but be sure to leave room for some of the excellent desserts. Lower prices can be found in the adjoining trattoria, known as the Vineria Cibreino, but the atmosphere here is somewhat muted. Don't forget the other parts of the Cibreo – the delicatessen and café (▶ 78). Making reservations several days in advance is essential for the main restaurant.

➕ 201 E1 ☒ Via de' Macci 118r ☎ 055 234 1100 ⌚ Tue.–Sat. 12:50–2:30, 7:30–11; closed Aug.

Danny Rock $

There's a young, lively and non-Florentine look and atmosphere to this modern-looking pub-restaurant-pizzeria. The pizzas, crepes, burgers and generous salads are of excellent quality, and prices are good, too. You can also eat or drink here late in the evening – if you do, you'll have plenty of company, for it's wildly popular with young visitors and Florentines alike. There's a long bar under an airy vaulted ceiling, plus places to sit outside in summer.

➕ 200 C1 ☒ Via Pandolfini 13r ☎ 055 234 0307 ⌚ Sun.–Fri. 7:15 p.m.–1 a.m., Sat. 7:15 p.m.– 2 a.m.

Enoteca Pinchiorri $$$

An *enoteca* is usually an inexpensive wine bar, but not here. Pinchiorri is Florence's best and most expensive restaurant, with one of the finest wine cellars in Europe. The prices for the highly refined and elaborate Italian dishes and international food are high – very high – while the service and the surroundings are uncompromising in their formality (men should wear a jacket and tie to feel comfortable). Yet there's nowhere better if you want the Florentine gastronomic treat of a lifetime

🗺 204 C5 ✉ Via Ghibellina 87
☎ 055 242 777 🕓 Tue.–Sat. 12:30–2, 7:30–10; closed Aug.

Osteria dei Benci $$

This is one of Florence's new breed of bright, informal restaurants, distinguished by a single attractive dining room painted in warm colors and with a pretty medieval brick vault. The staff are young, the service relaxed and the Tuscan food well-prepared and imaginative without being too daring. Dishes might include tasty vegetable soups and broiled meats (lamb in season is excellent). Menus change regularly to take advantage of season and availability of fresh produce.

🗺 204 B4 ✉ Via de' Benci 13r
☎ 055 234 4923 🕓 Mon.–Sat. 12:45–2:30, 7:45–10:45

Osteria del Caffè Italiano $$–$$$

This combination wine bar, restaurant and trattoria just west of Santa Croce offers a choice of dining experiences and prices. All three eating areas have distinctive medieval Florentine decor – terracotta floors, whitewashed walls and heavy beamed or vaulted ceilings – set in a restored 14th-century Palazzo Salviati. You can come here for a light lunch, a full meal or a glass of wine and snack at any time of the day. Food is typically Tuscan, whether it's salami and cheese or a main course of bistecca alla Fiorentina.

🗺 204 C5 ✉ Via Isole delle Stinche 11–13r ☎ 055 289 368 🕓 Tue.–Sun. 12:30–2:30, 7:30–11:30

Pizzaiuolo $–$$

Pizzaiuolo, opposite the chic Cibreo (▶ 77), has no pretensions to being other than what it is – a good, straightforward family-run pizzeria. The establishment has strong connections with Naples, birthplace of the pizza, and most Florentines rate the pizzas here as the best in the city. There are pastas and starters on the menu too, but the pizzas are what people come for: that and the lively atmosphere. The dining area is rustic, with huge beams and no-nonsense chairs and tables. Be certain to make reservations.

🗺 201 E1 ✉ Via de' Macci 113r
☎ 055 241 171 🕓 Mon.–Sat. 12:30–2:30, 7:30–midnight

BARS AND CAFÉS

Amon $

If you want a change from Italian food, try this moderately priced place, whose Egyptian-style frescoes provide a clue to the type of food available. Virtually all the snacks are based around pita bread and a variety of Arab and Middle Eastern fillings. Delicious cakes and sweet pastries are also available.

🗺 198 C2 ✉ Via Palazzuolo 28r
☎ 055 293 146 🕓 Tue.–Sun. noon–3, 6–11

Caffè Cibreo $

It's hard to think of a prettier café in Florence. The lovely wood-paneled interior dates from 1989 but it could just as easily have been lifted from somewhere at least 200 or 300 years older. Although the café is a distance from the city center, it is close to the Sant'Ambrogio market and is a civilized and cozy place, with the added incentive that snacks and cakes (including a famed chocolate torte with bitter orange sauce) come from the celebrated kitchens of the co-owned Cibreo restaurant nearby (▶ 77). There's outside dining for those long, hot summer days, but the street is not terribly pretty.

➕ 201 E1 ⊠ **Via Andrea del Verrocchio 5r** ☎ **055 234 5853** ⏰ **Tue.–Sat. 8 a.m.–1 a.m.**

Caffè Italiano $

After you visit the Uffizi, head to this stylish and little-known café just a few paces off the busy Via dei Calzaiuoli. You can stand in the pretty, wood-panel bar downstairs or while away a rainy afternoon in the cozy little hideaway of dark wood and red velvet seats upstairs. Light lunches – pastas, grilled meats, salads and similar tempting selections – are served 1–3.

➕ 203 F5 ⊠ **Via della Condotta 56r** ☎ **055 291 082** ⏰ **Mon.–Sat. 8–8**

Caffetteria Piansa $

If you've come this far north, you may well wish to push on to Cibrèo for your refreshment break (▶ 78). If not, this is a quiet place for cakes, snacks, sandwiches, self-service light meals, lunch and

coffee, for Piansa is a cafe outlet for one of the city's best coffee roasting and blending companies. Few visitors know about the place, which is generally only busy at lunch, when students and local office workers fill the wooden tables.

➕ 200 C1 ⊠ **Borgo Pinti 18r** ☎ **055 234 2362** ⏰ **Mon.–Sat. 8 a.m.–8:30 p.m.**

Cantinetta dei Verrazzano $

Cantinetta dei Verrazzano, a superb place in a central location just a few paces off Via dei Calzaiuoli, is ideal for a snack or light meal. When you walk in, all manner of sandwiches and other tasty delights such as pizza and focaccia (most freshly baked on the premises) immediately catch your eye under the huge glass-fronted display on your left. You can buy this food to take out or nibble on the bench by the door, or settle down for a more leisurely drink or meal in the café-wine bar to the rear. The place is owned by

the Castello di Verrazzano estate, one of Chianti's leading vineyards, so the wine here is also good.

➕ 199 F1 ⊠ **Via dei Tavolini 18-20r** ☎ **055 268 590** ⏰ **Mon.–Sat. 8 a.m.–9 p.m.; closed Aug.**

Enoteca Baldovino $

This mellow *enoteca*, or wine bar, lies just across the street from the co-owned Baldovino (▶ 76), and makes a perfect stop if you simply want a snack. Light meals (including some hot dishes), coffee and cakes are on offer, not to mention a wide selection of wines by the glass. Its stylish rooms have a bright, modern and vaguely Moorish look, thanks to the patterned tiles fronting the bar. The bar also sells an intriguing variety of excellent wines by the bottle and a selection of tempting oils, sauces and other foodstuffs.

➕ 205 D4 ⊠ **Via San Giuseppe 18r** ☎ **055 234 7220** ⏰ **Daily noon–midnight, Jun.–Sep.; Tue.–Sun. noon until late, Oct.–May**

Perchè No! $

Perchè No! (Why Not!) has been selling superlative ice cream since 1939 and provides central Florence's only serious rival to Bar Vivoli (▶ 73). The selection of flavors usually numbers more than 50, and varies according to the season.

➕ 199 F1 ⊠ **Via dei Tavolini 19r** ☎ **055 239 8969** ⏰ **Daily 10 a.m.– 1 a.m., but earlier closing in winter**

Rivoire $-$$

It's hard to resist settling down at one of Rivoire's outside tables over-looking Florence's principal square – Piazza della Signoria. When the café was founded in 1872, it specialized in hot chocolate, but these days most drinks are available. Prices are high and the food rarely more than average. But it's worth paying the high prices at least once just for the view.

➕ 203 F5 ⊠ **Piazza della Signoria 5r** ☎ **055 214 412** ⏰ **Tue.–Sun. 8 a.m.–midnight**

Where to... Shop

Shopping in eastern and central Florence requires a sense of adventure. Apart from one or two key streets with many varied shops – notably Via dei Calzaiuoli and Borgo degli Albizzi – this is an area of the city where the more individual and interesting stores are scattered far and wide. Some of the quirky, offbeat shops lie in the Sant'Ambrogio district, which is also home to a good local food market, surrounded by lively cafés and restaurants. It is also worth spending time exploring the streets around Santa Croce: here you'll find the occasional old-fashioned artisan's workshop.

DEPARTMENT STORES

Coin

Coin offers the best one-stop shopping in Florence, partly because it has a central location, and partly because the quality across its wide range of clothes, linens and other household goods is outstanding. Clothes include label and designer items, conservative Italian classics (for men and women), and younger and more modern fashion items in a dedicated area on the first floor. Towels, kitchenware and other household goods can be found in the basement. Note the Sunday hours, useful if you're in Florence for a long weekend.

✛ 199 E1 ⌧ Via dei Calzaiuoli 56r ☎ 055 280 531 Ⓖ Mon.–Sat. 9:30–8, Sun. 11–8

FOOD AND WINE

Pane & Co

This shop just south of the Bargello (▲ 62) sells a range of Tuscan breads, wines and other specialties; everything from the celebrated pecorino (sheep) cheeses of Pienza and San Gimignano to the *brutti ma buoni* (ugly but good) biscuits of Siena and the mountain hams of the Pratomagno region.

✛ 203 F5 ⌧ Piazza di San Firenze 5r ☎ 055 213 063 Ⓖ Daily 8–8 (except Sat. 8–1, Jun.–Aug.; Wed. 8–1 rest of year)

Pegna

Florentines have been visiting this temple to fine food in a little street just south of the Duomo since 1860. You can buy excellent cheeses, salamis, coffees, teas, olive oils, wines, cakes, chocolates and other gastronomic treats – 7,000 different items in all – from Italy and many other countries around the world.

✛ 199 F1 ⌧ Via dello Studio 26r ☎ 055 282 701 or 055 282 702; www.Pegna.it Ⓖ Mon.–Tue., Thu.–Sat. 9–1, 3:30–7:30, Wed. 9–1; closed Sat. afternoon in summer

HOUSEHOLD GOODS

Mazzoni

Mazzoni has been a byword in Florence for fabrics, linens, towels, pajamas, handkerchiefs and the like for more than 100 years. This central shop lies just off the busy Via dei Calzaiuoli and is one of the three Mazzoni outlets in the city.

✛ 199 E1 ⌧ Via Orsanmichele 14r ☎ 055 215153 Ⓖ Tue.–Sat. 9:30–1, 3:30–7:30, Mon. 3:30–7:30; closed Sat afternoon in summer

Mesticheria Mazzanti

Since 1930 Mazzanti has sold a colossal range of household and garden items, everything from nails, cleaning materials and flower pots to coffee-makers, cutlery and saucepans.

✛ 201 E1/F1 ⌧ Borgo La Croce 101r ☎ 055 248 0663 Ⓖ Mon.–Fri. 9–1, 3:30–7:30, Sat. 9–1

Patti & Co

This small shop sells interesting carpets, textiles, ceramics and other customers over the years have included Napoleon, writer Stendhal, composer Giacomo Puccini, opera diva Maria Callas and English poets Shelley and Lord Byron. All in their time have been beguiled by the company's exquisite pens, stationery, diaries and other items – actress Elizabeth Taylor once ordered blue-violet stationery to match her eyes.

✚ 203 E5 ⊠ Piazza della Signoria 13r ☎ 055 284655 ⏰ Tue.–Sat. 10–7:30

Zecchi

Artists won't be able to drag themselves away from this superb emporium just south of the Duomo, which sells every art-related raw material and accoutrement imaginable. It's worth a look even if you're not an artist or don't intend to buy.

✚ 199 F1 ⊠ Via dello Studio 19r ☎ 055 211470 ⏰ Mon.–Fri. 8:30–12:30, 3:30–7:30, Sat. 8:30–12:30

ethnic and exotic *objets d'art* from around the world.

✚ 200 B1/C1 ⊠ Borgo degli Albizi 64r ☎ 055 243610 ⏰ Tue.–Sat. 10–1, 3:30–7:30, Mon. 3:30–7:30

JEWELRY

Lapini

This historic shop is definitely a cut above most of Florence's many jewelers, as stones and jewelry here are of the very highest quality. Lapini uses the finest materials, often rare, and has unusual designs (both modern and traditional). The shop also sells a fascinating range of contemporary and antique watches.

✚ 199 F1 ⊠ Via de' Cimatori 34r ☎ 055 277 6452 ⏰ Mon.–Fri. 10–7, Sat. 10–1, Jul.–Aug.; Tue.–Sat. 10–7, Mon. 3–7, rest of year

Torrini

It's hard to argue with the reputation or quality of a jeweler that first registered its trademark –

a distinctive half clover-leaf with spur – as long ago as 1369. This is still one of the best places in Florence to buy jewelry, and gold jewelry in particular.

✚ 199 F2 ⊠ Piazza del Duomo 10r ☎ 055 230 2401 ⏰ Tue.–Sat. 9:30–1, 3:30–7:30, Mon. 3:30–7:30

MARKETS

Piazza dei Ciompi

The small collection of bric-à-brac stalls at Florence's flea market, or Mercato delle Pulci, in Piazza dei Ciompi, just north of the Casa Buonarroti (▶ 74), is modest by the standards of most city flea markets. However, it becomes more worth a visit on the last Sunday of each month, when a larger bustling antiques market fills the piazza and crowds into the many surrounding streets.

✚ 201 D1 ⊠ Piazza dei Ciompi, off Via Pietrapiana ☎ No phone ⏰ Mon.–Sat. 9–7

Sant'Ambrogio

Sant'Ambrogio is the city center's main food market after the Mercato Centrale (▶ 111), but looks and feels more like a neighborhood market than its bigger and more central rival. It mostly serves the residents of the surrounding Sant'Ambrogio and Santa Croce districts. It is also becoming the focus of a rejuvenated quarter that's home to small specialist stores, cafés and restaurants. One such is Arte Alimentare Meridionale at Piazza Lorenzo Ghiberti 33 (tel: 055 2342696), which specializes in fresh mozzarella and other southern Italian foods.

✚ 201 E1 ⊠ Piazza Lorenzo Ghiberti, off Via de' Macci ⏰ Mon.–Sat. 7–2

PAPER AND STATIONERY

Pineider

Pineider is Italy's – and possibly Europe's – ultimate stationery maker, founded in 1774. Its

Where to...
Be Entertained

Eastern Florence contains the headquarters of several of the city's major orchestras and classical music associations, as well as several of its trendiest bars, its best jazz club and one or two of its most popular clubs.

CLASSICAL MUSIC

Tuscany's regional orchestra, the **Orchestra Regionale Toscana**, has its headquarters at Via de' Benci 20 (tel: 055 242 767 or 055 234 7355) and offers concerts (main season Dec.–May) at the nearby **Teatro Verdi** (Via Ghibellina 101, tel: 055 212 320 or 055 239 6242). Tickets are available from the Teatro Verdi box office or the Box Office ticket agency outlets (▲ 46).

Florence's official city orchestra, the **Filarmonica di Firenze "Giacchino Rossini,"** performs at various venues during its main season (Jan.–Feb.), but also presents a series of outdoor concerts in Piazza della Signoria in summer months. Consult tourist information centers for details (▲ 39). The **Orchestra da Camera Fiorentina**, or Florence Chamber Orchestra (Via Enrico Poggi 6, tel: 055 783 374; www.videosoft.it/orchest) is based in the north of the city, but performs regular concerts in the central church of **Orsanmichele** (▲ 72). Tickets are available from the number above, from Box Office outlets (▲ 46), or from Orsanmichele an hour before each performance. The **Amici della Musica**, one of the city's leading classical music associations, is based at Via G Sirtori 49 (tel: 055 608 420 or 055 607 440), but organizes concerts at the Teatro della Pergola (Via della Pergola 18, tel: 055 247 9651) – built in 1656 and reputedly Italy's oldest surviving theater – northeast of the Duomo.

JAZZ

For a different sort of music, head for the long-established and informal **Jazz Club** (Via Nuova de' Cacciani 3, tel: 055 247 9700, closed Mon. and Jun.–Sep.), scene of live jazz most nights; it is located in a tiny side street a block south of Via degli Alfani at the corner of Borgo Pinti. You need to buy a "membership" as a formality to enter the club, which is based in a medieval cellar.

NIGHTCLUBS

You'll hear occasional live music at **Pongo** (Via Verdi 57r, tel: 055 234 7880, opening hours vary, usually Thu.–Sat. 10 p.m.–3 a.m., closed Jun.–Sep.). It's better known as an unpretentious club that has no dress code, good music, and a refreshingly relaxed air. Not as good is the area's other main club, **Full-Up** (Via della Vigna Vecchia 23–25r, tel: 055 293 006, open Tue.–Sat. 11 p.m.–4 a.m., closed Jun.–Sep.), which has a small dance floor and mainstream music. A more hip set head instead for **Maramao** (Via de' Macci 79r, tel: 055 244 341, open Tue.–Sat. 11 a.m.–2 a.m.), a sleek disco (arguably the city's trendiest) that changes its look frequently but is never less than cutting edge. If this sounds too intimidating, relax in the nearby, ever-popular **Rex Café** (Via Fiesolana 23r, tel: 055 248 331, open daily 5 p.m.–2:30 a.m.; closed Jul.–Aug.), easily the best of the bars in eastern Florence, for an early evening drink or small-hours nightcap. The interior looks striking and alarming – lots of mosaics, mirrors and strange lamps – but the atmosphere and clientele are easy-going.

Northern Florence

In Two Days 86 – 87
Don't Miss 88 – 101
At Your Leisure 102 – 107
Where To 108 – 112

Getting Your Bearings

This noble district was once home to the Medici family, long-time rulers of Florence who commissioned the greatest architects of the time to create such landmarks as the Palazzo Medici-Riccardi (the first Medici residence and seat of political power), the churches of San Marco and San Lorenzo, and lavish Cappelle Medicee, the last resting place for generations of Medici grand dukes.

The Duomo, one of the world's largest cathedrals and the first port of call for most visitors, lies at the heart of the district. As you explore the surrounding streets, you'll frequently catch glimpses of its multicoloured marble cladding and the massive dome that dominates the entire city.

★ Don't Miss

At Your Leisure

Above right: Detail of the ceiling frescoes in the Sala di Luca Giordano, Palazzo Medici-Riccardi

Today, the area around San Marco (once leafy, open countryside beyond the city walls, well-suited to the needs of the monks of San Marco and Santissima) is a lively student quarter, full of good bars, restaurants and the huge, colorful San Lorenzo market. It is also home to Florence's most celebrated resident – Michelangelo's *David* – the original resides in the Galleria dell'Accademia.

Previous page: Michelangelo's *David*, in the Galleria dell'Accademia

Right: Piazza della Santissima Annunziata, considered one of the city's most elegant squares

From churches, museums and viewpoints to lively markets, cafés and wine bars, this area embraces some of the city's most spectacular sights.

Northern Florence in Two Days

Day One

Morning

Start your day at the striking **Museo dell'Opera del Duomo** (below, ➤ 103), and spend a couple of hours admiring the many treasures from the Duomo, Campanile and Battistero that are sheltered here for safekeeping.

Sit at one of the café-terraces edging the traffic-free Piazza del Duomo and marvel at the monstrous proportions of the mighty marble-coated Duomo (➤ 88–94), then explore its vast interior.

Lunch

Head north to the district of San Lorenzo. Buy a picnic at the Mercato Centrale (➤ 111) to eat on the steps of San Lorenzo, or grab a light lunch at Trattoria Mario (➤ 109) or Trattoria Sergio Gozzi (Piazza San Lorenzo 8, tel: 055 28194, open only for lunch).

Afternoon

The plain, unfinished facade of **San Lorenzo** (➤ 95–97) belies the many artistic and architectural jewels within. Be sure to see the Sagrestia Vecchia, then join the lines of people waiting to enter the dazzling **Cappella dei Principi,** made entirely of marble inlay, and the **Sagrestia Nuova,** with its celebrated Michelangelo sculptures.

Evening

Return to the Duomo and climb the dome (right) for a bird's-eye view of the city at sunset. Remember to take plenty of film for your camera.

Day Two

Morning

The simple, spiritually uplifting masterworks of Fra Angelico (below) housed in the monastery of **San Marco** (➤ 100–101) provide a gentle start to the day. Once you're within the peaceful cloisters, you'll see why American novelist Henry James said of Fra Angelico, "Immured in his quiet convent, he never received an intelligible impression of evil."

The nearby **Museo dell'Opificio delle Pietre Dure** (➤ 105), a workshop and museum of marble inlay, provides a fascinating insight into this unique Florentine art, and makes the craftsmanship in the Cappella dei Principi (➤ 96) seem all the more remarkable.

Lunch

You'll be spoiled with the choice of inexpensive, cheerful cafés around here as this is the heart of the university quarter.

Afternoon

After lunch, while away a couple of hours at the **Galleria dell'Accademia** (➤ 98–99). Established in 1563 with Michelangelo among its founders, the world's oldest art school is today home to a priceless collection of fine art, including Michelangelo's *David*.

Then, make your way down Via Cavour to the **Palazzo Medici-Riccardi** (➤ 104–105). The building was to set the standard for Renaissance villas throughout Europe, and the tiny chapel within, adorned with richly colored frescoes, is a little-known jewel of the Medici crown.

Evening

Enjoy an early evening aperitif at one of the district's traditional wine bars, Zanobini (Via Sant'Antonino 47r) and Casa del Vino (Via dell'Ariento 16r) are both highly recommended. Then round off your day with some traditional Tuscan fare at Antichi Cancelli (Via Faenza 73r, tel: 055 218 927, open Tue.–Sun. 11–3, 7–midnight), one of the most popular trattorias in town.

Duomo, Campanile di Giotto and Battistero

The Duomo (Cathedral) was the grandest building project ever undertaken in Florence, and the vast russet-colored dome that dominates the cityscape is considered the greatest engineering feat of the Renaissance. At the time of its construction, the dome aroused disbelief and delight. Today, visitors still marvel at this magnificent creation "which soars to the sky and has a shadow wide enough to cover all the people of Tuscany" (Leon Battista Alberti, architect).

Work on the Duomo was begun by the city architect Arnolfo di Cambio in 1296, at a time when medieval Florence was at the height of major political, economic and urban expansion. The Republic wanted it to be one of the largest cathedrals in Christendom, "a building of the highest and most sumptuous magnificence so that it is impossible to make it better or more beautiful with the industry and power of man." They weren't disappointed: the result was the world's fourth largest church (after St. Peter's, Rome; St. Paul's, London; and the Duomo in Milan). Its sheer size was typical of the Florentine desire for supremacy. To this day it remains the tallest building in the city.

Building Stages

The Duomo was conceived as a vast, covered piazza where the entire church-going population of Florence could assemble. It has a capacity of more than 20,000 people. Various buildings were demolished (including the old

---

🔲 199 F2　✉ Piazza del Duomo
☎ Dome and Campanile: 055 230 2885; Duomo: 055 294 514
🕐 Duomo: Mon.–Fri. 10–5, Sat. 10–4:45, Sun. 1:30–5. Services daily 7:30, 8:30, 9, 9:30, and 10:30 a.m., noon, 6 and 6:30 p.m.
Dome: Daily 8:30–7. Last tickets at 6:20
Campanile: Daily 8:30–7:30. Last tickets at 6:50

Battistero: Mon.–Sat. noon–6:30, Sun. 8:30–4, Jul.–Sep.; Mon.–Sat. 8:30–7, Oct.–Jun. Masses on weekdays at 10:30 and 11 a.m. Crypt: Mon.–Sat. 10–5
🚌 Many routes including 1, 6, 14, 17, 23, 36 and 37
💰 Dome: moderate. Campanile: moderate. Battistero: inexpensive. Crypt: inexpensive

Brunelleschi's dome – one of the architectural wonders of the world

Above left: Statue on the Duomo's marble-clad facade

Vital Statistics

Duomo Length: 505 feet
Width: 125 feet at the aisles;
300 feet at the transept
Dome Height: 350 feet
including the lantern
Diameter: 140 feet
Campanile Height: 280 feet

Church of Santa Reparata) to make room for
it, entire forests provided timber, and huge
slabs of marble were transported along the
Arno river in flotillas. Its foundation stone was
laid in 1296, but it took more than 100 years
to complete.

Arnolfo died soon after the project started
and Giotto took over as city architect. He,
however, devoted most of his time to the
Campanile (► 92), and as a consequence

Frescoes depicting the Last Judgement decorate the interior of the dome

work on the Duomo ceased for almost 20 years. By 1418, the massive base was in place, but the problem of how to construct the dome to cover it remained unresolved.

Finally, a competition was organized to find a solution. The prize, a princely sum of 200 gold florins (more than a skilled craftsman could earn in two years of work), attracted proposals from craftsmen, masons and cabinet-makers from all over Europe. One of the many bizarre ideas put forward was to build a mound of earth and coins over which the dome could be molded; then the citizens of Florence would be free to gather up the coins and take the earth away with them at the same time! Eventually, Florence's own architectural genius, Filippo Brunelleschi, came up with the successful design.

Brunelleschi's Dome

Brunelleschi made it his life's work to find a solution to this architectural puzzle, and the erection of the world's largest masonry dome was to be his most extraordinary and daring achievement. The key to his success lay in his revival and adaptation of classical building techniques – which by the 15th century were largely forgotten and to this day are not fully understood. Combining this knowledge with both medieval and Renaissance principles, he built the dome up by setting stones and bricks of varying sizes and densities in a self-supporting herringbone pattern – a technique copied from the Pantheon in Rome.

Brunelleschi involved himself in every detail of the construction, from the baking of the bricks to the invention of a complex rainwater drainage system. New tools and devices had to be created: for example, to enable bricks to be raised such considerable heights, he called in a group of clockmakers to design a series of hoists and pulleys that were powered by a pair of horses.

One of the principal difficulties that Brunelleschi faced in construction was to ensure that the dome was built with the correct curvature in every phase of the work so that it would ultimately converge at the center. To prevent the dome from buckling under its own weight, he designed a series of wooden rings to encircle the dome in the same way that iron hoops contain the staves of a barrel. These rings were invisible, buried in the dome's masonry.

It was this vision – of a massive dome that seemed to rise heavenward without any visible means of support – that both inspired and frustrated everyone involved with the project until its eventual completion in 1436, 16 years after construction had begun.

The small, octagonal lantern erected on top of the dome (again by Brunelleschi) completed his creation. One of the highlights of any visit to the Duomo is the climb up to it, via the steps between the inner and outer skins of the dome. At over 300 feet, it offers the loftiest panorama of the city.

The Interior

Inside, the cathedral is gloomy and plain, as many of its finest art-works were removed to the Museo dell'Opera del Duomo (▶ 103) in the 19th century. Brunelleschi wanted the interior of the dome to be decorated with mosaics, but in the 16th century it was decided that a painting of the Last Judgement by Giorgio Vasari and Federico Zuccari would be more appropriate. The result is undeniably beautiful but somehow rather too gaudy for Brunelleschi's simple, rational design.

The apse consists of four tribunes and three

The Pigeon Loft
Before entering the Duomo, look up at the dome and you'll see there is a ring around its base – an arcaded gallery – which suddenly stops. It is said that Michelangelo strolled past and remarked "What's that? A pigeon loft?" That same day work ceased and the gallery was never completed.

After the lavish facade, the Duomo's interior is surprisingly austere

minor apses, each crowned by a miniature copy of the dome and housing five chapels. The 15th-century stained glass is by Brunelleschi's great rival, Lorenzo Ghiberti.

A stairway in the aisle near the south door leads down to the crypt, which contains the excavated remains of the fifth-century Church of Santa Reparata, a bookshop and, behind an iron grille, a plain stone slab inlaid in the floor, inscribed "The body of a man of great genius, Filippo Brunelleschi, Florentine."

Campanile di Giotto

Beside the Duomo stands the elegant, square Campanile (bell tower), designed by Giotto in 1334 but not completed until 22 years after his death by Andrea Pisano and Francesco Talenti. Most of the Campanile's original sculptures and reliefs are now housed in the nearby Museo dell'Opera del Duomo (► 103).

Although the Campanile is not as high as Brunelleschi's dome, it nevertheless affords spectacular views of the Florentine rooftops from its summit. It is sheathed in ornate white, green and pink Tuscan marble. The neo-Gothic facade of the cathedral (added in the late 19th century) echoes its style but lacks its finesse and charm.

There is a climb of 414 steps to the terrace atop Giotto's campanile

Battistero

The Duomo is partnered by the Battistero (Baptistery), one of Florence's most important religious establishments and the oldest building in the city. It is dedicated to its patron saint, John the Baptist. According to medieval legend, a Roman temple to Mars, the pagan god of war, once stood here, later becoming a Christian church. Today's building – a characteristic example of Tuscan Romanesque style – dates from the 11th century and was used primarily for baptism ceremonies which, in those days, took place just twice a year. The exterior is clad in white and green marble, and its octagonal shape is said to symbolize the "eighth day" or "eternity."

The Baptistery's most famous features are its three sets of **bronze doors.** The **south doors,** designed

Top: Detail of
Ghiberti's door
panel *Moses
Receives the Ten
Commandments*

Above: Admiring
the *Gates of
Paradise*

by Andrea Pisano between 1330 and 1136, are the oldest. The 28 reliefs portray scenes from the life of St. John the Baptist.

Over a century later, to mark Florence's deliverance from the plague that struck Tuscany, the Guild of Cloth Merchants decided to commission another set of doors. To find an artist, a competition was staged, and leading craftsmen, including rivals Brunelleschi and Ghiberti, submitted trial bronze panels depicting Abraham's sacrifice of Isaac (now housed in the Bargello, ► 62–65). Much to Brunelleschi's consternation, he and Ghiberti won the commission jointly. Working together was not a proposition that Brunelleschi could countenance and he promptly gave up sculpture (leaving Ghiberti to work on the doors alone) and concentrated on outdoing him in architectural skill.

Ghiberti began work on the **north doors**, which depict scenes from the life of Christ, in 1403. They were so well received when they were finally completed in 1424 that he was commissioned to design another set of bronzes for the **east doors.** Ghiberti took nearly 30 years to complete these but the end result was a triumph of design, dubbed the **"Gates of Paradise"** by Michelangelo. The panels demonstrate the artistic ideas that led to the Renaissance: they are set in square frames and the buildings depicted in the 10 Old Testament scenes are in a new classical architectural style and show a confident line of perspective. Today's east doors are actually modern copies, but you'll find some of the original panels in the Museo dell'Opera del Duomo (► 103).

At the time of its construction, the **Baptistery's dome** was the largest in Europe. Its interior, covered in glittering mosaics created by Venetian craftsmen, with assistance from Giotto and Giovanni Cimabué, represented a dazzling display of Florence's wealth. The centerpiece shows Christ welcoming the arisen dead into heaven with his right hand and condemning damned souls to hell with his left hand. Beside him are the Apostles, Mary and John the Baptist, with angelic choirs above. Below the ensemble, the history of the world is portrayed in 59 scenes. The stories progress horizontally, starting above the entrance door: the highest band shows *The Creation*; the next is *The Life of Joseph*; then *The Life of Christ*; while the lowest band represents *The Life of John the Baptist*.

Sculptural detail adorning the Campanile

TAKING A BREAK

You'll find no airs and graces at **Le Mossacce** (Via del Pronconsolo 55r, tel: 055 294 361), a tiny local café with wooden tables, paper placemats and hearty home cooking.

DUOMO, CAMPANILE AND BATTISTERO: INSIDE INFO

Top tips Take binoculars with you to study the mosaics inside the Baptistery.
• Neither the dome nor the Campanile has an elevator. The dome has **463 steps** and the **Campanile 414.** Unless you're feeling particularly energetic, choose one or the other and climb it either early in the morning before it gets too hot or at sunset for spectacular photos. The dome is the more interesting (and higher) climb, as you get an insight into its construction and a bird's-eye view of the cathedral, but it usually has the longer line. Both offer **breathtaking views of the city** and its surrounding girdle of hills.
• Inside the Baptistery, ask for the free, highly informative **audio guide.**

One to miss The ruins of the **Church of Santa Reparata** in the crypt are confusing, and unless you are particularly interested, it is not worth paying to see them.

Hidden gems Domenico di Michelino's painting in the left aisle of the Duomo depicts Dante, Florence's greatest poet. *The Divine Comedy* was once read out loud to large, enthusiastic crowds in the cathedral.
• Look for Paolo Uccello's ***Clock for the Canonical Hours*** (1443), to your right as you enter the Duomo. It goes counterclockwise.
• In the Battistero, the **tomb of Baldassare Cossa** (deposed Pope John XXIII), sculpted by Donatello and Michelozzo, is one of the earliest Renaissance wall tombs (1421–27).
• The large **octagonal font** in the Battistero is where many famous Florentines, including Dante, were baptized.

San Lorenzo and the Cappelle Medicee

After the Duomo, San Lorenzo is the city's second most important church. Founded in the fourth century, the original church served as Florence's cathedral for 400 years. In the early 15th century it became the official church of the Medici family and was entirely rebuilt to designs by Brunelleschi. The facade remains unfinished to this day, despite various proposals, including one by Michelangelo.

Previous page:
Piazza di San
Lorenzo, site of
a popular daily
market

Brunelleschi's elegant interior is one of the supreme master-pieces of the early Florentine Renaissance. It is based on Gothic architectural principles, with a cross-shaped plan and three aisles, but has elements that later became typical features of Renaissance buildings: rounded arches, a coffered central ceiling, and *pietra serena* (gray sandstone from the quarries of Fiesole, ➤ 8–9). The treasure trove of precious artworks contained here was financed mainly by the Medici family. The Sagrestia Vecchia (Old Sacristy), also by Brunelleschi, is an architectural gem, consisting of a geometrically perfect cube topped by a dome. The apsidal ceiling represents the celestial hemisphere, showing the passage of the sun between the constellations above Florence on the night of July 4, 1442.

The cloisters lead to the Medici's great Biblioteca Laurenziana

(Laurentian Library), housing one of the world's most important collections of Italian manuscripts and featuring Michelangelo's highly original *pietra serena* staircase, formed of three separate flights.

Cappelle Medicee

The Cappelle Medicee (Medici Chapels), the family mausoleum of the Medici, consists of three distinct parts, the crypt, the Cappella dei Principi and Sagrestia Nuova.
The remarkable **Cappella dei Principi (**Chapel of the Princes) was begun in 1604 and took 300 years to complete. It consists entirely of marble and precious stones, painstakingly pieced together by craftsmen of the Opificio delle Pietre Dure (➤ 105).

The opulent
Cappella dei
Principi

San Lorenzo
🚼 199 E2
✉ Piazza di San Lorenzo
☎ 055 216 634
🕐 Church: daily 7:30–11:50, 3:30–5:40. Services: Mon.–Sat. 8, 9:30 and 10 a.m., Sun. 8, 9:30 and 11 a.m. and 6 p.m.
Sagrestia Vecchia: Mon., Wed., Fri.–Sat. 10–11:45, Tue. and Thu. 4–5:45.
Biblioteca Laurenziana: Sat. 2–7:30, Sun. 8:30–1:30
🚌 Many routes including 1, 6, 14, 17 and A
💷 Free

Cappelle Medicee
✉ Piazza Madonna degli Aldobrandini
☎ 055 238 8602
🚌 Many routes including 1, 6, 14, 17 and A
🕐 Daily 8:30–5, public holidays 8:30–1:50; closed first, third and fifth Mon. and second and fourth Sun. of the month. Last entry 30 mins before closing; the chapel is locked at 4:40
💷 Expensive

The end result was so spectacular that the Medici family used the chapel (intended as a mausoleum) to receive foreign ambassadors and hold marriage ceremonies.

A narrow corridor leads to the **Sagrestia Nuova** (New Sacristy), designed by Michelangelo along similar lines to Brunelleschi's Old Sacristy, to house the Medici tombs. With clever use of white marble and dark gray stonework, he created an appropriately solemn atmosphere. Michelangelo also produced some of his finest, most famous sculptures for the tombs, including the monumental funerary figures of **Night** (a young woman asleep) *and* **Day** (a strong, muscular man whose face is roughly hewn), and, on the opposite side of the sacristy, ***Dawn and Dusk,*** who together symbolize the passage of time.

Night and Day, Michelangelo's celebrated tomb statues in the Sagrestia Nuova

TAKING A BREAK

At lunch time, try **Palle d'Oro** (Via Sant'Antonino 45r, tel: 055 288 383) and choose between a quick snack at the bar, a sandwich to take away or a meal in the simple restaurant at the back.

SAN LORENZO AND THE CAPPELLE MEDICEE: INSIDE INFO

Hidden gems In the nave of the church, look for the *bronze pulpits,* depicting scenes from Christ's Passion and Resurrection. These were the last works of Donatello.

• *The Martyrdom of St. Lawrence* (1659), in the north aisle, is a vast Mannerist fresco by Bronzino (Agnolo di Cosimo Tori).

• *St. Joseph and Christ in the Workshop* by Pietro Annigoni (1910–88), at the end of the north aisle, is notable as one of few modern works to be seen in Florence.

• Today, the *Marriage of the Virgin* altarpiece (1523) by Rosso Fiorentino is used for the blessing of engagement rings. Fiorentino later left Florence to live and work in France.

• Michelangelo's *Madonna and Child* (1521) in the Sagrestia Nuova is considered one of his most beautiful statues.

Galleria dell'Accademia

Florence's Academy of Fine Arts was founded in 1563 as the first school in Europe devoted to teaching the techniques of drawing, painting and sculpture. Its art collection was formed in the 18th century to provide students of the academy with inspirational models.

Nowadays, everyone comes here to see *David* (1501–04), the city's most celebrated sculpture. Created by Michelangelo from a single block of marble when he was just 29 years old, the 13-foot masterpiece established him as the foremost sculptor of his time. As Giorgio Vasari remarked: "There has never been seen a pose so fluent, or a gracefulness equal to this, or feet, hands and head so well-related to each other with quality, skill and design." The statue shows David in meditative pose preparing for his fight with Goliath – a young man aware that the salvation of his people depends upon him and his skill, rather than in the traditional pose of triumph (with one foot on the severed head of the defeated giant). Placed in Piazza della Signoria (▶ 60–61) on completion, *David* soon became a symbol of civic pride and liberty for the Florentine Republic. Amid growing concerns that he was losing his balance and leaning forward, *David* was eventually moved to the Accademia in 1873 for safekeeping. It was a massive undertaking: streets were widened, arches demolished, and the move took 40 men five days to accomplish.

Facing page: *David* – a legend in marble

Below: Michelangelo's *Quattro Prigioni*, four dramatic *non-finito* works

Other classic works by Michelangelo include the dramatic *Quattro Prigioni*, four muscular *non-finito* men struggling to free themselves from the stone. It was intended for the tomb of Pope Julius II. The Accademia is not, however, just the "Museum of Michelangelo," so be sure to see the rest of the collection, including such treasures as Pacino di Buonaguida's *Tree of Life* (1310); Taddeo Gaddi's reliquary cupboard panels showing *Stories of Christ and St. Francis of Assisi* (1330–35) from Santa Croce; and (on the second floor) Jacopo di Cione's 14th-century embroidered altar frontal showing *The Coronation of the Virgin* from Santa Maria

🔢 200 B3
✉ Via Ricasoli 58–60
☎ 055 294 883

🕐 Tue.–Sat. 8:30–6:50, Sun. 8:30–7
Last tickets 30 min. before closing
🚌 1, 6, 11 and 17
💶 Expensive

GALLERIA DELL'ACCADEMIA: INSIDE INFO

In more depth Look for Giovanni di Scheggia's *Cassone Adimari*, an elaborately painted wooden chest dating from the 15th-century. Originally part of a bride's trousseau, it is covered with scenes depicting daily life in Florence.

• In Lorenzo Monaco's painting *Christ in Pietà* note the symbols of the Passion story: Pilate washing his hands (under the cross on the left); thirty pieces of silver, the ear of Malchus and the torch symbolizing Christ's arrest (under the cross on the right); St. Peter's denial (top left) and Judas's kiss (top right).

Novella. Finally, the 19th-century gallery contains plaster busts of key figures: Machiavelli, Dante, Byron, Liszt.... See how many you can identify.

TAKING A BREAK

A good choice for lunch is **Trattoria Mario** (► 109), where you can enjoy authentic Tuscan food.

San Marco

The monastery of San Marco is one of the most spiritually uplifting places in Florence. Fra Angelico, who lived and worked here, provided much of the decoration, and the beautiful, faded frescoes are some of his most important works. His use of pale colors and local landscapes as backdrops gives the paintings a mystical serenity. Fra Bartolomeo, St. Antonio (Bishop of Florence) and the religious fanatic Girolamo Savonarola also spent time here.

A church and convent stood on this site since the 13th century. In 1437 Cosimo de' Medici commissioned Michelozzo to enlarge them to house the Dominican monks from nearby Fiesole. In the 1580s the dark, lofty church was rebuilt, and a new facade by Agostino Nobili added some 200 years later.

But it is Fra Angelico's frescoes that are San Marco's real draw. As soon as you enter the first cloister in the museum, you see one of his most important frescoes, the ***Crucifixion with St. Dominic*** (Dominic can be identified by his white habit and black cape, typical of the order).

The door to the right of the entrance leads to a small gallery devoted to Fra Angelico's work. After World War I, all of his Florentine paintings were amassed here, including the ***Deposition*** (1432), containing a portrait of Michelozzo (the figure in the black hood behind Christ) and the ***Linaiuoli Tabernacle*** (1433), the most frequently reproduced of all his paintings. His magnificent ***Crucifixion*** fresco, which graces an entire wall of the chapter house, is unusual in that it contains figures not alive at the time of Christ, among them St. Dominic and St. Francis.

Continue up to the second floor to the dormitory. Fra Angelico's inspired ***Annunciation*** (1442), a masterpiece of Renaissance perspective, greets you at the top of the stairs. Beyond lie 44 tiny cells, which form the backdrop

The Church of San Marco, beside the monastery complex

➕ 200 B4
✉ Piazza di San Marco
☎ 055 238 8608 or 055 239 6950
🕐 Church: daily 7–noon, 4–8. Services Mon.–Sat. 7:30 a.m. and 6:30 p.m., Sun. 10:30 and 11:30 a.m., 12:30 and 6:30 p.m. Museo di San Marco: Mon.–Fri. 8:30–1:50, Sat.–Sun. 8:30–6:50; closed first, third and fifth Sun. and second and fourth Mon. of the month
🚌 Major intersection – many routes including 1, 7, 25, 33 and C
💶 Moderate

for a celebrated series of devotional frescoes; one per cell to aid the monks in meditation.

Fra Angelico used azurite and gold in his harmonious painting, *The Annunciation*

TAKING A BREAK

Directly opposite San Marco, **Ristorante Accademia** (Piazza San Marco 7r, tel: 055 217 343) is a lively trattoria serving simple Florentine dishes. The *menu del dia* is particularly good value.

SAN MARCO: INSIDE INFO

Top tips Arrive early to **beat the crowds,** and begin your visit on the second floor to appreciate the solitariness of the monks' cells.
• Allow at least **2 hours** in the museum.

Hidden gems In the first-floor gallery, look for the **35 scenes from the Life of Christ** by Fra Angelico. These masterpieces, originally cupboard panel decorations, are remarkably intricate in their design.
• Don't miss Domenico Ghirlandaio's *Last Supper* in the refectory (to the left of the stairs to the second floor).

In more depth Among the most beautiful of the **cell frescoes** are *The Deposition* (cell 2); *The Annunciation* (cell 3); *The Crucifixion* (cell 4); *The Transfiguration* (cell 6); *The Mocking of Christ* (cell 7); and *The Coronation of Mary* (cell 9).
• Cells 12–14, **Savonarola's quarters** when he was prior, contain various mementos and a portrait by Fra Bartolomeo.
• In cells 38–39, which were kept for **Cosimo il Vecchio** when on retreat, look for the *Adoration of the Magi* fresco.

At Your Leisure

1 Loggia del Bigallo

It's easy to miss the Loggia del Bigallo, an exquisitely carved Gothic porch on the corner of Piazza di San Giovanni and Via del Calzaiuoli. It was constructed in the 14th century for the Misericordia, one of Florence's great charitable confraternities, which still runs an ambulance service and has its headquarters in the square.

For years, the loggia served as a kind of lost-property office for unwanted babies. Abandoned children were displayed here for three days and if their parents didn't come forward to claim them within that time, they were sent to foster homes. In the 15th century, the Misericordia merged with a similar charitable concern called the Bigallo.

Today, a small gallery (open only during Christmas festivities) houses various works of art accumulated by both organizations, including Bernardo Daddi's fresco of the *Madonna della Misericordia* (1342), containing the earliest-known view of Florence.

🔢 199 E2 ✉ Piazza di San Giovanni
🚌 36, 37 🎟 Free

2 Museo di Firenze com'era

If possible, make this small museum one of your first ports of call. You will see the development and urban transformation of Florence from the Renaissance to the end of the 19th century, portrayed through a comprehensive series of maps, drawings, models, paintings and prints.

The museum is housed in a former convent surrounding a grassy courtyard near the Duomo. Its finest exhibits include the famous Pianta della Catena (Chain Map, 1470) showing a detailed panorama of the city (the original is in Germany); the exquisite lunettes (1599) by the Flemish artist Giusto Utens, cataloging all the Medici

The Medici *Villa di Cafaggiolo* lunette by Giusto Utens

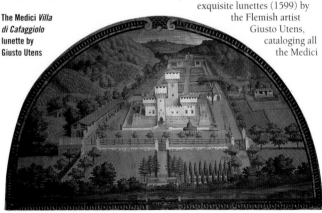

villas and gardens; and *Views of the City* by Giuseppe Zocchi, which provides a vivid impression of Florentine street life during the 18th century.

One room is devoted to the drawings of Giuseppe Poggi, the city architect who planned to remodel much of central Florence during its brief spell as the capital of Italy (1865–71). Fortunately, international opposition halted his schemes, but not before the 14th-century walls had been destroyed (together with numerous medieval buildings) to make way for Piazza della Repubblica (➤ 127).

🕂 200 C1 ✉ Via dell'Oriuolo 24
☎ 055 261 6545 🕓 Mon.–Wed., Fri.–Sat. 9–2, Sun 8–1 🚍 14, 23 and A 💷 Inexpensive

❸ Museo dell'Opera del Duomo

The Cathedral Works Museum, in a striking modern building just behind the Duomo, contains many precious items removed from the Duomo, Campanile and Battistero for purposes of preservation. Most notable are the Lorenzo Ghiberti panels from the Baptistery doors (➤ 92–93), which are displayed in the main courtyard (where Michelangelo carved *David*).

The first floor contains 14th-century sculptures from the facade of the Duomo, including an

The treasures housed in the Museo dell'Opera del Duomo once adorned the cathedral

unusual *Madonna and Child* by Arnolfo di Cambio, better known as the *Madonna with the Glass Eyes*. Halfway up the first flight of stairs is a beautiful *Pietà*, sculpted by Michelangelo when he was almost 80. It is an especially significant work as it was meant for his own tomb. He portrayed himself in the figure of Nicodemus, a sculptor and one of the two men who removed Christ from the cross.

Farther upstairs, you'll find sketches and models of different facades proposed for the Duomo, showing the change in architectural taste from the 15th to the 19th century. There is also a model of the dome and a picture of King Victor Emmanuel II laying the first stone of the present facade in 1860, together with his trowel and various other Duomo memorabilia. Brunelleschi's funeral mask (1446) and a reconstruction of his work-yard, showing the wooden scaffold-ing and types of tools he used, are also on display.

🕂 200 B2 ✉ Piazza del Duomo 9
☎ 055 230 2885 🕓 Mon.–Sat. 9:30–6:30, Sun. 8–2 🚍 14 and 23 💷 Moderate

6 Palazzo Medici-Riccardi

The innovative style of this massive palazzo, home to the Medici family for nearly 100 years, marked a turning point in Renaissance architecture. Within its bulky walls lies the Cappella dei Magi, one of Florence's most beautiful chapels, adorned with brilliantly colored frescoes.

Cosimo il Vecchio (the Elder), founder of the great Medici dynasty, had a passion for building and is considered among the great innovators of the Renaissance movement in Florence. Having dismissed Brunelleschi's original designs for the palace as too showy, he commissioned his favorite architect, Michelozzo di Bartolommeo Michelozzi, to build a more discreet symbol of his power. Michelozzi's rustic design, featuring large, rough-hewn blocks of stone, became the model for other Renaissance palaces.

During the time that the palace served as the Medici family home (1444–1540), the family gradually deprived the old Republican aristocracy of its power. The Duomo and the

Inside the vast Sala di Luca Giordano in the Palazzo Medici Riccardi

Palazzo Vecchio (key symbols of Republican Florence) diminished in importance, while the Medici palace became prominent as the real seat of political power. Nowadays, the Palazzo Medici-Riccardi (incorporating the later owner's name) houses offices of the Town Prefecture.

The **Cappella dei Magi** is the palace's greatest treasure. Its richly colored frescoes showing the *Journey of the Magi* were probably commissioned by Cosimo's eldest son, Piero the Gouty, and painted by Benozzo Gozzoli between 1459 and 1463. Set in an idealized Tuscan landscape, they have an almost fairy-tale quality, with magical scenes of exotic birds, animals, kings and castles. You can identify members of the Medici family by their ostrich-feather emblem – on the right wall, Piero's son, Lorenzo the Magnificent (on the central white horse), is followed by Cosimo (on another white horse), with Piero (hatless) between them, then his brother Lorenzo (in a conical hat, also riding). The artist can be seen in the crowd following the king, with his name inscribed on his small red cap. The Cappella dei Magi is hard to find. Proceed to the first courtyard, enter the door immediately to your left, then climb the stairs to the third floor, where a small door on the left will lead you into the chapel.

Only two more rooms in the palazzo are open to the public. The Sala di Luca Giordano on the second floor, with its lavish gilt stucco work, painted mirrors and chandeliers, is named after the Neapolitan artist who frescoed the ceiling with a splashy baroque *Apotheosis of the Medici*. In an adjoining room, you'll find a demure *Madonna and Child* painting by Filippo Lippi, which was once the altarpiece of the palace chapel.

➕ 199 F2 ✉ Via Cavour 1 ☎ 055 276 0340 🕓 Mon.–Tue., Thu.–Sat. 9–1, 3–6, Sun. 9–1 🚌 1, 6 and 17 💷 Moderate

⑦ Museo dell'Opificio delle Pietre Dure

The Medicis were the first to promote Florence's special craft of producing inlaid pictures by using *pietre dure* (marble and semi-precious stones). Ferdinando I de' Medici founded the Opificio in 1588 as a workshop for the craftsmen working on the family mausoleum – the Cappella dei Principi (► 96) – and the city's most spectacular example of the craft. Now located in the former convent of San Nicoló, the Opificio delle Pietre Dure is a national institute for the teaching of this ancient and unique Florentine art.

A small museum on the premises contains an exquisite collection of different marbles, tools of the trade, and a dazzling display of items – cabinets, tables, vases, picture frames, even portraits of the Medici grand dukes – all made with semi-precious stone inlay or *scagliola* (made with painted plaster rather than costly marble).

➕ 200 B3 ✉ Via degli Alfani 78 ☎ 055 265 111 🕓 Mon., Wed.–Sat. 8:15–2 (also second Sun. of the month), Tue. 8:15–7 🚌 C 💷 Inexpensive

⑩ Giardino dei Semplici

Although somewhat unkempt, the Semplici Gardens, Florence's botanical garden hidden off the popular tourist track beyond San Marco, provides a tranquil and rare green space. The gardens were founded in 1545 by Cosimo I de' Medici to grow herbs and other *semplici* (raw ingredients) used by medieval apothecaries in the preparation of medicines. Today it forms part of the University of Florence, containing about 7,000 species of plants. It is especially stunning in springtime.

➕ 200 C4 ✉ Via Micheli 3 ☎ 055 275 7402 🕓 Mon.–Fri. 9–1 🚌 1, 7 25, 33 and C 💷 Moderate

Left: Ornamental *pietre dure* work dating from the 17th century

Renaissance frescoes grace Santissima Annunziata's Cloister of the Votive Offerings

decoration by Giovanni Battista Foggini. The entrance porch was added to the church in 1601 and decorated by up-and-coming young artists Pontormo, Fiorentino, Baldovinetti and Sarto.

Outside, the piazza is considered among the city's most elegant squares, frequently described as "an extended Renaissance courtyard." An equestrian statue of Duke Ferdinando I by Giambologna graces the center of the square, together with two Mannerist bronze fountains. Each year a fair is held here to celebrate the Feast of the Annunciation (March 25), and on the Feast of the Rificolona (September 7) Florentines parade through the city with colorful paper lanterns to give thanks to the Madonna of Santissima Annunziata.

➕ 200 C3 ✉ Piazza della Santissima Annunziata ☎ 055 239 8034 🕐 Daily 7–12:30, 4–6:30 🚌 6, 31, 32 and C 🎟 Free

🔟 Santissima Annunziata

The most striking thing about this church is the feeling that you've entered it at the wrong end, as half the pews face the doorway!

Immediately to your left, above the silver altar, is one of the city's most venerated shrines – a painting of the Virgin Mary. The story says that in 1252 a monk, struggling to paint the Virgin's face, fell asleep and on waking found the fresco had miraculously been finished by an angel.

The church's interior, with its mass of colored marble, gilt and frescoed side chapels, is magnificent. The Feroni Chapel (Cappella Feroni) in particular (first on the left) is considered a jewel of Florentine baroque, with

🔢 Museo Archeologico Nazionale

The remarkable collections of ancient art in the Archeological Museum provide a refreshing change from the glut of Florentine Renaissance art. They include Italy's most important Etruscan artifacts and its second most important Egyptian collection. The museum was badly damaged during the 1966 flood (➤ 28–29), and numerous items are not yet on display.

This vase, one of the exhibits in the Museo Archeologico Nazionale, depicts the battle between the centaurs and the Greek lapiths

measurement (the slender columns are equal in height to the width of the arches), and enhanced by the alternation of light plaster and dark ribbing. The charming ornamental rondels by Andrea della Robbia on the facade show babies wrapped in swaddling clothes.

Open to visitors are two elegant cloisters and a gallery of paintings donated by benefactors of the orphanage, including Ghirlandaio's *Adoration of the Magi*, once in the adjoining church.

🕂 200 C3 ⊠ Piazza della Santissima Annunziata 12 ☎ 055 249 1708 🕐 Cloisters and Gallery: Mon.–Tue., Thu.–Sat. 8:30–2, Sun. 8:30–1. Last tickets 30 min. before closing 🚌 6, 31, 32 and C 📋 Inexpensive

Brunelleschi's arcaded loggia at the Spedale degli Innocenti, a beautiful example of Classical design

Star exhibits include an Egyptian chariot made of wood and bone (14th century BC, found near Thebes); the François vase, depicting scenes from Greek mythology (570 BC, found in an Etruscan tomb near Chiusi); and the Etruscan bronze chimera (fifth century BC), a peculiar mythical creature with a lion's body, a goat's head and a serpent for a tail.

🕂 200 C3 ⊠ Via della Colonna 38 ☎ 055 23575 🕐 Mon.–Fri. 9–7, Sat. 9–2, Sun. 2–7. Last entry 30 min. before closing 🚌 6, 31, 32 and C 📋 Moderate

🔟 Spedale degli Innocenti

Europe's first orphanage – the Hospital of Innocents – was founded here in 1445, following the delivery of Agatha Emerald on January 25. From that day forth, mothers could place unwanted children anonymously on the *rota* (a rotating stone wheel) here and ring the bell. The stone was then turned around and the child was taken in. Spedale degli Innocenti is still run as an orphanage, and there are offices of the United Nations Children's Fund, UNICEF, on the premises.

The building, designed by Filippo Brunelleschi, is a prime example of restrained classical design. The arcaded loggia is based on the repetition of the exact same

Where to...
Eat and Drink

Prices

Expect to pay per person for a meal, excluding drinks and service
$** under €20.65 **$$** €20.65–€41.31 **$$$ over €41.31

Northern Florence is an area with a wide choice of inexpensive cafes and restaurants, thanks to a large student population and the presence of the Mercato Centrale, the city's principal food market, which provides a focus for cheap trattorias and bars aimed at shoppers and market traders.

Blue Anchor $

The Blue Anchor has been described as a "Scottish bistro" (many Italians are enthusiasts for all things Scottish) and its decor does feature the odd splash of tartan. In truth, it is a rather good and easy-going bar-bistro that sells cakes, snacks and light meals, which include a variety of non-Italian dishes such as succulent roast beef, salmon, kedgeree, apple crumble and a delicious carrot cake. The selection of beers is especially good, too.

+ 199 E3 ☒ **Piazza del Mercato Centrale 44r** ☎ **055 265 4029** 🕑 **Wed.–Mon. 11 a.m.–1.30 a.m.** (also Fri.–Sat. 1:30 a.m.–2:30 a.m.)

Caffèlatte $

Caffèlatte is somewhat out on a limb, but it makes a convenient stop for coffee, cakes and snacks if you're close to Piazza Santissima Annunziata (▶ 106). Much of the produce is organic or has a healthy bias and a lot of the baking is done on-site. The walls are hung with contemporary art or used for exhibitions, and the old tables, covered with newspapers and magazines for customers to read, create an informal atmosphere.

+ 200 C2 ☒ **Via degli Alfani 39r** ☎ **055 247 8878** 🕑 **Mon.–Sat. 8 a.m.–midnight, Jan.–Nov.; daily 8 a.m.–midnight, Dec.**

Casa del Vino $

The Casa del Vino, or House of Wine, is just that – a place to come to drink or buy wine. It is often busy, thanks to its location close to the Mercato Centrale, but usually only with locals rather than visitors. You can choose wine to buy by the bottle to take home, or wash down crostini (toasts) or panini (rolls) at the bar with one of many wines available by the glass.

+ 199 E3 ☒ **Via dell'Ariento 16r** ☎ **055 215609** 🕑 **Mon.–Fri. 9–2, 4:30–8, Sat. 9–2**

Fiaschetteria $

A *fiaschetteria* is a traditional wine bar, a place that sells wine by the glass and an inexpensive selection of snacks, pastas and simple hot meals. This place is especially popular at lunch time, when it fills up with students. The dish of the day is usually good value for money.

+ 200 B3 ☒ **Via degli Alfani 70r, corner of Via dei Servi** ☎ **No phone** 🕑 **Mon.–Sat. 9–7**

Gradisca $

A simple bakery and shop that sells a wide variety of sandwiches, rolls and other breads with a good selection of fillings. Perfect for a take-out lunch or snack.

+ 200 A3/C5 ☒ **Via San Gallo 107r** ☎ **055 470 386** 🕑 **Mon.–Fri. 10:30–3, 5:30–9, Sat. 10:30–3; closed mid-Jul.–early Sep**

Nerbone $

There's no restaurant or café in Florence more authentic than this tiny place in a busy corner of the Mercato Centrale. Market traders and local shoppers crowd its tables and counters, filling up on a selection of tasty snacks and simple hot lunch dishes (pastas, stews, soups), whose range and recipes have been tried and tested since the place opened in 1872.

🚹 199 E3 ⊠ Mercato Centrale
☎ 055 219 949 ⓦ Mon.–Sat.
7–2

Taverna del Bronzino $$$

This is northern Florence's fashionable and expensive option, an elegant place with vaulted ceiling and terra-cotta floors. It has been around for years, but still seduces the great and the good (local and international alike) with its charming setting and refined regional cuisine – the meats and fresh fish are excellent. The regular menu is full of Florentine and Tuscan

staples such as *bistecca alla fiorentina*, but the daily menu is often more creative and adventurous. You might be able to sample imaginative and mouthwatering dishes such as *rombo al forno con olive* (oven-cooked turbot with olives) or *rigatoni al ragù bianco d'anatra* (pasta with duck sauce). The restaurant is located north of the city center, near the Museo di San Marco (▶ 100).

🚹 199 F5 ⊠ Via delle Ruote 25r
☎ 055 495 220 ⓦ Mon.–Sat.
12:30–2:30, 7:30–10:30;
closed Aug.

Trattoria Mario $

Mario is a Florentine institution that makes few concessions to interior decor or stylish dining. It's a rough and ready eating place just north of the Mercato Centrale that provides inexpensive, authentic and good-quality Tuscan food (lunch only) to students, shoppers and market traders.

You'll find tripe on Mondays and

Thursdays, fish on Fridays and just one pudding week-round – *cantucci* with *vin santo* (biscuits with dessert wine).

🚹 199 E3 ⊠ Via Rosina 2r-Piazza del Mercato Centrale ☎ 055 218
550 ⓦ Mon.–Sat. 12:30–3; closed
Aug.

Zanobini $

Zanobini is much like its neighbor, the Casa del Vino (▶ 108). It's a simple wood-paneled wine bar patronized almost entirely by locals (a good recommendation). Its local popularity is despite the fact that Zanobini lies just off streets filled with visitors crowding the San Lorenzo market (▶ 111). It makes a good place to eat a hunk of bread with cheese or salami and drink a glass of wine. There's also a good selection of wines by the bottle to buy in the back room.

🚹 199 E3 ⊠ Via Sant'Antonino 47r
☎ 055 239 6850 ⓦ Mon.–Sat. 8–2,
3:30–8; closed public holidays

Zà-Zà $

This long-established, once low-key place is in a convenient location, close to the Mercato Centrale. Za-Za is now patronized by the rich and famous, such as King Juan Carlos of Spain, U.S. actor Bill Cosby, and super-models Naomi Campbell and Linda Evangelista. Chances are you'll have to wait patiently for a table at busy times. You can see the appeal, however: low prices (you choose from one of several tempting set-price menus); a rustic stone dining room lined with pictures and fascinating old photographs (there is a larger eating area downstairs); and good, expertly cooked, basic food. Try the justifiably celebrated hot antipasti or the tasty *crostini* (toasts) with taleggio cheese, oil, pepper and vinegar.

🚹 199 E3 ⊠ Piazza del Mercato
Centrale 26r ☎ 055 215 411
ⓦ Mon.–Sat. noon–11, Easter–Oct.;
Mon.–Sat. noon–3, 7–11, Nov.–Easter

Where to... Shop

Shopping in northern Florence is dominated by two adjacent markets: the Mercato Centrale, a superlative covered food market, and San Lorenzo, a general street market selling clothes, leather and other goods. Individual shops of note are thinner on the ground, though the district is home to excellent bookshops and fine food and wine outlets.

BOOKS

Feltrinelli

Feltrinelli belongs to a nationwide chain of bookshops. Invariably busy, its various floors are filled not only with Italian titles, but also a sprinkling of English and other foreign-language books – though the sister store, Feltrinelli Internazionale, is a better bet for such titles. This branch just west of the Duomo has a particularly good selection of guides and maps in English and Italian.

➕ 199 E2 ☒ Via Cerretani 30r
☎ 055 238 2652 ⊛ Mon.–Sat. 9–7:30, Sun. 10–1, 2:30–7:30

Feltrinelli Internazionale

A short walk from the Duomo, this specialist branch of the excellent Feltrinelli chain of bookshops deals in English and other foreign-language titles, as well as maps, guides, magazines and good art and photography sections. It's a good place to buy the useful *Firenze Spettacolo* listings magazine (▲ 46).

➕ 199 F2 ☒ Via Cavour 12–20r
☎ 055 219 524 ⊛ Mon.–Sat. 9–7:30

Paperback Exchange

This secondhand bookshop at the northern end of Via Fiesolana is a good place to come if you run out

of vacation reading. It has a particularly good selection of English titles with an art, art history or Italian connection, and – as the name suggests – offers an exchange scheme for old paperbacks.

➕ 200 D2 ☒ Via Fiesolana 31r
☎ 055 247 8154 ⊛ Mon.–Fri. 9–7:30, Sat. 10–1, 3:30–7:30; closed Sat. afternoon Jul.–Aug.

FOOD AND WINE

Brunori

This tremendous bakery sells bread in just about every size, shape and type imaginable, as well as rolls, *focaccia*, pizza and other items ideal for picnics.

➕ 200 C1 ☒ Borgo Pinti 16r
☎ 055 248 0809 ⊛ Thu.–Sat. and Mon.–Tue. 8–1, 3:30–8, Wed. 8–1; closed Sat. afternoon in summer

I Sapori di Chianti

Although you'd be hard pressed to beat the food and wine available in the Mercato Centrale (▲ 111), this

small shop offers a more manageable selection of high-quality wines, grappas, oils, honey, hams, cheeses, preserves and other gourmet products from the celebrated Chianti region. Most products are attractively packaged, making this a good place to come for gifts to take home.

➕ 200 B2 ☒ Via dei Servi 10r
☎ 055 238 2071 ⊛ Daily 9:30–7:30

Robiglio

Robiglio is an old-fashioned *pasticceria*, or cake and pastry shop, with three outlets in Florence: this is the main one. It makes an elegant place to enjoy tea, coffee and other drinks – the hot chocolate is superb. It also sells exquisite cakes, many of which make excellent gifts to take home or eat elsewhere. Another central Robiglio outlet can be found just south of the Duomo on Via de' Tosinghi (tel: 055 215 013).

➕ 200 C3 ☒ Via dei Servi 112r
☎ 055 214 501 or 055 212 784 ⊛ Mon.–Sat. 7:30–7:30

Stenio del Panta

This fine delicatessen has been in business for several generations. It sells a wide range of food, but is best known for its many forms of preserved fish (salt cod and tins of tuna, sardines, anchovies). Sales assistants will also make up sandwiches with a filling of your choice.

🗺 199 E3 ☒ Via Sant'Antonino 49r
☎ 055 216 889 🕐 Mon.–Fri.
7 a.m.–7:30 p.m., Sat. 7–1, in summer;
Tue.–Sat. 8–7:30, Mon. 4–7:30, in winter

HOUSEHOLD

Bartolini

Bartolini was founded in 1921 and has become such a fixture that locals refer to the junction where it stands as the "Bartolini corner." It sells just about every item of kitchenware you could wish for, as well as fine china, porcelain and glassware from some of the best names worldwide (Alessi, Spode, Wedgewood, Riedel and so on).

🗺 200 B2 ☒ Via dei Servi 30r,
corner of Via Bufalini ☎ 055 289
223; www.dinobartolini.it 🕐 Tue.–Sat.
9–1, 3:30–7:30, Mon. 3:30–7:30

Giraffa

This shop offers a good selection of ceramics, fabrics, lamps, candle-holders and other similar products for the home.

🗺 199 E3 ☒ Via de' Ginori 20r
☎ 055 283 652 🕐 Mon.–Fri. 10–1,
3:30–7:30, Sat. 10–1, in summer;
Tue.–Sat. 9–1, 3:30–7:30, Mon.
3:30–7:30, in winter

La Ménagère

Founded in 1901 and run by the same family since 1921, this shop offers several floors of superb glassware, china, porcelain, furniture and many other irresistible contemporary and classic designer items for the home and office.

🗺 199 E2 ☒ Via de' Ginori 8r
☎ 055 213 875 🕐 Tue.–Sat. 9–1,
3:30–7:30, Mon. 3:30–7:30

MARKETS

Mercato Centrale

Florence's magnificent central food market deserves almost as much attention from visitors as the city's museums and galleries. Opened in 1874, it is Europe's largest covered food hall, a wonderful stone, iron and glass building designed by Giuseppe Mengoni, the architect responsible for Milan's celebrated covered shopping galleries. The market's upper level is devoted mostly to fruit and vegetables – the huge swathes of color and wonderfully fresh food provide a mouthwatering spectacle. On the first floor, stalls display cheese, ham, meats, dried goods, olive oils, pasta and a cornucopia of other basic and gourmet foodstuffs. This is a great place to come for treats and gifts to take home, for picnic provisions or for snacks and light meals in places such as Nerbone (▶ 109), but if you want to buy wine, you should visit wine bar-shops such as Zanobini or the Casa del Vino (▶ 108).

🗺 199 E3 ☒ Piazza del Mercato
Centrale ☎ No phone 🕐 Mon.–Sat.
7–2 (also Sat. 4–8 p.m. in winter)

San Lorenzo

The San Lorenzo market fills the area around the Church of San Lorenzo. Many stands sell mid-price leather jackets, shoes, ties, purses, luggage, T-shirts and inexpensive clothing. The quality of the leatherware can be surprisingly good, and prices correspondingly high given that this is a market. At the same time, the competition for buyers means you may be able to haggle over prices, but be warned that the vendors are hard-nosed. Note that goods are priced lower at the weekly market in Cascine Park (▶ 134). The streets can be uncomfortably crowded, with pickpockets operating, so keep your valuables safe.

🗺 199 E2 ☒ Via dell'Ariento–Piazza
di San Lorenzo–Via Canto de' Nelli
☎ No phone 🕐 Daily 7 a.m.–8 p.m.

Where to...
Be Entertained

Northern Florence may attract a sizable daytime population of students and visitors, but its nightlife is relatively quiet as most people prefer to head east or across the river to the Oltrarno. The area does have a handful of places to listen to live music or enjoy a late drink, as well as one or two churches and auditoria where you may catch a classical recital.

JAZZ AND FOLK

Classical, jazz and other musical recitals are occasionally held in the **Lyceum** (Via degli Alfani 48, tel: 055 247 8264). Churches such as San Lorenzo and the Duomo also sometimes host concerts, choirs or organ recitals – for details check with tourist information centers (▶ 39) or keep your eyes peeled for posters outside the venues.

For folk, solo musicians and other small-scale concerts, head for **Chiodo Fisso** (Via Dante Alighieri 16r, tel: 055 238 1290, open daily 7 p.m. until late) just south of the Duomo. Don't be put off by its low-key exterior – the club's been around for years and the music is good.

NIGHTCLUBS

If you want to dance, hunt out the **Apollo Bar** (Via dell'Ariento 41, tel: 055 215 672, open Mon. 9–9, Tue.–Sat. 7 p.m.–2 a.m., Sun. 5 p.m.–2 a.m.), a club and disco in the street on the western edge of the Mercato Centrale. It's cramped and the music is often too loud to hold any real conversation, but still attracts a hip Florentine crowd.

Nearby, **Caracol** (Via de' Ginori 10r, tel: 055 211 427, open Tue.–Thu., Sun. 5:30 p.m.–1:30 a.m., Fri.–Sat. 5:30 p.m.–2:30 a.m.) is a lively South American-style bar with a special line in tequila – happy hour (5:30–7 p.m.) is especially busy. There's little in the way of seating, so this is not the place for a restorative drink after a bout of sightseeing: think of it more as a good place to start an evening on the tiles.

For equally cheap and cheerful drinking in far from sophisticated surroundings, try the **Gap Café** (Via dei Pucci 5a, tel: 055 282 093, open daily 7 a.m.–1 a.m.; closed Mon. in Aug.) a few steps north of the Duomo. Its popularity has more to do with low prices and late hours than any intrinsic atmosphere. Close by the Duomo, **Genesi** (Piazza del Duomo 20r, tel: 055 287 247, open Tue.–Sun. 9 p.m.–2 a.m.) is rather more upscale. There's a basement bar – usually decorated in a fairly outrageous style – and a more comfortable and sedate first-floor bar. The latter usually has live jazz most evenings. Prices for drinks are higher than elsewhere.

Somewhere that doesn't have to worry about a high-rent central location is **Tenax** (Via Pratese 46, tel: 055 308 160), which lies out in the northern suburbs near Peretola airport. This large, long-established disco and live music club is one of the city's most celebrated nightspots. It's worth the trip on the nights when there is live music if you want to catch good local bands or the occasional big-name international act. See listings in newspapers or posters around the city for details of forthcoming events. At other times DJs, music – everything from house to Latin – and theme-nights change nightly. There is plenty of room, with lots of bars and seating.

Sᵛˢ THOMAS DE AQVITO

Getting Your Bearings

This is the oldest, most eclectic district of Florence. Traces of Roman *Florentia* can still be seen, together with the ancient grid of medieval lanes – today graced by the impressive buildings of the city's Renaissance heyday when the wealthiest families vied to create the most beautiful palazzi, churches and monuments.

This area stretches from the main train station, a rare example of modern architecture in town, to the Ponte Vecchio, the oldest bridge in Florence and a veritable jewel in its crown. Between these two extremes, you'll find a mixed bag of attractions. Santa Maria Novella, for example, is one of the city's largest and most prestigious churches, overflowing with sacred art; Palazzo Davanzati provides a fascinating insight into the luxurious lifestyles of medieval merchants; while grandiose café-lined Piazza della Repubblica harks back to Florence's brief spell as capital of Italy.

It is also among the best shopping districts, with the likes of Gucci, Prada and Bulgari in Via de' Tornabuoni – the city's prime shopping street.

Left: The western district boasts the finest in Florentine fashion

★ Don't Miss
2 Santa Maria
  Novella ➤ 118
7 Ponte Vecchio ➤ 122

At Your Leisure
1 Officina Profumo-Farmaceutica di
  Santa Maria Novella ➤ 126
3 Ognissanti ➤ 126
4 Palazzo Strozzi ➤ 127
5 Piazza della Repubblica ➤ 127
6 Mercato Nuovo ➤ 128
8 Palazzo Davanzati ➤ 128
9 Santa Trinita ➤ 129

Stazione
Centrale di
Santa Maria
Novella PIAZZA DELLA
STAZIONE

PIAZZA
DELL'UNITÀ
ITALIANA

Cappellone
degli
Spagnoli **2** Santa Maria
Novella

VIA DE' PANZANI

VIA DE' GIGLIO

Museo di
Santa Maria
Novella

VIA
DELLA
SCALA

1
Officina
Profumo -
Farmaceutica
Santa Maria
Novella

PIAZZA
SANTA MARIA
NOVELLA

VIA D BANCHI

Ognissanti

PALAZZUOLO

PIAZZA
OTTAVIANI

PIAZZA
ANTINORI

VIA DE' VECCHIETTI

VIA DE' CALZAIUOLI

NISSANTI

BORGO
OGNISSANTI
A VESPUCCI

VIA DE FOSSI

VIA D SPADA

VIA DE' TORNABUONI

**Piazza
della
Repubblica**

VIA D STROZZI **5** VIA D CORSO

PIAZZA
C GOLDONI

VIA D VIGNA NUOVA

4
Palazzo
Strozzi

VIA DE'
SASSETTI

VIA DEI

PONTE ALLA CARRAIA

LUNGARNO CORSINI

**Santa
Trinita**
9

PIAZZA
S TRINITA

VIA PORTA ROSSA

VIA D CONDOTTA

8

6

PIAZZA DELLA
SIGNORIA

Arno

PONTE SANTA TRINITA

**Palazzo
Davanzati**

**Mercato
Nuovo**

VIA POR SANTA MARIA

LUNGARNO GUICCIARDINI

VIA DI SANTO SPIRITO

LUNGARNO ACCIAIUOLI

Galleria
degli
Uffizi

BORGO SAN JACOPO

**Ponte
Vecchio** **7**

Corridoio
Vasariano

Top left: Early evening on
the Ponte Santa Trinita

Previous page: Stained-glass window
depicting St. Thomas Aquinas in Santa
Maria Novella

0   200 metres
0   200 yards

Spend a couple of hours admiring the treasures of Santa Maria Novella and Santa Trìnita, indulge in some serious shopping at the designer shops at Via de' Tornabuoni and stroll across the Ponte Vecchio, one of the city's most celebrated landmarks.

Western Florence in a Day

10:00 a.m.

Allow plenty of time to visit the Gothic church of **Santa Maria Novella** (▶ 118–121). It contains an astonishing wealth of sacred treasures, including some of the most important works of art in Florence (frescoes in the Spanish Chapel, left). The adjoining **Museo di Santa Maria Novella** (▶ 121) in the cloisters is also worth a glimpse.

11:30 a.m.

Relax with a coffee in one of the popular cafés fringing **Piazza della Repubblica** (▶ 127), an imposing square centered on a bombastic arch. It was laid out as part of the grandiose plans to remodel Florence during the city's brief stint as the nation's capital. Pause awhile and consider how different Florence might have looked today had architect Giuseppe Poggi been allowed to continue with his plans, which would have destroyed a large number of Florence's finest buildings.

12:00 noon

No visit to Florence is complete without indulging in some shopping. After all, this is the home of such legendary names as Gucci and Ferragamo (▶ 24–27 and 135). You'll find everything in this part of town from top couturiers to markets, including a flower market on Thursday mornings under the portico in Piazza della Repubblica. In the narrow lanes, look out for local artisans who continue Florence's tradition of fine craftsmanship. Their skills range from textile-making and pottery production to stone-cutting and restoration work.

1:30 p.m.

Head to the small but frenetic **Mercato Nuovo** (➤ 128) and join local market-workers in a traditional lunch of *trippa* (tripe). Or try Caffè Gilli in nearby Piazza della Repubblica.

3:00 p.m.

Continue your shopping spree as you head down the crowded Via Por Santa Maria to marvel at the **Ponte Vecchio** (above, ➤ 122–125), one of the most picturesque sights in Florence. Aglitter with jewelry shops, the bridge you see today presents a scene that has hardly changed since 1593.

4:00 p.m.

Take time to visit the church of **Santa Trìnita** (➤ 129). Compared to Santa Maria Novella, it receives surprisingly few visitors, yet it contains one of Florence's most fascinating frescoes – *Scenes from the Life of St. Francis* by Domenico Ghirlandaio. As with many Renaissance frescoes, important personages of the era can be identified within the painting, but here Ghirlandaio goes one step further and includes several Florentine landmarks, including the church itself.

5:30 p.m.

You should have time for a bit more shopping in Via de' Tornabuoni (➤ 132–135), the most elegant street in Florence. The glamorous window displays lining this majestic avenue are a delight to behold, but take a look at the prestigious palaces – the former homes of wealthy Renaissance bankers and merchants. There are also several tempting tearooms along the way.

8:00 p.m.

Round off the day with dinner at Oliviero (➤ 131), where you can enjoy innovative Tuscan cuisine.

Santa Maria Novella

The strikingly beautiful Gothic church of Santa Maria Novella contains some of Florence's most important artworks by such masters as Giotto, Brunelleschi, Domenico Ghirlandaio and Filippino Lippi, while the adjoining cloisters form a fascinating museum of precious frescoes.

Right: the elegant facade of Santa Maria Novella

The mighty church you see today had very humble beginnings. In 1221 Dominican friars established a small chapel called Santa Maria delle Vigne (of the vines) set among vineyards beyond the city walls, but with a large open space in front of it, ideal for preaching to large congregations. In 1278 two friars, Fra Sisto and Fra Ristoro, started to convert the original chapel into the largest monastery complex in Florence. The buildings were completed in the mid-14th century and the church was consecrated in 1420, but the delicate marble facade remained incomplete until 1458, when architect Leon Battista Alberti was commissioned to finish it. Rather than start anew, he cleverly blended the existing Gothic elements with new Renaissance features – such as the two large volutes (spiral scrolls) in the upper section of the facade designed to conceal the side chapel roofs – creating an elegant and well-balanced whole.

The Interior

The interior of Santa Maria Novella is one of the finest examples of Florentine Gothic architecture. Light and lofty, it was designed not only for silent meditation but also as a meeting place for large congregations. At first glance, the nave appears to be exceptionally long, but this is an optical illusion, created by spacing the pillars closer together as they approach the chancel. The walls were once smothered by frescoes, but many were lost in the 16th century when the interior was whitewashed and the windows shortened to make way for side chapels.

Halfway down the left aisle you'll find one of the church's most influential works of art – Masaccio's pioneering canvas *Trinità* (1427). In the center is Christ on the Cross, at the bottom are the Madonna and St. John, and at

The Piazza
In 1563 Cosimo I de' Medici initiated horse and carriage races in the spacious piazza outside the church. The obelisks supported by bronze turtles, which stand at either end of the square, marked the turning points of the race track.

✚ 198 C2
✉ Piazza di Santa Maria Novella
☎ Church: 055 210 113 or 055 215 918. Museo di Santa Maria Novella: 055 282 187
🕐 Church: Mon.–Sat. 7–noon, 3:30–6, Sun. 3:30–5.
Museo di Santa Maria Novella: Mon.–Thu. and Sat. 9–2, Sun. 8–1
🚌 Many routes including 6, 11, 12, 36, 37 and A
💰 Inexpensive

the top God the Father with the Holy Spirit in the form of a dove beneath his beard. The two extra figures in the bottom corners are members of the Lenzi family, who commissioned this work of masterful perspective.

Continue to the raised **Cappella Strozzi** in the left transept. The 14th-century frescoes here were based on Dante's epic poem, *The Divine Comedy*. At the center is the **Last Judgement,** on the left *Paradise* and on the right **Hell.** Dante himself is portrayed in the Paradise fresco amid angels, saintly figures and members of the Strozzi family.

The sanctuary's main chapel, the **Tornabuoni Chapel** (behind the high altar), was financed by the Tornabuoni family, following the Black Death of 1348. Giovanni Tornabuoni was the uncle of the great Medici Grand Duke

Ghirlandaio's magnificent frescoes in the Tornabuoni Chapel provide an insight into life in 15th-century Florence

Lorenzo the Magnificent. The frescoes (1485–90) here by Domenico Ghirlandaio include *Scenes from the Life of the Virgin* (on the left wall) and *Scenes from the Life of St. John the Baptist* (on the right). They also provide an invaluable record of life in Florence in the 15th century, with portraits of important dignitaries and the blatant glorification of the Tornabuoni family (shown worshipping on the far wall). Their representation in the frescoes, combined with the fact that they were related to the Medici, so outraged Girolamo Savonarola (► 13) that he condemned the cycle as an example of frivolous and profane art.

The next chapel to the right – **Cappella de Filippo Strozzi** – contains further dramatic frescoes (1489–1502) by Filippino Lippi, one of Florence's earliest Mannerist painters. The chapel's stained-glass window is also attributed to him.

Museo di Santa Maria Novella

The cloisters form a small museum
with a separate entrance alongside the
church. It has two main attractions: the
Cappellone degli Spagnuoli (Spanish
Chapel) and the **Chiostro Verde**
(Green Cloister), named after the
greenish hue of Paolo Uccello's fading
frescoes of the early 15th century. The
Spanish Chapel was built as the chapter house of the monastery, but in the
16th century, Eleonora of Toledo, wife
of Cosimo I, designated it a place of
worship for her Spanish entourage.
The walls are completely covered in
frescoes by Andrea di Bonaiuto (known
as Andrea da Firenze), exalting the role
of the Dominicans in the struggle
against heresy. In one section they are
portrayed as hounds of God (in Latin
Domini canes, a pun on the order's
name), leading their followers, the
stray sheep, back to the fold.

The dramatic
frescoes in the
Spanish Chapel
portray themes
of salvation and
damnation

The decoration of the chapel represents one of the largest
painted areas of the late 14th century. As the influential writer
and critic John Ruskin wrote: "It will literally seem to you one
of the grandest places roofed without a central pillar that you
ever entered. And you will marvel that human daring ever
achieved anything so magnificent."

TAKING A BREAK

Buca Mario (Piazza Ottaviani 16r, tel: 055 214 179) is a
hugely popular restaurant in the cellars of an ancient palazzo.
It serves homemade pasta dishes and mouthwatering *bistecca
alla Fiorentina* at affordable prices.

SANTA MARIA NOVELLA: INSIDE INFO

Top tips **Arrive early** to avoid the worst of the crowds.
• Bring **loose change** to illuminate the frescoes and **binoculars** to see the details
of the frescoes.

Hidden gems Filippo Brunelleschi dismissed Donatello's wooden crucifix in
Santa Croce (▶ 66) as resembling "a peasant on a cross," so Donatello
challenged him to do better: the **wooden *Crucifix*** (1420) in the Cappella Gondi
was the result.

In more depth Paolo Uccello's **frescoes in the Chiostro Verde** depict stories
from Genesis, including *The Creation of the Animals, Adam and Eve, The
Original Sin, The Labors of the Prisoners, Cain and Abel, Lamech and Noah's
Ark, The Flood* and *The Drunkenness of Noah*. Uccello was obsessed with
perspective and the frescoes are remarkable for their figures and perspective
devices. Unfortunately, some were irreparably damaged by the 1966 floods.

An unchanging aspect. Saved from destruction in World War II, the bridge today (below) looks much as it did in the 19th century (right)

Ponte Vecchio

The Ponte Vecchio (Old Bridge), located at the heart of the city, is one of Florence's most famous landmarks. Lined on both sides with shops supported over the river with timber brackets (*sporti*) and painted in vivid shades of orange and yellow ochre, it is particularly photogenic and lively at sunset when Florentines gather for their evening *passeggiata*. The bridge's three stone arches cross the Arno river at its narrowest point, linking the historic city center with the Oltrarno (► 137).

➕ 203 E4
✉ Ponte Vecchio
🚌 B and D
💶 Free

A peaceful moment away from the busy shops that line the bridge

The Ponte Vecchio was the only bridge in the city to escape destruction in World War II, spared by retreating Nazi forces in 1944, possibly on Hitler's orders. There has been a bridge here since Roman times, but the current Ponte Vecchio dates from 1345 when it was built to replace the former wooden structure that was swept away when the river flooded. It was probably designed by Taddeo Gaddi. In 1565 an elevated walkway, the Corridoio Vasariano (► 54), was built along the eastern side of the bridge.

Today the bridge is lined with glitzy jewelry shops, but in the Middle Ages it was a very different scene. Butchers and fishmongers had their shops here, as did leather-workers who

A Devastating Flood

Over the years the Ponte Vecchio has withstood floods, battles and bombing. However, it didn't fare so well on November 4, 1966, when a freak cyclone swept across the region, destroying part of the bridge and washing a fortune of gold downstream. This was Florence's worst flood, and the damage to the city's artistic heritage was immense. Treasures in the Museo Archeologico, the Biblioteca Nazionale and 8,000 Renaissance paintings stored in the basement of the Uffizi were damaged, and Santa Croce was submerged beneath 15 feet of mud and water.

hung hides in the water for up to eight months before tanning them with horse's urine. A gap was created in the row of shops on one side to make the bridge easier to clean.

These trades were eventually banished by Grand Duke Ferdinando I, who would cross the bridge daily en route to the Palazzo Pitti. The Duke found the stench so offensive that in 1593 he replaced the tradesmen with the jewelers and goldsmiths who have been there ever since.

TAKING A BREAK

Buca dell'Orafo (Volta de' Girolami 28r, tel: 055 213 619), a tiny basement restaurant, has long been a Florentine favorite.

A Fateful Murder – Guelphs vs. Ghibellines

In 1215, nobleman Buondelmonte de' Buondelmonti was murdered at the entrance to the bridge following a quarrel between two Florentine *consorterie* (groups of noble families). The event sparked a bitter conflict between the Guelph middle classes, who had played an important role in promoting the economic development of Florence, and the old Ghibelline nobles, who wished to maintain their feudal privileges. Despite periods of Ghibelline power, the city was predominantly controlled in the 13th century by the Guelph faction.

Divisions within the Guelph faction between the Blacks (who supported the Pope) and the Whites (who were opposed to papal influence) eventually led to civil war. In 1302, numerous Whites were forced into exile, including Dante, who was convicted for alleged corruption.

Once butchers and tanners occupied the shops on the Ponte Vecchio (left), but now jewelry shops crowd the bridge (below)

PONTE VECCHIO: INSIDE INFO

Top tip For the **best photos** of the bridge, stand either on the Ponte Santa Trinita, or on one of the river embankments nearby at sunset.

Hidden gem In 1900 **Benvenuto Cellini**, one of the most famous of Florence's Renaissance goldsmiths, was comemmorated with a bust that stands in the middle of the bridge.

At Your Leisure

❶ Officina Profumo-Farmaceutica di Santa Maria Novella

Just behind Santa Maria Novella is one of the oldest pharmacies in the world. It was set up by Dominican friars soon after 1221, the year of their arrival in Florence. Here the monks grew the herbs they needed for medicines and ointments used in the monastery's little infirmary, including a rosewater disinfectant – considered useful in times of plague.

In 1612, the pharmacy was opened to the public. Its reputation rapidly grew and its products soon became known throughout Europe. Today, the beautiful hand-wrapped cosmetics, potpourri and fragrances are still made to ancient recipes.

➕ 198 C2 ✉ Via della Scala 16
🕐 Tue.–Sat. 9:30–7:30, Mon. 3:30–7:30
🚌 6, 11, 12, 36, 37 and A 🎫 Free

Designer Shopping
- **Via de' Tornabuoni** is the place to go for designer-label shopping: choose from Prada, Trussardi, Beltrami, Bulgari, Ferragamo, Tiffany, Vuitton and Hermés.
- **Via della Vigna Nuova** is equally sophisticated but has more choice of home-grown talent, including Gucci, Pucci and, the new kid on the block, Enrico Coveri.

This ancient herbalist's shop adjoins the cloisters of Santa Maria Novella

The wealthy Vespucci family gave their patronage to the church of Ognissanti, which is decorated with many frescoes

❸ Ognissanti

The church of Ognissanti (All Saints) was established by a Benedictine order of monks in the 13th century. In later years it came under the patronage of the Vespuccis, a wealthy merchant family whose most famous member, Amerigo, gave his name to the New World (➤ 17).

Amerigo can be seen in Domenico Ghirlandaio's beautiful fresco, *Madonna della Misericordia* (1472), in the second chapel on the right. He is the young boy immediately to the left of the Virgin Mary. Halfway down the nave on the right, an intense fresco of *St. Augustine* (1480) by Sandro Botticelli is complemented by Ghirlandaio's *St. Jerome* (1480) on the opposite wall. Other treasures include Botticelli's tomb, a monk's habit reputedly worn by St. Francis when he received the stigmata, and, in the adjoining refectory, a moving *Last Supper* (1480) by Ghirlandaio.

➕ 198 B2 ✉ Borgo Ognissanti 42
☎ 055 239 8700 🕐 Mon.–Sat.
7:45–noon, 4–7, Sun. 8:45–1,
4–7:30 🚌 12
🖐 Free

4 Palazzo Strozzi

The Palazzo Strozzi is the largest palace in Florence. It was built by the egocentric banker Filippo Strozzi in the 15th century in an attempt to outdo the Medici family, his archenemies. Determined to prove that he was the richest and most influential man in the city, Strozzi purchased and demolished 15 buildings to make way for this monumental palace. Leaving nothing to chance, he even called in astrologers to determine the most favorable day on which to lay the foundation stone!

Unfortunately, he never lived to see the end result – an astonishing masterpiece of Renaissance art. Although only three stories high, each floor is as tall as a normal palazzo. As with many contemporary palazzi, the exterior is heavily rusticated, according to Michelozzo, "to unite an appearance of solidarity and strength with the light and shade so essential to beauty under the glare of the Italian sun." Today, the palace contains various cultural institutes, and the second floor is used for major art exhibitions.

➕ 199 D1 ✉ Piazza degli Strozzi
☎ 055 239 8563 🕐 Opening hours vary with each exhibition 🚌 A

5 Piazza della Repubblica

Piazza della Repubblica has long been at the heart of Florentine history. It was once the site of the Forum, the main square of the Roman city of *Florentia*, and in medieval times the city's principal food market was held here. A single column topped by a statue of Abundance – all that remains of the ancient market – still stands in the square. Later the square became the center of the Jewish ghetto.

Today's piazza, with its triumphal arch, was laid out in the 19th century as part of Giuseppe Poggi's grandiose plans to remodel Florence. Many locals consider the square an eyesore, but its cafés have always been hugely popular.

➕ 199 E1
✉ Piazza della Repubblica 🚌 A 🖐 Free

The grand entrance to Florence's most modern square –19th-century Piazza della Repubblica

6 Mercato Nuovo

There has been a market here since the 11th century, but the New Market you see today was constructed in the mid-16th century as a place for gold and silk merchants and bankers to conduct their business. Today's vendors sell leatherware, knick-knacks and souvenirs, and the lovely loggia is a popular venue for street muscians on summer evenings. You'll also usually find a couple of *tripperie* – mobile stands selling traditional market delicacies of *trippa* (tripe) and other offal cuts in a *panini* (bread roll), which can be washed down with a glass of local wine.

Under the loggia, a marble wheel in the middle of the floor marks the spot where dishonest merchants were put into the stocks to be bombarded with rotten fruit and vegetables. On the southern edge of the market stands a bronze of a wild boar, *Il Porcellino* (a 17th-century copy of the Roman marble original, now in the Uffizi). The base of the small fountain beneath him is smothered in minute bronze flowers, frogs, snails, a bee and other enchanting details. Rub the nose of the boar. It will bring you luck and ensure a return visit to Florence.

➕ 203 D5 ✉ Via Calimala 🕐 Daily 9–7, Apr.–Oct.; Tue.–Sat. 9–7, rest of year
🚌 A
💲 Free

Cafés and Cake Shops

- **Giubbe Rosse** (Piazza della Repubblica 13–14r). A stylish early 20th-century café, once a popular haunt of artists and intellectuals.
- **Giacosa** (► 130). This elegant café and cake shop on Via de' Tornabuoni, was the birthplace of the Negroni cocktail (Martini, gin and Campari).
- **Procacci** (► 134). A chic place full of shoppers carrying their designer purchases. Try the delicious *tartufati* (truffle rolls).

8 Palazzo Davanzati

This stately 14th-century palace and former home of the wealthy Davizzi family has been converted into the Museo della Casa Fiorentina Antica (Museum of the Old Florentine House), providing a rare and vivid insight into the life of city merchants, artists and noblemen during the Middle Ages. The palazzo has been closed for long-term restoration, but is due to reopen soon. Check with the tourist office for the latest information.

➕ 203 E5 ✉ Via Porta Rossa 13 🕐 Currently closed for renovation
🚌 6, 11, 36, 37 and A

Il Porcellino – a city emblem

9 Santa Trìnita

With so many noble palazzi in the streets surrounding Santa Trìnita, it's hardly surprising the local parish church contains private chapels dedicated to wealthy Florentines, among them the Strozzi, Davanzati, Spini and Doni families. Each is embellished with elaborate frescoes, reliquaries and tombs in an attempt to outdo its neighbors. Built in the 11th century, the original church was plain and austere but, over the years, it gradually became more ornate. The baroque facade was added in 1593.

The second chapel of the left transept boasts one of Florence's most beautiful tombs, a marble monument of Benozzo Federighi, Bishop of Fiesole (1454–57), by

Ghirlandaio's *Nativity* in Santa Trìnita's Cappella Sassetti

Luca della Robbia. It is framed by a simple border of painted floral terra-cotta tiles.

The undisputed *pièce de résistance* of Santa Trìnita, however, is the **Cappella Sassetti** (second chapel of the right transept) with its delightful frescoes by Domenico Ghirlandaio depicting scenes from the life of St. Francis of Assisi (1483–86). They tell the story of a child who fell out of a window (in the background on the left side), and how St. Francis (in the foreground) came to resurrect him. The backdrop for this miracle is 15th-century Florence and it is possible to identify the buildings (including the earlier Gothic facade of Santa Trìnita), as well as some contemporary figures (among them Sassetti's friend, Lorenzo the Magnificent). The donors of the chapel, Francesco Sassetti and his wife, are portrayed praying on either side of the altar.

✚ 199 D1 ☒ Piazza Santa Trìnita
☎ 055 216 912 ◷ Daily 8–noon, 4–6. Services Mon.–Sat. 7:30 a.m. and 6:30 p.m., Sun. 7:30 and 11 a.m. and 6:30 p.m. ◻ 6, 11, 36, 37 and A
✋ Free

For Kids

- Rubbing the nose of *Il Porcellino* (► 128) and spotting the different types of insects around him.
- Palazzo Davanzati (► 128), which gives a vivid insight into the lifestyle of medieval merchants and nobles.
- Hide-and-seek on the Ponte Vecchio (► 122–125).

Where to...
Eat and Drink

Prices
Expect to pay per person for a meal, excluding drinks and service
$ under €20.65 $$ €20.65–€41.31 $$$ over €41.31

Western Florence does not have the number or variety of restaurants you'll find elsewhere in the city. Only two or three places are worth a special journey – Oliviero for dinner and Rose's, Caffè Amerini or Belle Donne for lunch – but there are several other excellent cafés for snacks or drinks. If you are on a tight budget, head for the area around the Santa Maria Novella railroad station where there is a plethora of fast food and other cheap eating places.

Belle Donne $

On entering Belle Donne you will be immediately struck by the huge piles of fruit, vegetables and flowers laid out in almost sculptural arrangements. The place is small, turnover quick and the setting relaxed – you share wooden tables with fellow diners, eat off paper tablecloths, and choose from a list of daily Florentine specials on a blackboard. It makes an excellent place for lunch, but is rather too informal for all but an early or impromptu dinner.

🚻 199 D2 ⊠ Via delle Belle Donne 16r ☎ 055 238 2609 🕐 Mon.–Fri.

12:30–2:30, 7:30–10, Sat. 12:30–2:30; closed Aug.

Caffè Amerini $

Like the not-so-distant Rose's (▶ 131), Caffè Amerini is a little different than most Florentine eating places. While it has the familiar medieval brick-arched ceiling found in many city bars or restaurants, its walls, furniture and fittings provide a far more modern and slightly eccentric edge. It's an easy-going place, good for breakfast or lunch. You simply point out which of the sandwiches, salads or other good snacks you want from the glass-fronted bar just inside the door and then take a seat to be served – you pay only a small premium for sitting down.

🚻 198 C1 ⊠ Via della Vigna Nuova 63r ☎ 055 284 941 🕐 Mon.–Sat. 8:30–8:30

Garga $$–$$$

Garga is patronized almost entirely by Florentines, but don't let that

intimidate you. The atmosphere and appearance of the place are pleasant and welcoming with pastel-colored walls, soft lighting, wooden ceilings and some curious frescoes. The food is Tuscan, with a mixture of fish and meat. Dishes might include *pesce spada* (swordfish), broiled meats such as lamb served with rosemary or red currants, risotto with asparagus or *baccalà* (salt cod) with a tomato and basil sauce. The wine list features good Tuscan wines.

🚻 199 F1 ⊠ Via del Proconsolo 31r ☎ 055 238 8123 or 055 239 8762 🕐 Tue.–Sun. 12:30–2:30, 7–11

Giacosa $$–$$$

If you have been to Rivoire in Piazza della Signoria (▶ 79), you'll know what to expect in the co-owned Giacosa. Both are equally refined, and both have an illustrious pedigree. The café was favored by 19th-century nobility, and the celebrated Negroni aperitif cocktail, a combination of gin, Campari and Martini, was invented here. Take a break in the café while shopping on Via de' Tornabuoni (▶ 131). It offers light snacks, a tremendous selection of cakes and high-quality chocolates.

🚹 199 D1 ⊠ Via de' Tornabuoni 83r ☎ 055 239 6226 🕐 Tue.–Sun. 7–11

Caffè Gilli $

Piazza della Repubblica is not an attractive square, and is redeemed only by its four large and historic cafés – Gilli, Giubbe Rosse, Donnini and Paszkowski – of which the Caffè Gilli is the most notable. The original Gilli opened in 1733 on Via degli Speziali, but moved to its present site in 1910. Today, it still preserves its stunning *belle époque* interior – worth seeing in its own right – but on warm days you should choose the large outside terrace. In cold weather, Gilli's famous hot chocolate is the drink to go for – it comes in five flavors: almond, coffee, orange, gianduia and cocoa. If you enjoy this type of

large and old-style café, try the Giubbe Rosse (founded in 1897), the next-best of the square's quartet.

🚹 199 E1 ⊠ Piazza della Repubblica 36–39r ☎ 055 213 896 🕐 Wed.–Mon. 8 a.m.–midnight

Latini $–$$

Latini used to be as perfect an old-style trattoria as you could wish for: simple food, low prices, generous portions, lots of locals and a rustic interior. Sadly, while the place still looks the part and still attracts some die-hard old regulars, it has become far too well-known for its own good. Chances are you'll have to wait in line (making a reservation can be difficult) for food that is rarely more than okay (the main-course meats are an honorable exception) but at prices that are a little steep. It's still a good option if you want to come here in the off-season or avoid the crowds.

🚹 199 D1 ⊠ Via dei Palchetti 6r ☎ 055 210 916 🕐 Tue.–Sun. 12:30–2:30, 7:30–10:30

Oliviero $$$

Oliviero is the best restaurant in this part of the city, its only minus mark being the slightly unusual and somewhat dated interior. The food, however, more than makes amends. The cooking embraces Tuscan and other Italian influences, but often adds an innovative touch. Fresh fish – unusual for a Florentine restaurant – is also often available.

🚹 203 E5 ⊠ Via delle Terme 51r ☎ 055 287 643 🕐 Mon.–Sat. 7 p.m.–midnight

Rose's $

There may come a time when you want a change from the classic Florentine restaurant or café. In this respect, Rose's is a breath of fresh air, a bright, modern and stylish bar-restaurant that wouldn't be out of place in New York or Sydney. The food is similarly diverse, and while there are plenty of Italian dishes, you can also eat sushi or inventive salads and snacks.

🚹 199 D1 ⊠ Via del Parione 26r ☎ 055 287 090 🕐 Mon.–Sat. 7 a.m.–1 p.m.

Uvafragola $

Uvafragola is a result of curious cross-cultural influences. For many years it was a Chinese restaurant. Now its young Italian-born Chinese owners have opened a busy pizzeria-trattoria whose convenient Piazza di Santa Maria Novella location attracts a lot of passing trade. Something of the owners' Chinese heritage is hinted at by the distinctly un-Florentine decor, but if all you want is a basic meal at good prices, the Tuscan food is as good and authentic as any comparable restaurant in the city. Much of the pasta is fresh and homemade and pizzas are served at lunch time – not always the case elsewhere, as many pizzerias only fire up their ovens in the evening.

🚹 198 C2 ⊠ Piazza di Santa Maria Novella 9–10 ☎ 055 215 387 🕐 Thu.–Tue. noon–3, 7–midnight

Where to… Shop

Western Florence has bigger and broader streets than many other parts of the city. Streets that are ideally suited to larger shops and the free movement of shoppers. Via de' Tornabuoni and surrounding streets such as Via della Vigna Nuova still boast the lion's share of Florence's designer and other fashion, shoe and accessory shops. Note that virtually all of these shops are closed on Monday mornings.

Streets such as Borgo Ognissanti also have an overflow of smarter stores and discreet individual designers' ateliers, not to mention the furniture and other workshops tucked into streets such as Via del Porcellana. Finally, around the Santa Maria Novella train station, you'll find a predictable rash of budget souvenir and clothes shops.

BOOKS

Seeber

Seeber is one of Florence's best bookshops, and rated *the* best by purists who object to the more modern approach of rivals such as Feltrinelli (▶ 110). It's especially good for books on art and antiques – with more than 10,000 titles – and also has a good selection of English and other foreign-language titles. This is also the place to come for the full range of the much-respected Touring Club of Italy guides and books, as well as other local and Italian guides available in English.

➕ 199 D1 ⊠ Via de' Tornabuoni 68–70r ☎ 055 215 697 🕒 Mon.–Sat. 9:30–7:30

CLOTHES AND ACCESSORIES

Armani

Giorgio Armani's understated and elegant clothes need little introduction. The designer's Via della Vigna Nuova shop is his flagship Florentine store. The less expensive Emporio Armani outlet is nearby in Piazza degli Strozzi.

➕ 198 C1 ⊠ Via della Vigna Nuova 51r ☎ 055 219 041 🕒 Tue.–Sat. 10–7:30, Mon. 3:30–7:30

➕ 199 D1 ⊠ Piazza degli Strozzi 16r ☎ 055 284 315 🕒 Tue.–Sat. 10–7:30, Mon. 3:30–7:30

Enrico Coveri

Coveri was born in nearby Prato, but before his death he became known for loud and vividly colored clothes that were at odds with the naturally classic and sober inclinations of most Florentines. His designs found favor nonetheless, and his bold style has been continued by the label's current in-house designers. The Via de' Tornabuoni address is the company's principal Florentine outlet; the Via della Vigna Nuova store stocks the less expensive range.

➕ 199 D1 ⊠ Via de' Tornabuoni 81r ☎ 055 211 263 🕒 Mon. 3:30–7:30, Tue.–Sat. 10–1:30, 3:30–7:30

➕ 199 D1 ⊠ Via della Vigna Nuova 27–29r ☎ 055 211 263 🕒 Tue.–Sat. 10–1:30, 3:30–7:30, Mon. 3:30–7:30

Ermenegildo Zegna

This long-established men's wear label has been well-known and respected in Italy for some time, but has only recently achieved greater prominence abroad. The suits and other clothes are quintessentially Italian – beautifully cut and crafted from exquisite and often exclusive fabrics. Shoes, ties, sportswear and other accessories are also available.

➕ 199 D1 ⊠ Via della Vigna Nuova-Piazza Rucellai 4–7r ☎ 055 283 011 🕒 Tue.–Sat. 10–7:30, Mon. 3:30–7:30

Gucci

The famous Gucci label was founded at this Florentine address, which still acts as a prestigious showroom for the revitalized company's clothes, shoes and accessories. Prices are high, but quality and cutting-edge cool are assured.

🚻 199 D1 🖂 Via de' Tornabuoni 73r
☎ 055 264 011 🕐 Tue.–Sat. 9:30–7, Mon. 3–7

Louis Vuitton

Fake Louis Vuitton purses and luggage are probably some of the most common items to be found laid out by the hawkers on the Ponte Vecchio and Florence's streets. This is the place to come for the real thing.

🚻 199 D1 🖂 Via de' Tornabuoni 24–28r ☎ 055 214 344
🕐 Tue.–Sat. 9:30–7:30, Mon. 3–7:30

Prada

Prada may have Milanese roots, but Florentines aren't proud. They happily patronize the shop of what

is currently one of the most fashionable of all designer labels.

🚻 199 D1 🖂 Via de' Tornabuoni 67r
☎ 055 283 439 🕐 Tue.–Sat. 10–7, Mon. 3–7

Pucci

The aristocratic Marchese Emilio Pucci made his name in the 1950s and 1960s with his bright and hugely distinctive printed silks (▲ 24–27). His star waned somewhat until the 1990s, when the same silks again became fashionable. Today, Pucci is the doyen of Florentine designers and is much feted in the city's fashion circles. In addition to the Via della Vigna Nuova shops, there is a showroom just north of the Duomo at Via dei Pucci 6.

🚻 198 C1 🖂 Via della Vigna Nuova 97r ☎ 055 294 028 🕐 Tue.–Sat. 10–1, 3:30–7:30, Mon. 3:30–7:30

Trussardi

Niccolò Trussardi's clothes, purses and accessories pay unashamed

homage to the classic English gentleman's and gentlewoman's look, a style much favored by many Italians and suave elder Florentines in particular.

🚻 199 D1 🖂 Via de' Tornabuoni 34–36r ☎ 055 219 902 🕐 Tue.–Sat. 10–7, Mon. 3–7

DEPARTMENT STORES

Rinascente

Rinascente is one of a nationwide chain of department stores. It has a more upscale reputation and more spacious presence than its nearby rival Coin (▲ 80), yet in the flesh the choice of goods seems inferior and their presentation dowdier. That said, this is still a good place to come for one-stop shopping for Italian clothes, kitchenware, linens and other department store staples if you're in Florence for only a short time.

🚻 199 E1 🖂 Piazza della Repubblica 1 ☎ 055 239 8544
🕐 Mon.–Sat. 9–9, Sun. 10:30–8

FABRICS

Casa di Tessuti

Florence has a long tradition of sumptuous fabrics (as you would expect of a city which owed, and still owes, much of its prosperity to textiles). For over 50 years this conveniently located shop just west of Piazza del Duomo has been a place of pilgrimage for Florentines and visitors alike in search of the finest silks, cottons, velvets, damasks, woolens and other fabrics.

🚻 199 E2 🖂 Via de' Pecori
☎ 055 219 961 🕐 Mon. 3:30–7:30, Tue.–Sat. 9–1, 3:30–7:30

FOOD AND WINE

Bottega della Frutta

Look no farther than this fine fruit and vegetable shop if you need provisions for a delicious packed lunch or picnic.

🚻 199 E1 🖂 Via della Spada 58r
☎ 055 239 8590 🕐 Mon.–Tue., Thu.–Sat. 8–7:30, Wed. 8–1:30

Dolceforte

This tiny shop specializes in high-quality chocolates, other sweet-toothed treats and biscuits, honeys and preserves. It is also an excellent place to buy gifts to take home.

✚ 198 C2 ⊠ Via della Scala 21
☎ 055 219 116 ⓒ Mon.–Sat. 10–1, 3:30–7:30

Enoteca Murgia

This is a tempting shop for serious wine-buyers but also for those who simply want a bottle of grappa or *vin santo* to take home. Murgia also sells a good selection of Tuscan and other Italian olive oils.

✚ 199 D2 ⊠ Via dei Banchi 55–57r
☎ 055 215686 ⓒ Tue.–Sat. 9–1, 3:30–7:30, Mon. 3:30–7:30

Procacci

This is the place to buy truffles in season (October–March). At other times of the year, you can buy the bottled or canned versions or stop by for one of the shop's famous truffle-flavored rolls – un panino tartufato.

✚ 199 D1 ⊠ Via de' Tornabuoni 64r
☎ 055 211 656 ⓒ Tue.–Sat. 8–1, 4:30–7:30

Tassini

Many decades of experience lie behind this shop's selection of fine Tuscan foods and wines. Pastas, dried porcini mushrooms, the best olive oils and a host of other gastronomic treats are available, along with the best vintages from some of the region's premier wine-growing areas – notably Montalcino, Chianti and Montepulciano.

✚ 203 E5 ⊠ Borgo SS Apostoli 24r
☎ 055 282 696 ⓒ Mon.–Sat. 9–1, 3:30–7:30

MARKETS

Cascine

The Cascine is the biggest of Florence's markets and takes place every Tuesday morning in the Parco delle Cascine, a large park to the west of the city center. It's a long walk to get here, so take a taxi or catch the B electric bus to Piazza Vittorio Veneto and change there to the P electric bus – the latter runs through the park on Viale degli Olmi. The outdoor market consists of hundreds of stands of all descriptions, from inexpensive clothes and shoes to food and general household goods. Prices here are among the best in the city.

✚ 198 off A2 ⊠ Viale Abraham Lincoln, Parco delle Cascine
☎ No phone ⓒ Tue. 8–1

Mercato dei Fiori

The practical side of getting your blooms home may stop you buying anything from Florence's small weekly flower market, but it's still worth making a detour to admire the displays if you're in the vicinity of Piazza della Repubblica on a Thursday morning.

✚ 199 E1 ⊠ Via della Pellicceria-Piazza della Repubblica ☎ No phone
ⓒ Thu. 8–1

Mercato Nuovo

▲ 127 ✚ 203 E5 ⊠ Loggia del Mercato Nuovo ☎ No phone
ⓒ Mon.–Sat. 9–7

PAPER AND STATIONERY

Cozzi

Cozzi is primarily a book-binding business, but sells a selection of beautiful diaries, notebooks and other leather- or plain-bound books covered in marbled paper.

✚ 203 D5 ⊠ Via del Parione 35r
☎ 055 294 968 ⓒ Mon.–Fri. 9–1, 3–7

Pineider

The second Florentine outlet of Italy's most prestigious stationer: the company has been making superb pens, desk accessories, handmade paper, business cards and other writing materials since 1774. Note also the Piazza della Signoria shop (▶ 81).

✚ 199 D1 ⊠ Via de' Tornabuoni 76r
☎ 055 211 605 ⓒ Tue.–Sat. 10–1, 3:30–7:30, Mon. 3:30–7:30

Erboristeria Inglese

The English Herbalist occupies part of the 16th-century Palazzo Larderel, a suitably aristocratic setting for this elegant purveyor of natural beauty products and fine toiletries. This is a place to come for a special treat.

➕ 199 D1 ⊠ Via de' Tornabuoni
🕿 055 210 628 🟢 Tue. and Fri.
9:30–7:30, Wed. Thu. and Sat. 9:30–1,
3:30–7:30, Mon. 3:30–7:30

Sigillo

This shop sells a wide range of fine soaps, perfumes, bath oils and other gloriously scented toiletries from around the world.

➕ 199 D1 ⊠ Via Porta Rossa 23r
🕿 055 287 732 🟢 Tue.–Sat. 10–1,
3:30–7:30, Mon. 3:30–7:30

Ducci

This shop between the Carraia and Trinita bridges does not have the old-fashioned charm of Baccani (see below), but its selection of historical and other prints and engravings is good. In addition it sells a selection of other goods that make excellent gifts, notably a variety of *objects d'art* in marble, woodcraft items and Florentine boxes covered in gold leaf and marbled paper.

➕ 199 D1 ⊠ Lungarno Corsini 24r
🕿 055 214 550 🟢 Mon.–Sat.
9–1, 3:30–7:30, Sun. 10–1, Mon.
3:30–7:30

Giovanni Baccani

Florence is dotted with enticing shops selling prints and engravings, but none is quite as pretty or alluring as this beautiful old shop founded in 1903. There's a huge selection of framed and unframed prints on a range of subjects and at prices to suit every budget. Florentine and other Italian scenes and maps are particularly good buys.

➕ 198 C1 ⊠ Via della Vigna Nuova
75r 🕿 055 214 467 🟢 Tue.–Sat.
9–1, 3:30–7:30, Mon. 3:30–7:30

Bisonte

Italians like a designer label, and in Bisonte's shoes and leather goods they have one that is growing ever more popular both at home and abroad. All the company's products are stamped with a distinctive bison motif, and although you will pay a lot for goods with this trademark, the products are extremely durable and well made.

➕ 203 D5 ⊠ Via del Parione 31r
🕿 055 215 722 🟢 Tue.–Sat. 9:30–7,
Mon. 3–7

Bonora

This shop has made exquisite hand-made and ready-to-wear shoes in classic styles – especially for men – since 1878. The prices are high, but these are some of the best shoes in Florence, which is to say some of the best shoes in Italy.

➕ 199 D1 ⊠ Via del Parione 11–15
🕿 055 283 280 🟢 Mon. 3:30–7:30,
Tue.–Sat. 10–7:30

Ferragamo

Salvatore Ferragamo was born in Naples and made his name in the United States making shoes for Hollywood stars (▶27). His descendants still run the company, and their Via de' Tornabuoni shop has a tremendous showroom not only for shoes – on which Ferragamo's reputation still largely rests – but also for clothes and leather accessories.

➕ 199 D1 ⊠ Via de' Tornabuoni 14r
🕿 055 292 123 🟢 Tue.–Sat.
9:30–7:30, Mon. 3:30–7:30

J P Tod's

No one in Italy took much notice of J P Tod's until their distinctive driving shoes became must-have accessories in the United States. Now the label is broadening its range – prices here are generally lower for the same item than else-where in Europe or the U.S.

➕ 199 D1 ⊠ Via de' Tornabuoni
103r 🕿 055 219423 🟢 Tue.–Sat.
10–7:30, Mon. 3–7

Where to...
Be Entertained

Western Florence is home to a wide range of bars and clubs as well as the Teatro Comunale, the city's principal performance space for classical music, dance and theater productions. The district's farthest fringe is also the site of several major dance clubs.

THEATER

The **Teatro Comunal** (Corso Italia 16, tel: 055 27791) is a drab-looking building well to the west of the city center. Its appearance notwithstanding, it is Florence's main theater and auditorium and provides the stage for performances of its own orchestra, chorus and dance companies, together with visiting orchestras and performers.

It also hosts many of the performances of the annual Maggio Musicale, one of Italy's leading music festivals. For information and tickets, visit the box office in person (Tue.–Fri. 10–4:30, Sat. 9–1) or tel: 055 211 158 or 055 213 535 (e-mail: tickets@maggiofiorentino.com; www.maggiofiorentino.com). Outside the Maggio Musicale, the main season for concerts, opera and ballet runs from January through April and September through December.

NIGHTCLUBS

One of the area's best-known nightspots is **Space Electronic** (Via Palazzuolo 37, tel: 055 293 082, open daily 10–2; closed Mon. in winter), a huge and fairly trashy disco. It claims to be Europe's largest disco, but it doesn't have cutting edge music or style. Much the same can be said about the almost equally large **Meccanò** (Viale degli Olmi 1, tel: 055 331 371, open Tue.–Sat. 11 p.m.– 6 a.m.) in the Casine park. This is the city's most famous disco and the one to visit if you're only going to sample one Florentine club. People come from across Tuscany for a night out here, so it's likely to be crowded. In summer the action spills outdoors. Dress is fairly stylish and the music is safe and commercial.

The third of western Florence's trio of key dance clubs is **Yab** (Via Sassetti 5r, tel: 055 215 160, open Mon., Wed.–Sun. 9 p.m.–4 a.m.; closed Jun.–Sep.), which generally pursues a more adventurous music policy than its rivals, but also operates an insidious "card" system where admission is usually free but you have to spend a minimum amount on drinks – if you don't spend enough, you have to pay up before leaving.

BARS

If you want to start or finish the evening in a quieter place, try the **Art Bar** (Via del Moro 4r, tel: 055 287 661, open Mon.–Sat. 7 p.m.–1 a.m.), a discreet and select little bar decorated in the manner of an antique shop. It is a popular choice with Florentines anxious to indulge in an early evening cocktail.

At the other extreme are two bars on or just off Piazza di Santa Maria Novella, both popular with young people: **Chequers** (Via della Scala 7–9r, tel: 055 287 588, open daily 6:30 p.m.–1:30 a.m. or later), a raucous pub and the **Fiddler's Elbow** (Piazza di Santa Maria Novella 7r, tel: 055 215 056), a small "Irish pub" that is also very busy and only marginally less animated.

Getting Your Bearings

The name Oltrarno means "beyond the Arno," and this small district along the south bank of the river presents a different Florence. Quieter, greener, more relaxed and with less traffic, it is one of the most rewarding areas to explore.

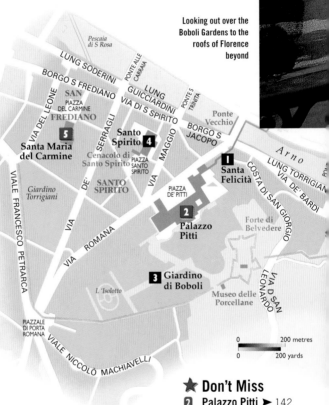

Looking out over the Boboli Gardens to the roofs of Florence beyond

Previous page:
Entering into San
Miniato al Monte

⭐ **Don't Miss**
2 Palazzo Pitti ➤ 142
5 Santa Maria del
Carmine – Cappella
Brancacci ➤ 148
6 San Miniato al
Monte ➤ 150

For a long time the Oltrarno was considered
an inferior neighborhood, inhabited only by
those with insufficient wealth to live in the
city center. This soon changed, however, when
the household of the Medici Grand Dukes
moved from the north bank to the Palazzo
Pitti in 1550, from where they ruled Tuscany
for the next 300 years. Several Florentine
aristocrats followed suit, building luxurious
palazzi near the Medici palace.

But to discover the true character of
Florence, step into the side streets, overflowing with tiny authentic restaurants,
boutiques, antique shops and artisans' studios.
Among the sights, Cappella Brancacci stands
out for its fabulous fresco cycle, while San
Miniato, on a grassy hilltop overlooking the
city, counts among Tuscany's finest
Romanesque treasures. Here, on the southern
fringes of the Oltrarno, you'll find city and
countryside merging together with quite
exceptional views.

At Your Leisure

This itinerary enables you to discover a most enchanting district of Florence, including its largest park and some of its finest museums, churches and viewpoints.

Oltrarno in a Day

9:00 a.m.

Make sure you arrive early at the **Palazzo Pitti** (below, ➤ 142–147) to get a head start on the hundreds of visitors who trail through the palace daily. You would be advised to devote most of your morning to the various museums here: take your time and be selective, but be sure to include the paintings of the Galleria Palatina in your itinerary.

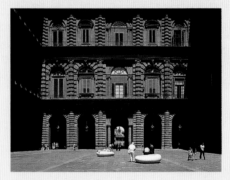

12:00 noon

Stroll through the magnificent **Giardino di Boboli** (detail below, ➤ 152–153), once the Pitti's private gardens, now Florence's largest public park and a foremost example of Italianate gardening.

1:00 p.m.

Grab a light lunch at Il Caffè (➤ 146) near the entrance to the Palazzo Pitti or head for the picturesque **Piazza di Santo Spirito** (➤ 153) to purchase a picnic lunch of antipasti, cheeses, cold cuts, salads and fruit from the daily market to eat on the steps of the church of Santo Spirito.

3:00 p.m.

Visit **Santa Maria del Carmine** (➤ 148–149) to see the beautiful, emotionally charged frescoes by Masaccio in the Cappella Brancacci (right), which had a profound influence on the direction of art in the early Renaissance. The church is located in a particularly individual part of the Oltrarno – the parish of San Frediano, once the wool-dyers' and leatherworkers' district which, together with the adjacent area around Santo Spirito, still has its own dialect. The side streets are packed with fascinating workshops, local stores and cafés.

4:30 p.m.

Save your visit to **San Miniato al Monte** (➤ 150–151) until the heat of the day subsides because it involves a lengthy uphill climb. Your efforts will be richly rewarded, however, by one of Florence's most beautiful churches, the picturesque countryside of the hinterland and outstanding city views.

7:30 p.m.

After a long and tiring day, treat yourself to a meal on the panoramic terrace at **La Loggia** (➤ 151).

Palazzo Pitti

The Palazzo Pitti, the most monumental of all Florence's palaces, was the chief residence of the Medici from the mid-16th century. Later it was home to their successors, the Lorraines, then briefly became the royal palace of the Savoy dynasty (1865–71), when Florence was the nation's capital. Today, its lavish rooms house several important museums of Medici treasures, including the Galleria Palatina with its prestigious collection of High Renaissance and baroque paintings.

The palace was originally built for Luca Pitti, a rich banker and rival of the Medici. It was begun in 1457, to a design by Brunelleschi, at a time when all eminent Florentine families were vying to build the biggest and best residences – symbols to reflect their standing in society. Determined to outdo even the great Medici, Pitti insisted that his palace windows were larger than the doors of the Medici palace (now the Palazzo Medici-Riccardi, ► 104–105). These grandiose ideas proved to be his downfall, however, as building costs bankrupted him and in 1465 construction was halted. Ironically, the palace was bought by the Medici in 1549.

It was Cosimo I's wife, Eleonora di Toledo, who, in ill health, persuaded her husband that she might benefit from the more rural setting of the Oltrarno, until then considered the "wrong" side of the river to live. She

✚ 203 D3
✉ Piazza Pitti
🚌 D

Luca Pitti intended that his residence rival the Medici palace and the sheer scale of the interior cannot fail to impress

Galleria Palatina and Appartamenti Monumentali
☎ 055 238 8614 ⏰ Tue.–Sat. 8:30–6:50, Sun. 8:30–1:50. Last tickets 45 min. before closing 🎫 Combined entrance fee: expensive

Grand Ducal Treasures Museum (Museo degli Argenti) and Costume Gallery
☎ 055 238 8709 ⏰ Daily 8:30–1:50; closed first, third and fifth Mon. and second and fourth Sun. of every month. Last tickets 30 min. before closing
🎫 Combined entrance fee with Costume Gallery: inexpensive

Galleria del Costume

Devotees of fashion should head for the Costume Gallery, where the changing tastes in courtly fashion are traced, from tightly trussed 18th-century corsets to frivolous party dresses of the 1920s. The gallery itself is closed for long-term restoration, but the collection is on display in the Palazzina della Meridiana, a wing of the palace accessed through the Giardino di Boboli (▶ 152).

employed Bartolommeo Ammannati to add two wings to the palace and a stately courtyard opening onto the magnificent Giardino di Boboli (▶ 152–153). The palace which you see today is three times its original size, due to subsequent enlargements and embellishment: the facade alone is more than 660 feet in length.

The Collections

Inside the palace, you'll find no less than six museums: the Galleria Palatina (Palatine Gallery), the Galleria d'Arte Moderna (Modern Art Gallery, see panel, page 146), the Museo degli Argenti (Silver Museum), the Appartamenti Monumentali (State Apartments), the Galleria del Costume (Costume Gallery, see panel above), and the Coach Museum, which houses a small collection of state carriages and sedan chairs, but is closed for long-term restoration. The Museo delle Porcellane (Porcelain Museum) can only be accessed through the Giardino di Boboli.

Don't be put off by the palace's immense size or daunted by its many museums and wealth of fine works of art. The secret is to be selective. Pick just one or maybe two collections that interest you and concentrate on those. If the going gets tough, seek retreat in the landscaped gardens.

The immense palace, viewed from the Boboli Gardens

Galleria Palatina

The Palatine Gallery was created by the Lorraine Grand Dukes at the start of the 19th century simply by converting the former

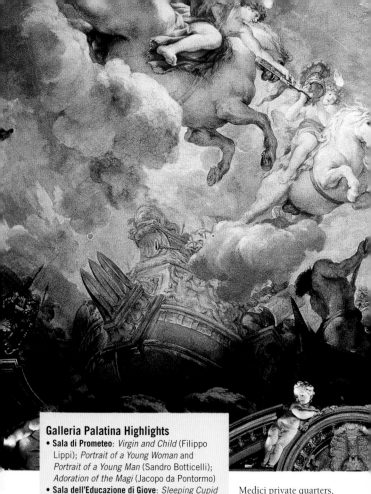

Galleria Palatina Highlights

- **Sala di Prometeo**: *Virgin and Child* (Filippo Lippi); *Portrait of a Young Woman* and *Portrait of a Young Man* (Sandro Botticelli); *Adoration of the Magi* (Jacopo da Pontormo)
- **Sala dell'Educazione di Giove**: *Sleeping Cupid* (Michelangelo Merisi da Caravaggio)
- **Sala dell'Iliade**: *La Gràvida – The Pregnant Lady* (Raphael)
- **Sala di Saturno**: *Madonna of the Chair* (Raphael)
- **Sala di Giove**: *La Velata – Veiled Woman* (Raphael); *Deposition* (Fra Bartolomeo)
- **Sala di Marte**: *The Consequences of War* and *The Four Philosophers* (Rubens)
- **Sala di Apollo**: *Mary Magdalene* (Titian); *The Holy Family* (Andrea del Sarto)
- **Sala di Venere**: *La Bella* (Titian)

Medici private quarters, packed with paintings, into public reception rooms. The display spans Florentine art from the early Renaissance to Mannerism (➤ 152), and includes key works from other contemporary Italian and European masters, including Raphael, Titian, Tintoretto, Rubens, Van Dyck. Unlike the Uffizi (➤ 52–59), the paintings are not displayed in a chronological order, but hung as the Medici Grand Dukes wished – in a purely decorative manner regardless of subject, style or date.

The ceilings in rooms 24 to 28 are painted with ebullient frescoes (1641–47) by Pietro da Cortona creating allegories of the education of young Cosimo III de' Medici by the gods. Start

from room 28 and work backward: in the Sala di Venere, Minerva (Knowledge) tears the prince from the love of Venus; in the following rooms he is taught science by Apollo (Sala di Apollo), war by Mars (Sala di Marte) and leadership by Jupiter (Sala di Giove); finally, the aged Cosimo is taken to Saturn, father of the gods, by Mars and Prudence and crowned by Fame and Eternity (Sala di Saturno).

Appartamenti Monumentali

The opulent state apartments on the second floor of the south wing are a must-see – home to the Medici, the Lorraine Grand Dukes and from 1865 to 1871, the official residence of King Vittorio Emanuele II. You can see his throne under a large canopy in the Sala del Trono. These princely rooms are extravagantly decorated with bold color schemes, ornate stuccowork ceilings and period furnishings, with the Sala Bianca (White Room), the palace ballroom, as the *pièce de résistance*.

Cortona's celebrated ceiling fresco in the Sala di Marte of Cosimo III de' Medici learning about war from Mars

One of the palace's exuberant state apartments

Galleria d'Arte Moderna

The Gallery of Modern Art (on the third floor of the palace) provides a complete panorama of Italian art from 1784 to 1924. Among the 2,000 paintings and sculptures are neoclassical and Romantic works (rooms 1–12); the Florence-based Macchiaioli (similar to French Impressionists, rooms 16–18); and Tuscan Postimpressionism (rooms 28–30).
Tel: 055 238 8616. Open daily 8:30–1:50; closed first, third and fifth Mon. and second and fourth Sun. of every month. Last tickets 30 min. before closing.

Museo degli Argenti

The Silver Museum is housed in the Grand Dukes' summer apartments (on the first and mezzanine floors beneath the Palatine Gallery) and contains an eclectic collection of Medici treasures. You'll find not only silverware, but a dazzling array of gold, amber, glass and other fine arts. Lorenzo the Magnificent's collection of 16 *pietre dure* vases in the Sala Buia includes Roman and Byzantine pieces and should certainly not be missed. The Medici jewelry collection, on the second floor, is also superb.

TAKING A BREAK

Il Caffé (Piazza Pitti 9, tel: 055 239 6241), virtually opposite the Palazzo Pitti, serves pasta, salads, snacks, cocktails and other refreshments. On some evenings, you can sit and enjoy live jazz.

Above: Canova's *Venus Italica* coyly watches visitors in the Sala di Venere, in the Galleria Palatina

Left: elaborate decoration in the Galleria Palatina

PALAZZO PITTI: INSIDE INFO

Top tips Try to **arrive early** and be prepared to wait in line.
• If you intend to visit three or more museums within the palace, consider buying a *Cumulativo* **ticket.** It's valid for three days and saves waiting in line at the ticket office each time you visit.

Hidden gems Galleria Palatina: Napoleon's bathroom, with its original neoclassical furnishings.
• Museo degli Argenti: Exquisite **pearl brooches,** modeled into various animal forms; frescoed state rooms, including an exuberant Medici allegory by Giovanni da San Giovanni and two staggering *trompe-l'oeil* "palace within a palace" frescoes in the Public Audience Chamber.
• Galleria d'Arte Moderna: Paintings from the **Staggia School,** the first school of landscape art in Tuscany (room 14).

Santa Maria del Carmine – Cappella Brancacci

The magnificent frescoes by Masaccio in the Cappella Brancacci, in the south transept of Santa Maria del Carmine, constitute the single most influential paintings of the Early Renaissance.

In 1423, Felice Brancacci, an important political figure in Florence and a wealthy silk merchant, commissioned two artists – Masaccio and Masolino da Panicale – to paint his family chapel with 12 scenes from the life of St. Peter (who is portrayed in orange robes throughout). However, work was interrupted in 1428 when Masaccio moved to Rome (he died a few months later, age just 27) and the Brancacci family was exiled from Florence by the Medici. The beautiful pastel-colored cycle was eventually completed by Filippino Lippi some 50 years later.

✚ 202 B4
✉ Piazza del Carmine
☎ 055 238 2195
🕐 Mon. and Wed.–Sat. 10–5,

Sun. 1–5. Last tickets 30 min. before closing
🚌 6 and D
💰 Moderate

The Frescoes: Who Painted What in the Cappella Brancacci

Left side
Top row: *Expulsion of Adam and Eve* and *The Tribute Money* (Masaccio);
St. Peter Preaching (Masolino)
Bottom row: *St. Peter Visited by St. Paul* (Lippi); *Resurrection of the Emperor's Son*
(Masaccio/Lippi); *St. Peter Enthroned* and *St. Peter Healing the Sick* (Masaccio)

Right side
Top row: *St. Peter Baptising the Converts* (Masaccio); *St. Peter Healing the*
Cripple, Raising Tabitha and *The Temptation of Adam and Eve* (Masolino)
Bottom row: *St. Peter and St. John Giving Alms* (Masaccio); *Crucifixion, Before the*
Proconsul and *The Release of St. Peter* (Lippi)

Left: Frescoes by Masaccio, Masolino and Lippi on the left wall of the Cappella Brancacci. Masaccio's depiction of Adam and Eve (top left) is noted for its intensity

An immediate contrast between the works of Masaccio and
Masolino is obvious in their two depictions of **Adam and Eve**
on the upper entrance piers. Masolino's portrayal is simple and
decorative, while the intensity of Masaccio's makes it one of the
most emotional images in Western art. It was this realism, in
particular, that set Masaccio's painting worlds apart from the
courtly, elegant style of his contemporaries. A strategically
placed fig leaf was added to his Adam at a much later date, but
this was removed during restoration work in the 1980s.

Also by Masaccio is the ***Tribute Money*** (left wall, top row),
unusual in that it contains three pictures in one: Christ (center)
instructing St. Peter to catch a fish (left) in whose mouth he will
find the tribute money to pay the tax collector (right). In ***The***
Resurrection of the Emperor's Son (left wall, bottom row, center),
Masaccio added various Brancacci family members to the scene,
but when they were exiled from Florence, their portraits were
eliminated. Filippino Lippi repainted them though, in 1481–82.

TAKING A BREAK

Try **Angiolino** (Via Santo Spirito 36r, tel: 055 239 8976), an
atmospheric trattoria serving such Florentine staples as
ribollita, tripe and broiled meats in rustic surroundings.

CAPPELLA BRANCACCI: INSIDE INFO

Top tips Santa Maria del Carmine is **closed to the public.** To reach the Cappella
Brancacci, go through a side door, along the peaceful late 16th-century cloisters,
then into the sacristy.
• Be prepared to **wait in line.** In peak season, visitors are sometimes **limited to just
15 minutes** inside the chapel.

Hidden gems The only known **contemporary portrait of architect Filippo**
Brunelleschi is in the scene of *St. Peter Enthroned* (left wall, bottom row). He can
be seen in the doorway on the right in a black hood.
• In the background of Masolino's *St. Peter Healing the Cripple* (right wall, top
row), you can see a lovely view of 15th-century Florence.
• The **two roundels** of ladies' faces behind the altar are remarkable for their depth
of color and delicate complexions.

San Miniato al Monte

One of Florence's oldest and most beautiful churches, and the most sublime example of Romanesque architecture in Tuscany, San Miniato was founded in 1013 near the tomb of Minias, a rich Armenian merchant who had traveled to Florence to spread Christianity. Minias was beheaded for his beliefs in AD 250 and, according to legend, picked up his severed head and marched up the hill with it, keen to be buried where he'd lived as a hermit.

After climbing the steep steps to the church's lofty hilltop terrace, you hardly know what to admire first: the dazzling facade with its geometric marble pattern typical of the Romanesque style, or the sweeping vistas of Florence. The mosaic in the pediment of **Christ with the Virgin and St. Minias** dates from the early 13th century. Atop the entire ensemble sits a gilded copper eagle clutching a bale of wool – the symbol of the Arte di Calimala, the powerful guild of wool importers who financed the church during the Middle Ages.

The interior is every bit as impressive as the exterior. It's strikingly arranged on three levels – the nave, a raised choir containing the main altar and, beneath it, the crypt, designed so the central altar could lie directly above St. Minias's relics. In the raised section, the intricately carved pulpit was set sideways so it could be seen by both the congregation and the monks segregated by the magnificent screen. The nave contains exquisite 13th-century **marble mosaic panels** depicting signs of the zodiac. The apse is dominated by a further Byzantine-style mosaic of **Christ with the Virgin and St. Minias.**

The vault of Michelozzo's 15th-century tabernacle is decorated with blue glazed-terra-cotta tondi

 205 D1
✉ Via del Monte alle Croci
☎ 055 234 2731
🕐 Daily 8–7:30, Apr.–Sep.; 8–5:30 rest of year
Services (usually in the crypt) Mon.–Sat. 8:30, 10 and 11:30 a.m. and 5:30 p.m., Sun. 8:30 a.m. and 5:30 p.m.
🚌 12 and 13
🎫 Free

The surrounding windows are covered with thin layers of alabaster to soften the light, enabling the monks to pray here with greater concentration. The oldest and most fascinating part of the church is the **12th-century crypt.** It rests on 36 marble columns, each one different and all salvaged from ancient Roman buildings. Services usually take place here and include an atmospheric vespers, often conducted in Gregorian chant.

Above: Michelangelo used to call San Miniato "my pretty country maid"

TAKING A BREAK

Enjoy gastronomic alfresco dining on the terrace of **La Loggia** (Piazzale Michelangelo, tel: 055 234 2832), a 19th-century neoclassical villa overlooking Florence.

Facing page, top left: detail of the 13th-century facade mosaic

SAN MINIATO AL MONTE: INSIDE INFO

Top tips Try to come when the church is at its quietest – either **early morning** or toward **the end of the day.**
• Visit the **monks' small shop** for lavender, honey, herbs and homeopathic remedies.

Hidden gems Cappella del Cardinale del Portogallo (Chapel of the Cardinal of Portugal), inspired by Filippo Brunelleschi's Sagrestia Vecchia in San Lorenzo (▶ 95–97), is striking in its simpicity of design.
• The Cappella del Crocifisso (Chapel of the Crucifix) is intricately carved and decorated with terra-cottas by Luca della Robbia.
• Sacristy with colorful fresco scenes from the life of St. Benedict.

At Your Leisure

❶ Santa Felicità

Santa Felicità's most precious treasure is the Cappella Capponi (to the right of the entrance), decorated by Jacopo da Pontormo with two of the greatest works of Mannerist art ever produced: the *Annunciation* and the *Deposition*. Painted between 1525 and 1528, these sophisticated frescoes have a strangely luminescent quality, which reflects the work's emotional intensity. *The Deposition*, with its iridescent palette of colors and its entwined yet graceful bodies, is widely acknowledged as Pontormo's greatest work, yet in many ways his *Annunciation* is even more moving in its simplicity.

As you leave the church, notice the unusual exterior. The edifice has been remodeled numerous times since its Romanesque origins and the dome was destroyed in the mid-16th century to make way for Giorgio Vasari's great Medici corridor (➤ 54), which is embedded into the rebuilt facade.

➕ 203 E4 ✉ Piazza di Santa Felicità
☎ 055 213 018 🕐 Mon.–Sat.
8:30–noon, 3–6, Sun. 9–11, 4–6. Services
Mon.–Sat. 6 p.m., Sun. 9 and 11 a.m.
🚌 D 🎟 Free

Mannerism

Mannerism was derived from the Italian word *maniere* (meaning style or elegance) and, as with the term Renaissance, it applies to a diverse movement of art characterized by exaggerated elegance, heightened color combinations, free-flowing lines and technical flair. It developed out of the Renaissance and lasted approximately 60 years (1520–80), with Pontormo's frescoes in Santa Felicità paving the way.

❸ Giardino di Boboli

The extensive Boboli Gardens climbing the hill behind the Palazzo Pitti are a magical retreat on a hot summer's day. Highlights include the Neptune Fountain and the unforgettable Bacchus Fountain (Cosimo I's court jester as the Roman god of wine seated astride a turtle); the Orangery, filled with sweet-smelling citrus plants; and the elegant avenue of cypress trees leading down to L'Isolotto (Little Island), a moated garden bedecked with statuary and fountains. There's even a *Kaffeehaus*, a rococo-style pavilion serving coffees and snacks, with exceptional views over the city and surroundings countryside.

At the top of the gardens, an 18th-century ballroom houses the Museo delle Porcellane (Porcelain Museum) with its important ceramic collection, including pieces from Sèvres, Vienna and Meissen. The views of Florence from the upper terraces are superb.

➕ 202 C2 ✉ Accessed from the
Palazzo Pitti ☎ 055 265 1816 🕐 Daily
9–7:30, Jun.–Aug.; 9–6:30, Apr.–May and
Sep.–Oct.; 9–5:30, Mar.; 9–4:30, Jan.,
Feb., Nov., Dec. Closed first and last
Mon. of every month. Last tickets 1 hour
before closing 🚌 D 🎟 Inexpensive

Cosimo I's court jester, immortalized in the
Bacchus Fountain in the Boboli Gardens

Museo delle Porcellane
✚ 203 D3 ✉ Accessed from the Palazzo Pitti ☎ 055 265 1816 🕐 Daily 9–1:50; closed first, third and fifth Mon., and second and fourth Sun. of every month 🎫 Combined entrance fee with Boboli Gardens: Inexpensive

4 Santo Spirito

Don't be put off by the austere, unfinished facade of Santo Spirito. This was Filippo Brunelleschi's last great church, described by Bernini as "the most beautiful church in the world" – light, airy and harmoniously proportioned with a colonnaded nave, graceful archways and 38 intimate side chapels, all in soothing gray and white stone.

But Santo Spirito is more than just a church: it is a splendid picture gallery filled with artistic masterworks. Each side chapel is a treasure trove of art, including several beautifully painted wooden altar frontals; Filippino Lippi's cherished *Madonna and Child with Saints* (1494) in chapel 11; and Raffaellino del Garbo's 16th-century interpretation of the same subject in chapel 30. Be sure to see the vestibule with its stylish barrel-vaulted ceiling, which leads to the sacristy – a veritable Renaissance gem designed by Antonio Giamberti da Sangallo – and a charming fountain-splashed cloister.

Next door, the **Cenacolo (Refectory) di Santo Spirito** is all that remains of the monastery that once stood here. It contains Andrea Orcagna's famous *Crucifixion* fresco, a rare example of high Gothic art in a predominantly Renaissance city, and a collection of Romanesque sculpture.

The atmospheric **Piazza di Santo Spirito,** dominated by the yellow facade of the church, resembles a cool garden with its plane trees and fountain. In the mornings, the tastes, fragrances and colors of the bustling market here (daily 8–2) provide a feast for all the senses. On Sundays there are interesting antiques and secondhand stands. By night it is a popular meeting place, its bars and

Santo Spirito's elegant colonnaded nave

cafés spilling out onto the cobbles and remaining lively until the early hours.

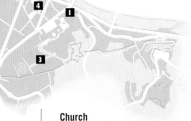

Church
✚ 202 C4
✉ Piazza di Santo Spirito 🚌 D ☎ 055 210 030 🕐 Daily 8:30–noon, 4–6 (closed Wed. afternoon). Services: Mon.–Fri. 9 a.m., Sat. 5:30 p.m., Sun. 9 and 10:30 a.m., noon and 5:30 p.m. 🎫 Free

Cenacolo
✚ 202 C4 ✉ Piazza di Santo Spirito 🚌 D ☎ 055 287 043 🕐 Tue.–Sun. 9–1:30 🎫 Inexpensive

Where to...
Eat and Drink

Prices

Expect to pay per person for a meal, excluding drinks and service
$ under €20.65 $$ €20.65–€41.31 $$$ over €41.31

The Oltrarno has always been a traditional and no-nonsense part of Florence, which is reflected in its straightforward and inexpensive restaurants. It is also an area with an up-and-coming reputation, which is reflected in several new, informal places to eat and drink, particularly on and around its two principal squares, Piazza del Carmine and Piazza di Santo Spirito. The San Frediano area is also becoming increasingly trendy, but it lies well to the east of the heart of the Oltrarno.

Angiolino $–$$

A traditional trattoria, this has a pretty interior: strings of tomatoes and plump pumpkins adorn the bar, and dried flowers and chilis hang from the old brick-vaulted main dining room. Checked tablecloths and wicker-covered wine bottles complete the picture. The menu offers simple Tuscan mainstream dishes – *crostini* (toasts), hams, salami, *ribollita* (vegetable soup), *bistecca*, *pappa al pomodoro* and other pastas, grilled meats and soups.

🚇 202 C5 ✉ Via di Santo Spirito 36r
☎ 055 239 8976 🕐 Tue.–Sun.
12:30–2:30, 7:30–10:30

Beccofino $–$$

Success often breeds success. This has certainly been the case with Beccofino, opened by David Gardner, the Scottish restaurateur responsible for Baldovino near Santa Croce (▶ 66). The atmosphere here is informal and welcoming; modern Italian food is excellent and fairly priced. The interesting and attractive setting combines comfort and style with panache (the building was previously a mosque and an art gallery). There's also an outside terrace, and a wine bar with a choice of snacks, sandwiches and wines by the glass. Food in the main restaurant might include homemade pasta with a sauce of zucchini or *una zuppa di pesce con i fagioli cannellini* (fish soup with cannellini beans).

🚇 202 C5 ✉ Piazza degli Scarlatti 1, off Lungarno Guicciardini ☎ 055 290 076 🕐 Wine bar: daily noon–3, 6–midnight. Restaurant: Tue.–Sun. 12:30–2:30, 7–11:30; Mon. 7–11:30

Borgo Antico $–$$

This is one of the Oltrarno's newer-style eating places. Its hugely popular, so becomes crowded and very noisy, though the noise and bustle is less of a problem if you can secure an outside table. Service can be slow and the food is huge. It runs the gamut of pasta, pizza, meat, fish, vegetables and salads – is rarely exceptional, though the portions are huge. Come to Borgo Antico for the convivial and lively atmosphere.

🚇 202 C4 ✉ Piazza di Santo Spirito 6r ☎ 055 210 437
🕐 Daily 12:45–2:30, 7:30–midnight

Caffè Pitti $

The piazza in front of the Palazzo Pitti offers several café options, of which this – the southernmost in the square – is by far the best thanks to its pretty and old-fashioned interior.

🚇 202 C3 ✉ Piazza Pitti 9r ☎ 055 239 6241 🕐 Daily 11 a.m.–2 a.m.

Caffè Ricchi $

Most big squares or neighborhoods have their pivotal bar, and in Piazza di Santo Spirito it's the Caffè Ricchi, a good place for breakfast, mid-morning coffee, a sandwich, a light lunch, an evening drink or a late nightcap. In good weather you can sit at outside tables on the traffic-free piazza.

➕ 202 C4 ☒ Piazza di Santo Spirito 9r ☎ 055 215 864 ⊘ Mon.–Sat. 7 a.m.–1 a.m., but earlier closing in winter

Casalinga $

This old-fashioned neighborhood trattoria still offers good basic Tuscan food, brisk service and an animated atmosphere you'd expect of a restaurant that's been run by the same family for a couple of genera-tions. Try eating here as an alterna-tive to the nearby Borgo Antico and Osteria Santo Spirito (▶ 154).

➕ 202 C4 ☒ Via del Michelozzi 9r, off Piazza di Santo Spirito ☎ 055 218 624 ⊘ Mon.–Sat. noon–2:30, 7–10

Fuori Porta $

Fuori Porta means "outside the door or gate," in this case the Porta San Miniato. This celebrated wine bar makes a good place to take a break if you're walking to or from the outlying church of San Miniato. The bar has 600 different wines, including 40 which are available by the glass, plus a wide selection of whiskeys, grappas and other unusual drinks from which to choose. The snack food is superb, and the menu also runs to a limited selection of delicious hot dishes.

➕ 204 C3 ☒ Via del Monte alle Croci 10r ☎ 055 234 2483 ⊘ Mon.–Sat. 12:30–3:30, 7–midnight

Hemingway $

Hemingway is a chic, modern little café just off Piazza del Carmine. It is unlike anything else in Florence, thanks to its specialties: tea, coffee and chocolate. You can choose from many different special teas, sample more than 20 types of coffee, try a tea-based cocktail; or gorge on the sensational cakes and chocolates. More conventional drinks and food are also available. This is a non-smoking café.

➕ 202 A5 ☒ Piazza Piattellina 9r ☎ 055 284 781 ⊘ Tue.–Sat. 4:30 p.m.–1 a.m., Sun. 11–8

Le Barrique $

After admiring the Cappella Brancacci, turn the corner into Via del Leone and try this small and attractive wine bar, where you can choose from several hot or cold dishes of the day or wash down bread, cheese and other snacks with a glass of wine.

➕ 202 A5 ☒ Via del Leone 40r ☎ 055 224 192 ⊘ Tue.–Sun. 4:30–midnight

Le Volpi e l'Uva $

This is a modern and first-rate enoteca, or wine bar, hidden in a small square just over the Ponte Vecchio. Its selection of wines by the glass is especially good –

with many unusual vintages – and changes every few days. The snack food offered, which includes crostini (toasts), panini (filled sandwiches), bread and cheese, is also excellent.

➕ 203 E4 ☒ Piazza dei Rossi 1r, off Piazza di Santa Felicità ☎ 055 239 8132 ⊘ Mon.–Sat. 10–8

Quattro Leoni $–$$

Relatively few casual visitors stumble across this trattoria, which lies in a quaint piazza just a few steps from the Palazzo Pitti. The interior is impressively rustic, with rough stone walls and colos-sal beams hung with dried flowers. The food is thoroughly Tuscan, and in summer can be enjoyed under vast umbrellas on the square outside.

➕ 203 D4 ☒ Via dei Vellutini 1-Piazza della Passera ☎ 055 218 562 ⊘ Daily noon–2:30, 7:30–11:30; closed Aug. and Wed. Oct.–May

Where to...
Shop

The Oltrarno is not an area blessed with many shops likely to interest visitors. Rather it is full of food and other stores designed to serve the local neighborhood.

ART AND ANTIQUES

Art and antiques to satisfy all tastes and budgets can be found in the fascinating medley of shops concentrated on Via Maggio and its surrounding streets. Via Maggio, in particular, has any number of well-stocked galleries and antique shops, notably **Mara Zecchi** (No. 34r, tel: 055 293368), filled with rare pieces dating from the Renaissance and earlier, and **La Malmaison** (No. 52, tel: 055 284060) and **Claudia Scalini** (No. 63r, tel: 055 216192), both excellent sources for various 19th-century artifacts. Note that all three shops are closed on Monday mornings. In a similar vein, be sure to visit **Castorina** (Via di Santo Spirito 13–15r, tel: 055 212885), remarkable for its huge numbers of decorative gilt picture frames, cherubs and ornate moldings, and browse among the many other original baroque or baroque-style items.

FOOD

Worth a journey in its own right is **La Bolognese** (Via dei Serragli 24, tel: 055 282318, open Mon.–Fri. 7–1, 4:30–7:30, Sat. 7–1), which offers a great selection of dried and fresh pastas. Or try **Torrefazione Fiorenza** (Via Santa Monaca 2r, tel: 055 287546, open Mon.–Tue., Thu.–Sat. 8–1, 4:30–7, Wed. 8–1), a lovely old aromatic shop that grinds and blends a wide range of coffees and sells spices and a variety of other goods.

Where to...
Be Entertained

Much of the entertainment in the Oltrarno is casual and offered by high-spirited restaurants, bars and cafes that stay open until the wee hours.

BARS

Dolce Vita (Piazza del Carmine, tel: 055 284 595, open Mon.–Sat. 10 a.m.–1:30 a.m., Sun. 5 p.m.–1:30 a.m.) is one of the city's most frequented bars. Forgo the over-slick interior in favor of a table outside on the piazza. **Cabiria** (Piazza Santo Spirito 4r, tel: 055 215 732, open daily 7 a.m.–1 a.m.; closed Tue. in winter) is altogether moodier and funkier, and appeals to an alternative clientele. It only really comes into its own in the evening. There are tables outside in summer.

LIVE MUSIC

For live jazz and other music, visit the popular **Il Caffè** (Piazza Pitti 9r, tel: 055 239 6241, open daily 11 a.m. until late. Alternatively, try **Zoe** (Via dei 13r, tel: 055 243 111, open Mon.–Sat. 8 a.m.–1 or 2 a.m., Sun. 6 p.m.–1 a.m.), a popular, elegant and relaxed bar (with dancing later on in the evening) in the Oltrarno's eastern margins just beyond the Ponte alle Grazie. In summer you can sit outside.

MOVIE THEATERS

Cinema Goldoni (Via dei Serragli 109, tel: 055 222 437) usually has an English-language screening once a week.

Excursions

The Tuscan countryside provides a perfect escape from the hustle and bustle and, in summer, the sheer heat of Florence. Should you tire of the capital's countless charms, why not set out to sample the rural pleasures of the region? Visit the magical cities of Lucca, Pisa, San Gimignano and Siena, all within easy reach.

Towns and Cities

As the critic Ervenat remarked, "The stones of cities mark the great hours of history," and nowhere is this more true than in Tuscany. Every Tuscan town, however humble, has at some point experienced a golden age, hence the abundance of beautiful palazzi, churches and grand piazzas – an artistic heritage that extends to even the remotest village.

You'll find that many of the towns and villages have similar features. Most have a main square flanked by their principal religious and civic buildings – the church, town hall, a loggia (built to provide shelter from the sun or rain, now commonly the site of the local market) and a towering campanile. These bell towers were built high so that the bells could be heard far and wide. They were rung to summon townspeople to Mass or to public meetings in the square, to sound the curfew and, when rung furiously (a *stormo*), to signal danger. Their

significance gave rise to the expression *campanilismo*, used to define the strong Tuscan character trait of parochialism.

The main square of most Tuscan towns and villages is also the scene of local festivities and the daily *passeggiata* when, following a lengthy siesta, the entire population promenades in their finery, gazing in shop windows and admiring each other. There are few places in Italy outside Rome and Milan where the art of *fare bella figura* (looking and being seen to look good) is more keenly practised than in the cities of Tuscany.

Tuscans are fiercely proud of their heritage, their countryside and their ancestry, which dates back to the Etruscans. But they are determined not to allow their great cities to become museum pieces given over entirely to tourism. Instead, they

Previous page: Tuscan landscape near Monticello

Above: Rolling Tuscan countryside near Monte Oliveto Maggiore

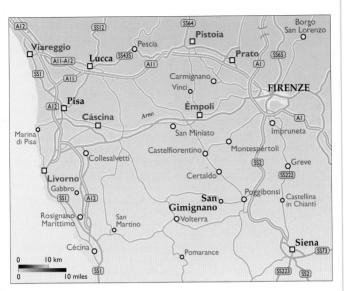

have cultivated thriving service sectors, especially in the fields of finance, architecture and conservation. Glass, marble and motorcycles count among the main industrial products, while Tuscany's crafts, olive oil and wines are respected worldwide. Living in a hard-working and economically independent region, the locals scorn the government in Rome, with its ceaseless bureaucracy. Many of them would prefer to revert to the autonomy they enjoyed before the unification of Italy in 1870.

The Countryside

Don't just visit Lucca, Pisa, San Gimignano, Siena and Tuscany's many hilltop towns and villages. The region's true identity is to be found in its beautiful countryside – its seductive, softly hued landscapes of undulating green hillsides splashed with wildflowers, hiding sun-bleached farms within their folds; picturesque lemon- and apricot-colored villas; olive groves; vineyards; fields of lavender, corn and bare terracotta earth; and single lines of cypresses. For this is quintessential Tuscany – an intoxicating backdrop to the cities that harbor the greatest art treasures of the Italian Renaissance; the archetypal Italian countryside, which for centuries has had a bewitching effect on visitors.

Siena

Siena is arguably the most beautiful city in Tuscany. Its appearance is distinguished from Florence by its hilltop site, its predominance of rich red brick as the main building material rather than honey-coloured stone, and its plethora of medieval monuments, which are a perfect foil to Renaissance Florence. As an alderman of the city once remarked: 'For those involved in governing the city, the main problem is one of beauty.'

View from the Duomo over Siena's main square, the Campo

According to folklore, Siena was founded by Senius, son of Remus, one of the two legendary founders of Rome – hence the abundant statues of the she-wolf who suckled Romulus and Remus. Since then the city has played a distinguished role in history, which is reflected in its rich cultural heritage. Its heyday came in the Middle Ages, when it was one of Europe's wealthiest cities. Not only did it boast a thriving textile trade but, much to the envy of Florence, it established the first international banks ever, raking in money from the whole of

Christendom on behalf of the papacy. Sienese painters (including Andrea Pisano, Simone Martini, Duccio di Buoninsegna and the Lorenzetti brothers) were at the forefront of Italian art. Their minute attention to detail and their early experimentation with techniques of perspective were widely respected and they were in constant demand throughout Tuscany.

However, the Black Death of 1348 dealt Siena a cruel blow: three-quarters of the population died, and the city never really fully recovered. For centuries it languished in the shadows of the then-thriving Florence and even in the late 19th century Henry James found it a 'cracking, peeling, fading, crumbling, rotting' city. But today, Siena is an elegant, old-fashioned provincial city, grown rich on banking and tourism, with plentiful art treasures, stylish shops and fantastic cellar restaurants – all encased within ancient city walls. There's a charming, almost medieval atmosphere in its uneven cobbled lanes, its dark stepped alleyways and the way in which the city is still divided into ancient districts called *contrade*, a system unique to Siena.

Coffee time in the Campo

At the height of its power, the city was split into more than 40 such districts, but since the 17th century there have been just 17. Each is still a village at heart, with its own symbols, traditions, social club, museum, church and fountain, where newborn babies are baptized into the *contrada*. The inhabitants are fiercely proud of their wards, leading to inevitable competition that reaches its climax each year at the Palio (▶ 164), Tuscany's best-known festival.

Piazza del Campo

No matter which way you turn in the labyrinth of medieval streets, even the darkest, most tortuous alleyway seems to lead back to Siena's main square, undoubtedly one of the most striking designs of Italian town planning. This vast, fan-shaped open space of red brick is divided into nine segments by long spokes of white marble and tilts with the natural slope of the hillside. Even the semicircle of elegant, rose-colored palazzi flanking the square was built according to strict 13th-century regulations, laid down to preserve the dignity of the city's great showpiece. The majestic Palazzo Pubblico and its bell tower, the second highest medieval tower in Italy, dominate the square. By day, the Campo is a popular meeting place, but by night it has an almost magical atmosphere, abuzz with crowds dining al fresco in the restaurants and cafés which fringe the uniquely seashell-shaped square.

Above: Cathedral treasures in the Museo dell' Opera del Duomo

Left: Palio celebrations outside the Duomo

Below: The distinctive cathedral campanile, with narrowing windows

Tourist Information Office
✚ 206 B4
✉ Piazza del Campo 56
☎ 0577 280551

Museo Civico and Torre del Mangia
✚ 206 B4 ✉ Piazza del Campo 1
☎ 0577 292263
🕐 Daily 10 a.m.–11 p.m., Apr. to mid-Sep.; Mon.–Sat. 10–7, Sun. 10–1:30, rest of year

Duomo
✚ 206 A3 ✉ Piazza del Duomo
☎ 0577 47321
🕐 Daily 9–7:30, mid-Mar. through Oct.; 9–1:30, 2:30–5, rest of year

Museo dell'Opera del Duomo
✚ 206 A3
✉ Piazza del Duomo
☎ 0577 283048
🕐 Daily 9–7:30, mid-Mar. through Sep.; 9–6 Oct.; 9–1:30, rest of year

The Palio

The Palio, a fiercely contested bareback horse race between the *contrades* of the city, takes place in the Campo each year on July 2 and August 16. It was first recorded in 1283, although it most likely had its origins in Roman military training. Each horse is blessed by the priest of the local *contrada*, then by the bishop at the Duomo, amid parades of drummers, trumpeters and flag-throwers all dressed in medieval costume. The massive crowds cram into the Campo, where straws are drawn to decide the heats. The actual races are over in a flash – each lost and won in just three laps of the square. The victor is awarded a *palio* (banner) and, in the evening, the winning horse takes a place of honor at an enormous open-air candlelit banquet in the square. It's a wonderful spectacle. You can see the Palio for free if you're prepared to stand, but you'll need to arrive early and be prepared for a long, hot wait. Tickets for numbered seats and balcony places are expensive and sell out many months in advance. Advance bookings can be made through Palio Viaggi, Piazza Gramsci 7 (tel: 0557 280 828).

Palazzo Pubblico

The Palazzo Pubblico, at the lower end of the Campo, has been the seat of government since the 13th century. Part of it (the Museo Civico) is open to the public and contains some of Tuscany's finest Sienese paintings. Ambrogio Lorenzetti's dazzling pair of frescoes, *The Allegories of Good and Bad Government* (1338), in the Sala della Pace are considered among the world's most important medieval secular paintings.

The 340-foot Torre del Mangia bell tower was built as a symbol of the freedom of the city-state to mark the end of the feudal era. It was named after its first bell-ringer, nicknamed *Mangiaguadagni* (literally "eat the profits") because of his idleness. Climb the 505 steps to the top. You'll be rewarded by unforgettable views.

Duomo

The spectacular black-and-white striped marble cathedral (built between 1215 and 1376) and matching campanile stand proud atop Siena's highest hill. The Sienese had hoped to make it the largest church in Christendom, intending the vast nave we see today to be merely the transept of a far greater building. In 1339, with this in mind, they began to build a new nave to the south, but plague struck the city, wiping out not only the funds but the congregation, too, so the church remained unfinished.

The incomplete nave now houses the **Museo dell'Opera del Duomo**, containing the sculptures by Giovanni Pisano that once adorned the facade of the cathedral, and Duccio's masterwork, a multi-paneled *Maestà* (enthroned Madonna). The abandoned wall of the Duomo, accessed through the museum, affords great views of Siena and the surrounding countryside.

The facade is a lavish confection of pink and white marble with an intriguing (and, some say, tasteless) blend of medieval statuary and 19th-century mosaic. The interior is equally ornate, described by writer John Ruskin as "overstriped, over-crocketed, over-gabled … a piece of faithless vanity." Highlights include Pisano's carved pulpit panels depicting scenes from the life of Christ; the inlaid marble pavement illustrating stories from the Bible; and Duccio's magnificent stained-glass windows in the apse.

SIENA: INSIDE INFO

Top tips The city center is **closed to traffic,** so be prepared to do a lot of walking! Thankfully, all the main sights are within easy reach of each other.
• Climb the Torre del Mangia or the old cathedral wall to get a feel for **Siena's size and layout.** The city, encircled within medieval city walls, is built on three ridges that all meet at Piazza del Campo.
• Try the delicious **local specialties,** *panforte di Siena* (a dark, dense cake made with candied fruit, nuts, cinnamon and cloves) and *ricciarelli* (sweets made from ground almonds, orange peel and honey).

One not to miss The **Enoteca Italiana Permanente** (National Wine Library) in the former munition cellars of the Fortezza promotes Italian wines. It claims to hold every variety of wine the country produces. What's more, its bar (open daily 3–midnight) offers all the wines by the glass or bottle. *Salute!*...

Hidden gems The **Pinacoteca Nazionale** (Via San Pietro 29, tel: 0577 281161, open: Mon.–Sat. 8:15–7:15, Sun. 8:15–1:15) contains a precious collection of paintings from the Sienese School.
• The **Ospedale di Santa Maria della Scala** (Piazza del Duomo, tel: 0577 224811, open: Mon.–Thu. 10–6, Fri.–Sun. 10 a.m.–11 p.m., Jul.–Sep.; daily 10:30–4:30, rest of year), housed in the ancient medieval hospital building, boasts a fascinating collection of **15th–century frescoes**.
• The only known **authentic portrait of St. Catherine of Siena** hangs in San Domenico (Piazza San Domenico, tel: 0577 280204, open: daily 7:30–1, 3–6:30).

Getting there In the early 19th century it took two days to travel the 70 km (43 miles) from Florence to Siena, and those who undertook the journey would write their wills before setting out! Today, it's much easier.
• The **fastest route from Florence is by car** (about 1 hour) on the toll-free Superstrada de Palio. The scenic Chiantigiana SS222 takes longer but passes through "Chianti Country"and some of Tuscany's most beautiful countryside. Cars are prohibited in the city center, but there are plenty of clearly signposted parking lots.
• SITA operate a regular **bus service** (approximately one an hour) from Florence's train station to Piazza San Domenico in Siena (tel: 055 214721 for information).
• **Trains** run from Florence most hours and take about 90 minutes. Some involve changing at Empoli. The station is 1.5 km (about a mile) from the city center so you'll need to catch a bus from the station to Piazza Matteotti, near the city center.

San Gimignano

Perched on a hilltop beyond olive groves, cypresses and vineyards, San Gimignano is one of the most picturesque towns in Tuscany, famous for its elegant, soaring towers. These *belle torri* were the skyscrapers of the medieval Tuscan world, hence the town's popular epithet, "Manhattan of the Middle Ages."

In San Gimignano's prime, there were a staggering 72 towers in the town, of which just 14 survive. They were built mainly in the 12th and 13th centuries as much as status symbols as for defense, with every noble family eager to demonstrate its prestige. The town thrived as an important trading post on the Via Francigena pilgrim route from northern Europe to Rome, and its population was double the size of today. But the plague of 1348, followed by the diversion of the pilgrim route, led to its decline. In later years many of the towers were demolished and the stone used to build citadels.

Sidewalk terraces are a trademark of San Gimignano's bustling piazzas

André Suares, on his Grand Tour of Europe at the turn of the 19th century, considered San Gimignano the most fascinating town in Italy. During his visit he also noted, "there is hardly a foreigner to be seen on this beautiful, languid August afternoon of torrid heat." This is no longer the case. The town's picturesque setting and proximity to Florence and Siena have made it into something of a tourist trap, with daily invasions of bus-tours thronging the immaculately maintained streets and souvenir shops. However, at sunset, after the last of the day-trippers have left, the town takes on a magical, timeless atmosphere.

Tourist Information Office
✉ Piazza del Duomo 1
☎ 0577 940008

Museo Civico
✉ Piazza del Duomo
☎ 0577 940008
🕐 Daily 9:30–7; closed Mon., Nov.–Feb.
🎫 Moderate (including entry to the Torre Grossa)

Collegiata
✉ Piazza del Duomo
🕐 Daily 9:30–7 (5:30 in winter)
🎫 Moderate

The Piazzas

Since the 1960s, San Gimignano has been under the auspices of
UNESCO. Walking through the two interlocking main squares
– **Piazza del Duomo** and **Piazza della Cisterna** – is rather like
walking onto a stage set, such is the magnificence of the surrounding buildings. Pause for an espresso or an ice cream,
absorb the atmosphere and marvel at the medieval palazzi
surrounding you. The Piazza della Cisterna is named after the
well at its center, the focal point of activity for more than eight
centuries. On the stone parapet you can see the ancient grooves
made by the taut ropes once used to draw water.

In Piazza del Duomo you'll find the **Palazzo Vecchio del
Podestà**, whose tower (1239) is probably the town's oldest, and
the grand town hall, **Palazzo del Popolo,** which houses the
Museo Civico on the upper floors.

Museo Civico

Here in the frescoed Sala del Consiglio, Dante, acting as ambas-
sador for the Guelph cause (▶ 125), tried to persuade the
town to join an alliance with Florence in 1300 against Pisa,
Siena, Arezzo and Volterra. San Gimignano's "reward" for
cooperation was the loss of its independence and a gradual
tightening of Florentine control. Today, the hall is dominated

Startling skyline
– the city of
beautiful towers

by a glorious *Maestà* by Lippo Memmi. The remaining galleries contain treasured paintings by Filippino Lippi, Benozzo Gozzoli, Pinturicchio (Bernardino di Betto Vagio), Taddeo di Bartolo and Memmo di Filippuccio.

The museum also affords access to the **Torre Grossa,** with memorable views across the pantiled roofs to the surrounding countryside and to the distant hills beyond.

Collegiata

The plain Romanesque facade of San Gimignano's former cathedral belies the extravagant interior, modeled on Siena's cathedral and decorated with four major fresco cycles. Those to look out for include Bartolo di Fredi's amazingly detailed

A bird's-eye view from the Torre Grossa

Old Testament Scenes (1367), 26 scenes which describe the stories from Genesis; Lippo Memmi's *Scenes from the Life of Christ* (1333–41); and Taddeo di Bartolo's *Last Judgement, Paradise and Hell* (1410), notable for its luridly graphic and entertaining detail.

The adjoining **Cappella di Santa Fina** is a veritable Renaissance masterpiece, with frescoes by Domenico Ghirlandaio describing some of the miracles worked by Fina (a young girl) from her sick bed.

SAN GIMIGNANO: INSIDE INFO

Top tip If you are short of time, concentrate on the frescoes in the Collegiata, and bypass the paintings in the Museo Civico, making your way instead straight to the top of the Torre Grossa to enjoy the impressive views.

Hidden gems The **garden at the "Rocca" fortress** at the top of the town, with fig and olive trees and wonderful views, is an ideal spot to write postcards or have an afternoon siesta.
• Look for **Benozzo Gozzoli's detailed fresco cycle** depicting the life of St. Augustine (1464) in the church of Sant'Agostino in Piazza Sant'Agostino.

Getting there The easiest way to reach San Gimignano, 57 km (35 miles) southwest of Florence, is **by car.** On arrival, you'll find there are plenty of parking spaces outside the main walls.
• By **public transportation,** catch a train or a bus (contact SITA, Via Santa Caterina di Siena 15, tel: 055 483651 for information) to Poggibonsi, then a TRA-IN bus (tel: 0577 204245) to San Gimignano. Allow at least 2 hours.

Lucca

There's an undeniably special charm about Lucca. Secure within splendid Renaissance ramparts lies an enthralling tangle of perfectly preserved medieval streets and squares graced by exquisite churches, gardens and palazzi. For Henry James (*Italian Hours*, 1909), Lucca was "overflowing with everything that makes for ease, for plenty, for beauty, for interest and good example."

Atmospheric Piazza del Mercato, surrounded by tall, irregular, medieval houses

In 180 BC, the town became a colony of ancient Rome, and the legacy of this era is still evident in the regular grid pattern of its streets. For years the two cities fought against Pisa and Florence, hence the handful of fortified palaces (the former homes of feudal lords) with watchtowers such as Torre Guinigi – one of the last towers in Italy to retain the old custom of having a

Tourist Information Office
✉ Piazzale Verdi ☎ 0583 419689

Duomo di San Martino
✉ Piazza del Duomo ☎ 0583 957068 🕐 Mon.–Sat. 9–5:30, Sun. 1–5:30, Apr.–Sep.; Mon.–Sat. 9–4, Sun. 1–4:30, rest of year

San Michele in Foro
✉ Piazza di San Michele in Foro 🕐 Mon.–Sat. 9–5:30, Sun. 1–5:30, Apr.–Sep.; Mon.–Sat. 9–4, Sun. 1–4:30, rest of year

tuft of holm oak crown its summit. The lords grew wealthy from olive oil and silk, and they used diplomacy rather than force to keep Lucca an independent republic, while other Tuscan powers succumbed to the Spanish and the French. Unlike their tourist-courting neighbors the Pisans and Florentines, the Lucchesi seem oblivious to their town's cultural heritage. As a result, Lucca remains remarkably unspoiled and relatively devoid of visitors.

Shopping in Lucca – a local craft market

Duomo di San Martino

To accommodate the adjoining belfry, Lucca's Duomo has an unusual, asymmetrical marble facade. Nevertheless, with its lace-like arcading and rich decoration, it remains a sublime example of the popular Pisan-Romanesque style. St. Martin, the Duomo's patron saint, is depicted on the facade in various scenes, including one where he cuts his cloak with a sword to share with a beggar.

The interior contains the *Volto Santo*, a revered 13th-century wooden effigy believed to have been carved by Christ's follower Nicodemus at the time of the Crucifixion, and one of Italy's finest pieces of funerary sculpture – Jacopo della Quercia's *Tomb of Ilaria del Carretto* (1406–13), depicting the youthful bride of Paolo Guinigi, a member of the powerful Guinigi family, which ruled the city in the 15th century.

Piazza del Mercato

During Roman times this was the site of the amphitheater, and its perfect oval plan has been preserved – even the entrances to the piazza are exactly where the gladiators would have entered. Today, this is Lucca's best-loved square, an evocative circle of old medieval houses in faded shades of terra-cotta and yellow, with laundry hanging out from the upper floors above the restaurants and cafés that spill out onto the square. There is a small market here on Wednesday mornings.

Elegant palazzi grace the narrow streets of Lucca

Cycling around the city walls

San Michele in Foro

This is the finest of Lucca's many churches built in the exuberant Pisan-Romanesque style. The facade is so lavishly decorated that you could be forgiven for mistaking it for the Duomo, with its riot of superimposed arcades, ornate pillars and barley-sugar columns. Unusually, the second arch is open to the sky, as is the light and airy two-stage pediment, surmounted by a statue of St. Michael (framed by a pair of trumpet-blowing angels) crushing the dragon.

Piazza di San Michele in Foro is Lucca's main square, more central than Piazza del Duomo. Its name "in Foro" indicates that it stands on the original site of the Roman forum – the city's main square, even in ancient times.

LUCCA: INSIDE INFO

Top tips For an **overview of Lucca,** do a circuit of the city walls, about 4 km (2.5 miles). The wide ramparts, which have been turned into a raised park, shaded by trees, offer a superb view of the surrounding countryside and the jagged Apuan Alps, their summits white with snow in winter.

Hidden gems Casa di Puccini (Corte San Lorenzo 8, Via di Poggio, tel: 0583 584028, open daily 10–6, summer; Tue.–Sun. 10–1, 3–6, winter) is the birthplace of the great Italian composer Giacomo Puccini and a must for music lovers.
• Look out for the **art nouveau shop-fronts and interiors** along Via Fillungo, and have an espresso in Caffè di Simo at No. 58.

Getting there There are a couple of **trains** an hour from Florence to Lucca. The journey takes around 1½ hours and the train station is outside the walls (south of the city) in Piazza Ricasoli.
• Regular **buses** (journey time 1 hour) run from Florence. They are organized by Lazzi (Piazza Stazione 47r, tel: 055 351061 for information).
• If you go by **car,** you may find **parking difficult** as cars are not permitted in the city center. The best parking lot is Le Tagliate, near Porta San Donato.

Pisa

Together with Venetian gondolas and the Colosseum in Rome, the gravity-defying Leaning Tower has become a symbol of Italy and is always the main port of call for first-time visitors to Pisa.

Yet, there's more to Pisa than the tower. It is the gateway to Tuscany, with an international airport (➤ 36), and the nation's second busiest port. From the 11th to the 13th centuries, at the height of its power, Pisa's formidable navy dominated the western Mediterranean and, until its harbor silted up 600 years ago, the languid Arno river was the city's lifeblood. Today, this bustling, industrious city still contains vestiges of its former glory – medieval towers, Romanesque architectural gems and mercantile palazzi, painted peach, yellow, terra-cotta and sepia.

If you stroll the narrow streets and wide cobbled piazzas, join in the *passeggiata* under the arcades of the main shopping street, Borgo Stretto, visit the elegant Piazza dei Cavalieri, the historic heart of Pisa, and shop with locals at the delightfully provincial market in Piazza Vettovaglie (Victuals Square), you will find a side of the city that many visitors overlook.

Campo dei Miracoli

Pisa's remarkable Field of Miracles, a great green swathe of lawn in its northwestern corner, boasts one of the most ambitious building programs of the entire Middle Ages. The four main elements – the Duomo, the Battistero, the Campo Santo cemetery and the legendary Torre Pendente (Leaning Tower) – complement each other perfectly, all dressed in dazzling white marble, with the city walls as a backdrop.

The legendary Torre Pendente and Duomo on the Campo dei Miracoli

Also in the Field of Miracles, you'll find two small museums: the **Museo delle Sinopie**, displaying sketches and fragmented remains of the fresco cycle from Campo Santo, and the **Museo dell'Opera del Duomo**, in the cathedral's chapter house,

Relax in one of Pisa's chic arcade cafés

Battistero and Campo Santo	Duomo	Museo delle Sinopie and Museo dell'Opera del Duomo
✉ Piazza dei Miracoli	✉ Piazza dei Miracoli	✉ Piazza dei Miracoli
☎ 050 560547	☎ 050 560547	🕐 Daily 10–7:40
🕐 Daily 8–7:40, Apr.–Sep.; 9–5, Mar. and Oct.; 9–4:40, Nov.–Jan.	🕐 Mon.–Sat. 10–7:40, Sun. 1–7:40, Mar.–Oct.; Mon.–Sat. 10–12:45, Sun. 3–4:45, Nov.–Jan.	

containing treasures from the Duomo and Battistero.

Visitors come in their millions to see the **Leaning Tower,** and marvel that gravity hasn't yet caused it to tumble. Indeed, the fascination of the tower is not its gleaming white marble, nor its six elegant registers of classical columns, but rather its defect. Pisa's tower has never stood upright. Eight centuries ago it was already tilting, probably as a result of an unstable water table, and the authorities believe the tilt is increasing by a third of an inch a decade. This accounts for the huge scaffolding of steel wires, struts, supports and counterweights – rather like a dentist's brace attempting to straighten a crooked tooth.

An Historic Tug of War

Every year special regattas and jousting competitions are organized in memory of Pisa's ancient maritime prowess. The grandest spectacle takes place on June 27 on the Ponte di Mezzo, when the ancient rivalry between north and south is reenacted in the highly contested *gioco dei ponte* (tug of war) across the bridge.

Left: Pisa was once a thriving port and vestiges of its former wealth and power can be found throughout the city

Pisa's **Battistero** is the largest in Italy and a veritable jewel, blending elegant Romanesque arcades with a Gothic crown. The interior is austere with simple, striped walls. Climb up to the gallery (and if you're feeling really energetic, up to the superior gallery) for a bird's-eye view of the piazza.

Behind the Baptistery, the **Campo Santo** cemetery is an ideal place for meditation. Unfortunately, Allied bombing destroyed most of the frescoes in the cloister, leaving its white marble bare.

The 300-foot-long **Duomo**, begun in 1063, took two centuries to complete. Its lace-like facade, made of white Carrara marble with superimposed registers of columns, set the pattern for the Romano-Pisan style of architecture that spread to the rest of Tuscany and beyond.

PISA: INSIDE INFO

Top tips The **tourist information office** (Piazza Stazione, tel: 050 42291) just outside the central station provides useful maps. There is a second office at 2 Via Cammeo (tel: 050 560464).

• Consider **renting a bicycle** to tour the town. They are available from the parking lot in Via Battisti, near the railroad station.

• It works out less expensive to **buy a combined ticket** for the sights of the Campo dei Miracoli: the Leaning Tower, the Duomo, the Battistero, the Campo Santo cemetery and the two museums.

Getting there The easiest way to reach Pisa from Florence is to travel by **train.** There is a regular service (two or three trains an hour) and the journey takes approximately 1 hour.

Walks

1 SAN MINIATO
Walk

Among Florence's many charms is its proximity to the Tuscan countryside. This walk starts from the Ponte Vecchio and takes you into the chain of hills that frame the southern perimeter of the city beyond the Oltrarno, with unforgettable views not only of Florence but also of the surrounding rural landscape.

1–2
Begin on the southern bank of the Arno, with the **Ponte Vecchio** (▶ 122–125) immediately behind you. Walk straight ahead up Via de' Guicciardini. The elevated **Corridoio Vasariano** (▶ 54), with its distinctive circular windows called *occuli* (eyes), will be on your left. Turn left into **Piazza di Santa Felicità** (▶ 152). Santa Felicità is believed to stand on the site of a late Roman church. In the square, a fountain combines a 16th-century bronze Bacchus with a Roman marble sarcophagus.

DISTANCE 4.5 km (3 miles) **TIME** 2½ hours (including visits)
START/END POINT Ponte Vecchio ✚ 203 E4
WHEN TO GO? The walk is long and hilly, so it's best avoided in the heat of the midday sun. Take a sun-hat, your camera and plenty of water.

2–3
Take the right fork out of the piazza, signed Costa di San Giorgio. This narrow lane winds steeply uphill, quickly leaving the city behind. House No. 19 was once Galileo's home.

Soon the small houses give way to large villas and beautiful gardens hidden behind high stone walls on either side of the lane. The road flattens out at Porta San Giorgio, the city's oldest surviving gate. Built in 1260, it is decorated with frescoes and carvings of St. George and the dragon. Go through the gate and to your immediate right is the Forte di Belvedere (currently closed for restoration). The Medici family added this once impregnable fortress to the city defenses in 1590, with just one means of access – a secret door in their palace gardens. Its ramparts command extensive views over Florence and the **Giardino di Boboli** (▶ 152).

Make the steep climb to San Miniato for sweeping city views
Previous page: Dawn of a new day, near San Quirico d'Orcia

3–4

Return to Porta San Giorgio. With the gateway behind you, turn immediately left along Via di Belvedere, a picturesque lane that follows the walls of the city's 14th-century defenses. The vista of olive groves, cypress trees and lush terraced hillsides to your right is broken only by the occasional peach-colored villa. Follow the road as it drops rapidly downhill to the small gate-way of Porta San Miniato.

4–5

Turn right at the gateway onto Via del Monte alle Croci (there is a small café here on the left side for refreshment), which gently snakes its way uphill to the Viale Galileo Galilei. Alternatively, you can take the more direct (but considerably steeper) "Way of the Cross,"

involving more than 100 stone steps, which begins soon after the bar, on your left. Continue up to the church of **San Miniato** (▶ 150–151) with its dazzling patterned marble façade and panoramic terrace.

San Miniato has always been held close to Florentine hearts. In 1530, during the Siege of

Taking a Break

You'll find bars and cafés near San Miniato and also toward the end of the walk in Via di San Niccolò and Via de Bardi.

Decorated with reproductions of Michelangelo's most celebrated sculptures and packed with souvenir stands, the square is always abuzz with visitors, here to enjoy the exceptional views over the terra-cotta roofs of Florence to the hilly countryside beyond.

6–7
Several stairways descend from Piazzale Michelangelo. Take the flight that leaves the square center-left, and zigzag your way down toward the Arno on the footpath through acacia groves to Porta San Niccolò, the imposing 14th-century gateway in the city wall at the bottom.

7–8
Turn left along Via di San Niccolò. Majestic buildings line the street, among them the 13th-century Palazzo Mozzi in Piazza de' Mozzi and Museo Bardini opposite (closed for restoration). The latter, the home of the 19th-century antiquarian and collector Stefano Bardini, is built almost entirely from medieval and Renaissance masonry.

8–9
From Piazza de' Mozzi, head toward the Arno and make your way back to the Ponte Vecchio along the riverbank.

Piazzale Michelangelo – a favorite with photographers

5–6
Leave San Miniato by an archway in the buildings to the west (beside the monks' shop) and start your gradual descent back to the city. Before long you will pass the

Florence, the bell tower was used as a watchtower. It was installed with cannon to shoot at the Medici troops and wrapped in mattresses to absorb the impact of enemy fire. In 1600 it was used as a hospital for plague victims and, later, as a hospice for the poor. The cemetery contains a splendid array of funerary monuments, including family tombs the size of miniature houses and the grave of Carlo Collodi, creator of *Pinocchio*.

apricot-colored church of San Salvatore al Monte, a charming Franciscan church with sober *pietra forte* decoration and early panel paintings dedicated to martyrs Cosmas and Damian, twin-brother physicians who refused to charge any fee for their services.

Continue downhill to Piazzale Michelangelo, laid out in 1869 by Giuseppe Poggi (who also converted the fortified area around the church into a grand cascade of terraces and stairways).

2 FIESOLE

Walk

DISTANCE 3 km (2 miles) **TIME** Minimum 2 hours (including visits) **GETTING THERE** It's an easy 30-minute bus ride to Piazza Mino da Fiesole. Catch the frequent bus No. 7 from the train station or Piazza di San Marco
START POINT Piazza Mino da Fiesole **END POINT** Piazza di San Domenico
WHEN TO GO? Choose a clear day to enjoy the breathtaking views of the city

This walk around the ancient hilltop town of Fiesole offers a taste of the lush, rolling countryside surrounding Florence. With its cooling breezes and unforgettable views, it also provides welcome respite from the constant crowds in the city.

1–2

Start in the main square, Piazza Mino da Fiesole. This hilltop site has been inhabited since the Bronze Age, and around 600 BC it was one of the most important Etruscan cities. In the third century BC it became a Roman city, but it began to decline after the Romans founded *Florentia* in the first century BC (▶ 8–9). The **Duomo**, dedicated to Romulus, the martyred Bishop of Fiesole, dominates the piazza. It was founded in the 11th century and its spartan interior bears much resemblance to San Miniato (▶ 150–151), with a wooden roof, three-tiered structure and columns topped with reused

Roman capitals. After visiting the church, head uphill to the 14th-century Palazzo Comunale, a beautiful yellow building with columns, stone crests and an attractive second-floor loggia. Here too is a bronze equestrian statue of King Vittorio Emanuele II and Giuseppe Garibaldi, hero of Italian nationalism.

2–3

Return toward the Duomo and take the first turn to the right, around the back of the church into Via Dupré. At a fork in the road, go through the archway straight ahead into the **Museo Fiesole**, an open-air

The Museo Fiesole is a rich repository of ancient remains

archeological site set into the hillside containing important Etruscan and Roman remains. Highlights include the Etruscan temple, some partly restored Roman baths and the beautifully preserved Roman theater, capable of holding 3,000 people. It is still used for ballet, theater and concert performances during the Estate Fiesolana (Fiesole Summer Festival).

3–4
When exiting the museum, turn left along Via Portigiani past the tourist information office and continue along Via Marini to admire the typically Tuscan landscape stretching into the distance.

4–5
Backtrack past the tourist office to the archway. Straight ahead, you will see the entrance to the **Museo Bandini**, worth a visit for its collection of 13th- to 15th-century paintings of the Tuscan School, which were bequeathed to Fiesole by local aristocrat Angelo Bandini.

5–6
Return to the main square. Turn right out of Via Dupré and follow the main road around to the left along Via Fra' Giovanni Angelico. Bear first right onto Via Vecchia Fiesolana, then descend

steeply, curving around to the right past the church of San Girolamo. Following a brief stretch with high walls on either side, you will reach Villa Medici on the left. This impressive cream-colored mansion with dark green shutters was one of the earliest of the family's country retreats, built in 1461 by Michelozzi for Cosimo il Vecchio de' Medici.

6–7
Follow the road as it swerves around to the left beneath the villa. Turn left at the fork in the road down Via Bandini. When you arrive at the junction with Via San Ansano (a grass track) beside a pretty apricot-

colored church, bear right past olive groves and down a roughly surfaced lane, which twists and turns steeply past numerous attractive villas and gardens. At the bottom you will reach a T-junction. Turn left, by more country houses, and continue until you reach the main road.

(although the bell tower and arcade were added two centuries later). The interior contains several works by Fra Angelico, who was prior here, and a painting attributed to Zanobi Poggini depicting Girolamo Savonarola (► 70) showing Florence to Christ and the Virgin Mary.

The church marks the start of the hamlet of San Domenico with its scattered houses, café and pizzeria. From the bus stop opposite the church, the No. 7 bus runs frequently back to the center of Florence.

The Romanesque facade of Badia Fiesolana

7–8

Turn immediately right (off the main road) and continue a short distance until you reach the **Badia Fiesolana**, a 15th-century church with a pretty Romanesque facade of inlaid marble and a magnificent Renaissance interior, decorated with the local gray sandstone called *pietra serena*. Once the residence of the Bishop of Fiesole, it is without doubt the most important religious building on the outskirts of Florence, allegedly built on the spot where St. Romulus was martyred.

8–9

Retrace your steps back to the main road. Facing you is the large apricot-colored church of **San Domenico**, built in the early 15th century

Taking a Break

You'll be spoiled for choice of restaurants, cafés and bars in Fiesole. Try Etrusca for pizzas or dine alfresco on the panoramic terrace of upscale Ristorante Aurora.

Opening Times

Tourist Information Office
⊠ Via Portigiani 3–5
☎ 055 5978373
🕒 Mon.–Sat. 9–8, Sun. 10–7

Duomo
⊠ Piazza Mino da Fiesole
🕒 Daily 8–noon, 3–6

Museo Fiesole
⊠ Via Portigiani 27
🕒 Daily 9:30–6:30
💶 Expensive

Museo Bandini
⊠ Via Dupré 1
☎ 055 59477
🕒 Daily 9:30–6:30

3 EAST OF THE DUOMO

Walk

This circular route takes you away from the frenetic city center to explore the atmospheric workers' quarter of Florence – an area few tourists penetrate. Its neighborhood shops, its colorful markets and its bustling narrow alleys reverberate to the beat of day-to-day Florentine life.

DISTANCE 3 km (2 miles) **TIME** 1½ hours (excluding visits)
START/END POINT Piazza del Duomo ⊞ 199 F2
WHEN TO GO? Mornings are best, when the two daily markets are at their liveliest

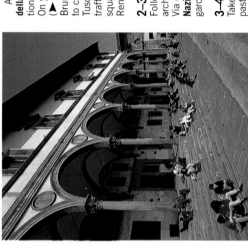

1–2

Leave Piazza del Duomo along Via dei Servi, the busy street that starts behind the cathedral's apse, to the left of the **Museo dell'Opera del Duomo** (▶ 103) and head in a northeasterly direction. This road was once the old processional route from the Duomo to the Church of Santissima Annunziata. At the first crossroad (with Via de' Pucci), notice the enormous Palazzo Pucci on your left, the former ancestral home of the famous fashion designer Marchese Emilio Pucci (▶ 26). Look back periodically for impressive views of the cathedral's dome.

Brunelleschi arches – Piazza della Santissima Annunziata

After one more crossroads, you'll reach **Piazza della Santissima Annunziata** (▶ 106), an exceptionally fine square, flanked by graceful arcades. On your right, the **Spedale degli Innocenti** (▶ 107), with its elegant loggia by Brunelleschi, was the first Renaissance building to combine classical proportions with traditional Tuscan Romanesque architecture. Except for the traffic racing across the north side of the square, it would still have the feeling of a Renaissance courtyard.

2–3

Follow the flow of the traffic through the archway beside the Spedale degli Innocenti onto Via della Colonna. **The Museo Archeologico Nazionale** (▶ 106–107), set in picturesque gardens, is on your left.

3–4

Take the second turning right onto Borgo Pinti, past the church and former convent of Santa Maria Maddalena dei Pazzi at No. 58 (now a

4–5

Cross Piazza di Sant'Ambrogio, and head south a short distance down Via de' Macci.

The first road on the left leads to the local market – **Mercato Sant'Ambrogio**, a smaller version of the city's main cast-iron-and-glass **Mercato Centrale** (➤ 111) – selling clothes, fruits and vegetables, meat, pasta, cheeses, olives, antipasti and regional wines.

5–6

Return to Piazza di Sant'Ambrogio. A left turn onto Via Pietrapiana leads to Piazza dei Ciompi and a second market – the **Mercato delle Pulci** (flea market), with its ramshackle booths of bric-à-brac. Alongside it, you'll find the arcaded Loggia del Pesce, originally built by Giorgio Vasari for the fishmongers of the

school) and peer into the charming courtyard garden on the opposite side of the road at No. 55. Turn left at the next crossroads onto Via de' Pilastri. Straight ahead is the plain, cream-colored church of Sant'Ambrogio with its simple brick bell tower. This neighborhood church is little known to tourists but contains the tombs of the great Renaissance sculptors Mino da Fiesole and Andrea del Verrocchio.

Mercato Sant'Ambrogio

6–7

Head due south from Piazza dei Ciompi along Borgo Allegri toward the campanile of Santa Croce. At the end of the road, turn right along Via di San Giuseppe until Piazza di **Santa Croce,** a spacious square graced by the church of Santa Croce (▶ 66–69) and a picturesque row of medieval houses. In Florence's heyday, this piazza was the scene of grand Medici ceremonies, jousting tournaments, even public executions. Today it acts as a pitch for the annual **Gioco di Calcio Storico** (▶ 46), the period costume soccer match that was first played in 1530.

The Santa Croce district is the lowest-lying part of Florence and traditionally the artisans' quarter, for centuries packed with workshops of furniture-makers, weavers and cloth-dyers. However, the flood of 1966 (▶ 28–29) hit this part of the city the hardest. A small wall plaque in the square, set 20 feet up (on the corner of Via Verdi), shows the level the muddy water reached at its peak. Some buildings still have a watermark. Although many small businesses were ruined, the area remains full of small neighborhood shops and workshops.

7–8

Leave Piazza di Santa Croce along Via Torta, heading west toward the city center. Notice how this narrow road and its continuations, Via Bentaccordi and Piazza de' Peruzzi, form a curve – they are built along the line of the Roman amphitheater of *Florentia*. Turn right off Via Torta up Via Isola delle Stinche to buy an ice cream at the celebrated **Bar Vivoli Gelateria** (▶ 73).

8–9

The next road to the left – Via della Vigna Vecchia – leads to the **Museo Nazionale del Bargello** (▶ 62–65), the oldest surviving civic building in Florence. Today the fortress-like building houses a priceless collection of Renaissance sculpture.

9–10

When you reach the Bargello, turn right onto Via del Proconsolo. As you walk back toward the Duomo, be sure to glance along Borgo degli Albizi (the third road on your right). Lined with grand Renaissance palaces, it is one of the oldest streets in Florence, following the route of the ancient Roman road to Rome. Continue up Via del Proconsolo until you reach your start point in Piazza del Duomo.

Taking a Break

Put together a picnic at Mercato Sant'Ambrogio, or try the best pizzas in town at Pizzauolo in Via dei Macci.

Mercato Vecchio, but moved here in 1890 when the market was demolished to make way for **Piazza della Repubblica** (▶ 127).

Dante, though exiled from Florence in his lifetime, is commemorated by a statue outside Santa Croce

Websites
- Florence Tourist Office:
www.firenze.turismo.
toscana.it
- ENIT:
www.enit.it

- General information:
www.fionline.it
www.informacitta.net
- Museums and art:
www.uffizi.firenze.it
www.fionline.it

In the U.K.
Italian State Tourist Office
(ENIT)
1 Princes Street
London W1R 8AY
☎ 020 7408-1254

BEFORE YOU GO

WHAT YOU NEED

- ● Required
- ○ Suggested
- ▲ Not required
- △ Not applicable

	U.K.	Germany	U.S.A.	Canada	Australia	Ireland	Netherlands	Spain
Passport/National Identity Card	●	●	●	●	●	●	●	▲
Visa	▲	▲	▲	▲	▲	▲	▲	▲
Onward or Round Trip Ticket	○	○	●	●	●	○	○	○
Health Inoculations (tetanus and polio)	▲	▲	▲	▲	▲	▲	▲	▲
Health Documentation	●	●	○	○	○	○	○	▲
Travel Insurance	○	○	○	○	○	○	○	○
Drivers License (national)	●	●	●	●	●	●	●	●
Car Insurance Certificate	○	○	△	△	△	○	○	○
Car Registration Document	●	●	△	△	△	●	●	●

WHEN TO GO

Florence

High season   Low season

JAN	FEB	MAR	APR	MAY	JUN	JUL	AUG	SEP	OCT	NOV	DEC
50°F	52°F	59°F	64°F	73°F	78°F	84°F	82°F	78°F	74°F	57°F	53°F

☀ Sun   ☁ Cloud   🌧 Wet   🌦 Sun/Showers

Temperatures are the **average daily maximum** for each month. The most popular months to visit Florence and Tuscany are May, June and September when there are long, warm days and plenty of sunshine. These are also the busiest months, so be prepared to wait in line for main attractions. July and August are popular months, too, but the city can get extremely hot and sticky. July is the hottest, driest month. Spring and autumn are the best seasons for viewing the colors of the countryside, although autumn is generally the wettest time in Tuscany. When planning your trip, consider also the fashion shows held in Florence during June, July and September, and the grape harvest in October. Remember to make your hotel reservations well in advance.

GETTING THERE

By Air Three main airports serve Florence – Galileo Galilei Airport at Pisa (80 km, 50 miles west), Guglielmo Marconi Airport at Bologna (105 km, 65 miles northeast) and Florence's small Amerigo Vespucci Airport (4 km, 2.5 miles northwest). The airports at Pisa and Bologna cater to scheduled services and charter airlines, while Florence's airport handles mainly Meridiana flights.

Major carriers at Pisa include Alitalia, British Airways, Lufthansa and Ryanair. Major carriers at Bologna include Air France, Alitalia, British Airways, Go, Italair, KLM, Lufthansa, Sabena, SAS and TAP Air Portugal. Major carriers at Amerigo Vespucci Airport include Meridiana, Alitalia, Sabena, Air France, Crossair and Lufthansa. There are no direct intercontinental flights so visitors from outside Europe need to fly into Milan or Rome (or another major European hub) and then take a connecting flight. Some no-frills European airlines, such as Ryanair to Pisa and Go to Bologna, offer budget fares.

Approximate flying times London (2 hours), Dublin (2 hours), New York (10-plus hours via London, Brussels, Paris or Rome), West Coast U.S.A. (14-plus hours via London, Frankfurt or Paris), Vancouver (12-plus hours via Frankfurt or London), Montréal (9 hours via Brussels, London or Paris).

By Rail Florence's main train station, Ferrovia Santa Maria Novella, is one of the main arrival points for trains from Europe, with direct rail links with Paris, Frankfurt and Ostend. It is located near the city center. Italy's state railroad (Ferrovie dello Stato) operates a high-speed train service (*pendolino* trains) between major Italian cities.

TIME

Italy operates on Central European Time, 1 hour ahead of Greenwich Mean Time in winter, six hours ahead of New York and nine hours ahead of Los Angeles. Clocks are advanced an hour between April and October.

CURRENCY AND FOREIGN EXCHANGE

Currency Italy was one of 12 European Union countries to start using a single currency, the **Euro**. Euro bills and coins were issued on 1 January, 2002 and the lira, formerly the unit of currency, is due to be phased out by the end of June 2002. Coins are issued in denominations of 1, 2, 5, 10, 20 and 50 Euro cents and 1 and 2 Euros. Bills are issued in denominations of 5, 10, 20, 50, 100, 200 and 500 Euros. One Euro is L1936.27.

Credit cards Most **credit cards** (*carta di credito*) are accepted in larger hotels, restaurants and stores, and can also be used at ATMs.

Exchange Most banks and private exchange offices throughout the city will change cash and **travellers' checks**. All transactions are subject to a small commission charge. Remember to take your passport with you.

TIME DIFFERENCES

GMT
12 noon

Florence
1 p.m.

U.S.A. New York
7 a.m.

Germany
1 p.m.

Rest of Italy
1 p.m.

Australia
Sydney 10 p.m.

WHEN YOU ARE THERE

CLOTHING SIZES

U.K.	Rest of Europe	U.S.A.	
36	46	36	
38	48	38	
40	50	40	
42	52	42	Suits
44	54	44	
46	56	46	
7	41	8	
7.5	42	8.5	
8.5	43	9.5	
9.5	44	10.5	Shoes
10.5	45	11.5	
11	46	12	
14.5	37	14.5	
15	38	15	
15.5	39/40	15.5	
16	41	16	Shirts
16.5	42	16.5	
17	43	17	
8	34	6	
10	36	8	
12	38	10	
14	40	12	Dresses
16	42	14	
18	44	16	
4.5	38	6	
5	38	6.5	
5.5	39	7	
6	39	7.5	Shoes
6.5	40	8	
7	41	8.5	

NATIONAL HOLIDAYS

Jan. 1	*Capodanno* – New Year's Day
Jan. 6	Epiphany
Mar./Apr.	*Pasqua* – Easter
Mar./Apr.	*Pasquetta* – Easter Monday
Apr. 25	Liberation Day
May 1	*Festa del Lavoro* – Labour Day
Jun. 24	*San Giovanni* – St. John's Day
Aug. 15	Assumption of the Virgin Mary
Nov. 1	*Tutti Santi* – All Saints' Day
Dec. 8	Immaculate Conception
Dec. 25	*Natale* – Christmas Day
Dec. 26	*Santo Stefano* – St. Stephen's Day

OPENING HOURS

○ Shops   ● Post Offices
● Offices   ● Museums/Monuments
● Banks   ● Pharmacies

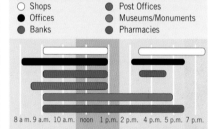

8 a.m. 9 a.m. 10 a.m. noon 1 p.m. 2 p.m. 4 p.m. 5 p.m. 7 p.m.

☐ Day   ■ Midday   ☐ Evening

Shops Some shops close on Monday morning in winter and on Saturday afternoon in summer. Summer opening hours are more flexible: some stay open at lunch time or in the evening. Many shops close for a few weeks around August 15.
Museums Times vary according to the season and many close Monday. Some Florentine museums have highly irregular opening hours, so check individual entries for details and phone ahead.
Post Offices The main post offices at 3 Via Pellicceria and 53 Via Pietrapiana are open all day. Stamps can also be bought from tobacco shops.
Pharmacies Every *farmacia* displays a list of nearby pharmacies open at night and on Sundays.

EMERGENCY 113

POLICE 112

FIRE 115

AMBULANCE 118

PERSONAL SAFETY

Petty crime, particularly pickpocketing, is fairly common in Florence. Be aware of scruffy, innocent-looking children selling flowers or begging: they may be in gangs, fleecing unwary tourists. Report any loss or theft to the *vigili urbani* (municipal police – blue uniforms in winter and white in summer). The *carabinieri* are the military police. They dress in red-striped trousers and deal with such offenses as theft and speeding. *La polizia* (the state police – blue uniforms with white belts and berets) deal with serious crime.

Police assistance:
☎ **112** from any phone

TELEPHONES

coins, tokens *(gettoni)* and phonecards *(una schede telefoniche)*, available from post offices, tobacco shops and bars. Break off the card's corner before use.
Lowest rates within Italy and Europe: Monday to Saturday 10 p.m.–8 a.m. and all day Sunday.

Public phones are indicated by a red or yellow sign, on the street, in bars and restaurants and in *Centri Telefoni* offices. Pay phones take

International Dialling Codes
Dial 00 followed by

U.K.:	44
U.S.A. / Canada:	1
Irish Republic:	353
Australia:	61
Germany:	49

MAIL

The main post offices in central Florence are at 71r Via Cavour, 53 Via Pietrapiana and 40r Via Barbadori. There are also red mail boxes, usually set into the wall, on most main streets and at the railroad station. Stamps are sold at post offices and tobacco shops.

ELECTRICITY

Current is 220 volts AC, 50 cycles. Plugs are two- or three-round-pin Continental types; North American visitors will require an adaptor. A transformer is likely to be needed for appliances operating on 110–120 volts.

TIPS/GRATUITIES

Restaurants include a service charge, but it is customary to round up the check. Leave loose change in bars: around €0.05 for drinks at the bar; €0.25 for drinking at a table; or €0.5 at an upscale hotel bar. Tipping is necessary elsewhere. As a general guide:

Tour guides	€1–€1.5
Taxis	10% of fare
Porters	€0.5–€1.3 per bag
Ushers	€0.5
Restroom attendants	€0.10–€0.15

CONSULATES and EMBASSIES

U.K.
☎ 055 284 133

U.S.A.
☎ 055 239 8276

Canada
☎ 06 445 981
(Rome)

Australia
☎ 06 852 721
(Rome)

New Zealand
☎ 06 440 2928
(Rome)

HEALTH

 Insurance It is essential to take out full travel insurance before you leave home.

 Doctors Ask at your hotel for details of English-speaking doctors.

Dental Services Travel insurance should also cover the cost of dental treatment.

 Weather Minor health worries include too much sun, dehydration or mosquito bites: drink plenty of fluids, and wear sunscreen and a hat in summer (particularly in July and August, which are the hottest months). Insect repellent may be useful if you have to sleep in rooms with windows open in summer.

 Drugs Prescription and other medication are available from a pharmacy (*una farmacia*), indicated by a green cross. Their highly qualified staff are able to offer medical advice on minor ailments, provide first-aid and prescribe a wide range of over-the-counter drugs. Hours are usually Mon.–Sat. 8:30–1 and 4–8 p.m., but a roster system ensures there are always some open.

 Safe Water Tap water is safe to drink throughout Italy, but most Italians prefer bottled water. Do not drink water that is marked *acqua non potablile*.

CONCESSIONS

Senior Citizens (over 60) are entitled to free admission into state museums and galleries.
Students under 18 are entitled to free admission into state museums. Be sure to carry some form of identification such as a passport.

TRAVELING WITH A DISABILITY

Florence and Tuscany do not cater well to travelers with disabilities, although more museums now have elevators, ramps and modified restrooms, and recent laws require restaurants, bars and hotels to provide facilities. Some intercity trains have special facilities for wheelchair users. There is an elevator at Santa Maria Novella station, but it must be booked 24 hours in advance, and the new intercity trains have special facilities for wheelchairs. Contact the tourist office at 1r Via Cavour for further details (055 290 832).

CHILDREN

Children are welcomed in most hotels and restaurants. Many attractions offer reductions. Baby-changing facilities are excellent in newer attractions but limited elsewhere.

RESTROOMS

There are few public restrooms in Florence, but most galleries, museums, bars, hotels, and department stores have facilities.

LOST PROPERTY

Contact the City Council Lost Property Office at 19 Via Circondaria (055) 328 3942.

SURVIVAL PHRASES

Yes/no **Sì/non**
Please **Per favore**
Thank you **Grazie**
You're welcome **Di niente/prego**
I'm sorry **Mi dispiace**
Goodbye **Arrivederci**
Good morning **Buongiorno**
Goodnight **Buona sera**
How are you? **Come sta?**
How much? **Quanto costa?**
I would like... **Vorrei...**
Open **Aperto**
Closed **Chiuso**
Today **Oggi**
Tomorrow **Domani**
Monday **lunedì**
Tuesday **martedì**
Wednesday **mercoledì**
Thursday **giovedì**
Friday **venerdì**
Saturday **sabato**
Sunday **Domenica**

IF YOU NEED HELP

Help! **Aiuto!**
Could you help me, please?
  Mi potrebbe aiutare?
Do you speak English? **Parla inglese?**
I don't understand **Non capisco**
Please could you call a doctor
quickly? **Mi chiami presto un
medico, per favore**

RESTAURANT

I'd like to reserve a table
  Vorrei prenotare un tavolo
A table for two please
  Un tavolo per due, per favore
Could we see the menu, please?
  Ci porta la lista, per favore?
What's this? **Cosa è questo?**
A bottle of/a glass of...
  Un bottiglia di/un bicchiere di...
Could I have the check?
  Ci porta il conto

DIRECTIONS

I'm lost **Mi sono perso/a**
Where is...? **Dove si trova...?**
  the station **la stazione**
  the telephone **il telefono**
  the bank **la banca**
  the restroom **il gabinetto**
Turn left **Volti a sinistra**
Turn right **Volti a destra**
Go straight **Vada dritto**
At the corner **All'angolo**
the street **la strada**
the building **il palazzo**
the traffic light **il semaforo**
the intersection **l'incrocio**
the signs for...
  le indicazione per...

ACCOMMODATIONS

Do you have a single/double room?
Ha una camera singola / doppia?
with/without bath/toilet/shower
  **Con/senza vasca/gabinetto/
  doccia**
Does that include breakfast?
  E'inclusa la prima colazione?
Does that include dinner?
  E'inclusa la cena?
Do you have room service?
  C'è il servizio in camera?
Could I see the room?
  E' possibile vedere la camera?
I'll take this room **Prendo questa**
Thanks for your hospitality
  Grazie per l'ospitalità

NUMBERS

0	**zero**	12	**dodici**	30	**trenta**	200	**duecento**
1	**uno**	13	**tredici**	40	**quaranta**	300	**trecento**
2	**due**	14	**quattordici**	50	**cinquanta**	400	**quattrocento**
3	**tre**	15	**quindici**	60	**sessanta**	500	**cinquecento**
4	**quattro**	16	**sedici**	70	**settanta**	600	**seicento**
5	**cinque**	17	**diciassette**	80	**ottanta**	700	**settecento**
6	**sei**	18	**diciotto**	90	**novanta**	800	**ottocento**
7	**sette**	19	**diciannove**	100	**cento**	900	**novecento**
8	**otto**	20	**venti**			1000	**mille**
9	**nove**			101	**cento uno**	2000	**duemila**
10	**dieci**	21	**ventuno**	110	**centodieci**		
11	**undici**	22	**ventidue**	120	**centoventi**	10,000	**diecimila**

MENU READER

acciuga anchovy
acqua water
affettati sliced
 cured meats
affumicato
 smoked
aglio garlic
agnello lamb
anatra duck
antipasti
 hors d'òeurves
arista roast pork
arrosto roast
asparagi
 asparagus
birra beer
bistecca steak
bollito
 boiled meat
braciola
 minute steak
brasato braised
brodo broth
bruschetta
 toasted bread
 with garlic or
 tomato
 topping
budino pudding
burro butter
cacciagione
 game
cacciatore, alla
 rich tomato
 sauce with
 mushrooms
caffè corretto /
macchiato
 coffee with
 liqueur/spirt, or
 with a drop of
 milk
caffè freddo
 iced coffee
caffè lungo
 weak coffee
caffellatte
 milky coffee
caffè ristretto
 strong coffee
calamaro squid
cappero caper
carciofo
 artichoke
carota carrot
carne meat
carpa carp

casalingo
 home made
cassata
 Sicilian fruit
 ice cream
cavolfiore
 cauliflower
cavolo cabbage
ceci chickpeas
cervello brains
cervo venison
cetriolino
 gherkin
cetriolo
 cucumber
cicoria chicory
cinghiale boar
cioccolata
 chocolate
cipolla onion
coda di bue
 oxtail
coniglio rabbit
contorni
 vegetables
coperto
 cover charge
coscia
 leg of meat
cotoletta cutlets
cozze mussels
crema custard
crostini canapé
 with savory
 toppings or
 croutons
crudo raw
digestivo after–
 dinner liqueur
dolci cakes /
 desserts
erbe aromatiche
 herbs
fagioli beans
fagiolini
 green beans
fegato liver
faraona
 guinea fowl
facito stuffed
fegato liver
finocchio fennel
formaggio
 cheese
forno, al baked
frittata omelette
fritto fried
frizzante fizzy
frulatto whisked

frutti di mare
 seafood
frutta fruit
funghi
 mushrooms
gamberetto
 shrimp
gelato ice cream
ghiaccio ice
gnocci potato
 dumplings
granchio crab
gran(o)turco
 corn
griglia, alla
 broiled
imbottito
 stuffed
insalata salad
IVA Value
 Added Tax (VAT)
latte milk
lepre hare
lumache snails
manzo beef
merluzzo cod
miele honey
minestra soup
molluschi
 shellfish
olio oil
oliva olive
ostrica oyster
pancetta bacon
pane bread
panna cream
parmigiano
 parmesan
passata sieved
 or creamed
pastasciutta
 dried pasta
 with sauce
pasta sfoglia
 puff pastry
patate fritte
 chips
pecora mutton
pecorino
 sheep's milk
 cheese
peperoncino
 chili
peperone red/
 green pepper
pesce fish
petto breast
piccione
 pigeon

piselli peas
pollame fowl
pollo chicken
polpetta
 meatball
porto port
 wine
prezzemolo
 parsley
primo piatto
 first course
prosciutto
 cured ham
ragù meat sauce
ripieno stuffed
riso rice
salsa sauce
salsiccia
 sausage
saltimbocca
 veal with
 prosciutto and
 sage
secco dry
secondo piatto
 main course
senape mustard
servizio compreso
 service charge
 included
sogliola sole
spuntini snacks
succa di frutta
 fruit juice
sugo sauce
tonno tuna
uova strapazzate
 scambled egg
uovo affrogato /
in carnica
 poached egg
uovo al tegamo /
fritto
 fried egg
uovo alla coque
 soft boiled egg
uovo alla sodo
 hard boiled egg
vino bianco
 white wine
vino rosso
 red wine
vino rosato
 rosé wine
verdure
 vegetables
vitello veal
zucchero sugar
zuppa soup

Picture credits

The Automobile Association wishes to thank the following photographers and libraries for their assistance with the preparation of this book.
Front and back cover: (t) AA Photo Library/S McBride; (ct) AA Photo Library/C Sawyer; (cb) AA Photo Library/J Edmanson; (b) AA Photo Library.

AKG, LONDON 10, 11 (Erich Lessing); 12t, 13t, 13c (S. Domingie); 15, 70 (Erich Lessing); ARCAID 33b (Richard Bryant); ART DIRECTORS AND TRIP PHOTO LIBRARY 167; AXIOM PHOTOGRAPHIC AGENCY 151t (J. Morris); BRIDGEMAN ART LIBRARY, LONDON 6/7 The 'Carta della Catena' showing a panorama of Florence, 1490 by Italian School (15th century) Museo de Firenze Com'era, Florence, Italy; 14t Gold florin with a fleur de lys, Florentine, 1252–1303 (verso) Bargello, Florence, Italy; 14b Scudo decorated with the Medici Coat of Arms (gold) by Benvenuto Cellini (1500–71) Bargello, Florence, Italy; 16t Giant catapult, c. 1499 (drawing) by Leonardo da Vinci (1452–1519) Biblioteca Ambrosiana, Milan Italy; 23 No. 192 The Arno in Florence with the Ponte Vecchio, (oil on canvas) by Bernardo Bellotto (1720–80) Fitzwilliam Museum, University of Cambridge, UK; 55 The Madonna di Ognissanti, c. 1310 (POST –restoration) by Giotto di Bondone (c. 1266–1337) Galleria degli Uffizi, Florence, Italy; 56t Portraits of Duke Federico da Montefeltro (1422–82) and Battista Sforza, c. 1465 (tempera on panel) by Piero della Francesca (c. 1419/21–92) Galleria degli Uffizi, Florence, Italy; 56b The Birth of Venus, c. 1485 (tempera on canvas) by Sandro Botticelli (1444/5–1510) Galleria degli Uffizi, Florence, Italy; 96 View of the interior showing the altar flanked by the Medici tombs of Cosimo I (1519–74) and Ferdinand I (1549–1609) by Matteo Nigetti (1560–1649), 1644 Chapel of the Princes, San Lorenzo, Florence, Italy; 105 Tile with Sunflower design (pietra dura) Museo Opificio delle Pietre Dure, Florence, Italy; 106b Red–figure vase depicting the battle between the Centaurs and the Lapiths, Greek (pottery) Museo Archeologico, Florence, Italy; 122t The Pontevecchio, Florence by Antonietta Brandeis (b. 1849), Gavin Graham Gallery, London, UK; EDIFICE 33t (Sayer); MARY EVANS PICTURE LIBRARY 9t, 12b, 14/5, 17t; TERESA FISHER 25r, 74; GETTYONE/STONE 3(v), 17b, 32/3, 52/3, 122/3, 160/1, 162, 164, 185; RONALD GRANT ARCHIVE 7; JOHN HESELTINE ARCHIVE 20b, 140t; REX FEATURES LTD 24, 25l, 26l, 26r; SCALA 57, 59t, 64, 102, 169; CHARLIE WAITE 3(iii), 3(iv), 157, 158/9, 175
The remaining photographs are held in the Association's own photo library (AA PHOTO LIBRARY) and were taken by SIMON MCBRIDE with the exception of the following:
J Edmanson 18/9ct, 32t, 128, 129, 143, 184; J Holmes 189br; E Meacher 21b; K Paterson 3 (i), 8b, 16b, 18/9t, 19c, 29, 62, 86b, 113, 119, 120, 124b, 138/9, 152, 161, 163b, 166, 168, 170t, 170b, 173, 174, 181; B Smith 150b, 153; C Sawyer 2(i), 3(ii), 5, 6b, 8t, 13b, 31t, 31b, 32b, 34t, 48, 49, 59b, 61, 66, 67t, 67b, 68, 68/9, 71, 72t, 72b, 73t, 75, 85t, 85b, 88, 88/9, 94t, 95, 106t, 107, 117, 124t, 126t, 126b, 127, 137, 150t, 163t, 165, 171, 172/3, 179, 182, 183, 189t; W Voysey 18/9b.

Author's acknowledgment

The author wishes to thank Victoria Riela of Room Service and Hotel Le Cascine for their assistance during the research of this book.

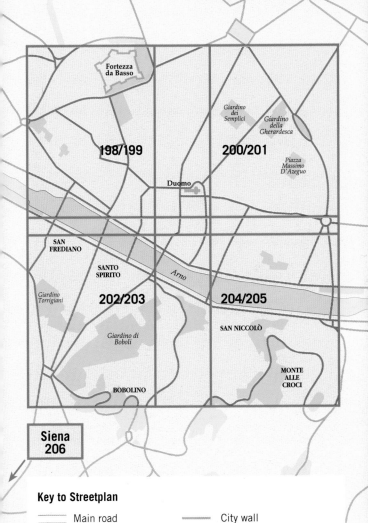

Streetplan

Fortezza
da Basso

198/199

Giardino
dei
Semplici

Giardino
della
Gherardesca

200/201

Piazza
Massimo
D'Azeguo

Duomo

SAN
FREDIANO

SANTO
SPIRITO

Arno

Giardino
Torrigiani

202/203

204/205

SAN NICCOLÒ

Giardino di
Boboli

MONTE
ALLE
CROCI

BOBOLINO

Siena
206

Key to Streetplan

Main road	City wall
Other road	Park
Pedestrian area	Important building
Rail line	Featured place of interest

0	100	200	300	400 metres
0	100	200	300	400 yards

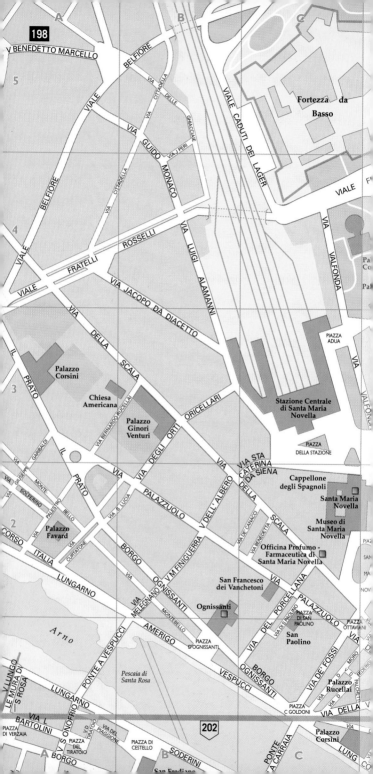

A
B
C

5

V BENEDETTO MARCELLO

BELFIORE

VIA CITTADELLA

VIA GUIDO MONACO

VIA DELLE GHIACCIAIE

VIA I PERI

VIALE CADUTI DEI LAGER

Fortezza da Basso

VIALE

VIA VALFONDA

4

VIALE

VIALE

BELFIORE

FRATELLI

ROSSELLI

VIA JACOPO DA DIACETTO

VIA LUIGI ALAMANNI

VIA VALFONDA

PIAZZA ADUA

3

IL PRATO

VIA DELLA SCALA

Palazzo Corsini

Chiesa Americana

VIA BERNARDO RUCELLAI

Palazzo Ginori Venturi

VIA DEGLI ORTI ORICELLARI

ORICELLARI

VIA STA CATERINA DA SIENA

VIA DELLA

Stazione Centrale di Santa Maria Novella

PIAZZA DELLA STAZIONE

Cappellone degli Spagnoli

Santa Maria Novella

2

VIA GIUSEPPE GARIBALDI

VIA MONTE BELLO

VIA SOLFERINO

VIA PALESTRO

IL PRATO

VIA S. LUCIA

PALAZZUOLO

BORGO OGNISSANTI

VIA DELL'ALBERO

V M FINIGUERRA

VIA DE CANACCI

VIA BENEDETTA

VIA DELLA SCALA

Museo di Santa Maria Novella

Officina Profumo - Farmaceutica di Santa Maria Novella

CORSO ITALIA

Palazzo Favard

VIA CURTATONE

LUNGARNO

VIA MELEGNANO

VIA MONTEBELLO

AMERIGO

San Francesco dei Vanchetoni

Ognissanti

VIA DEL PORCELLANA

PALAZZUOLO

PIAZZA DI SAN PAOLINO

VIA DI SAN PAOLINO

San Paolino

VIA OTTAVIANI

Arno

PIAZZA D'OGNISSANTI

Pescaia di Santa Rosa

VESPUCCI

BORGO OGNISSANTI

VIA DE FOSSI

VIA DEL MORO

VIA DEI FEDERIGHI

Palazzo Rucellai

V LUNGO LE MURA DI S ROSA

LUNGARNO

PONTE A VESPUCCI

V S ONOFRIO

V D TIRATOIO

VIA DEL PORCELLANA

PIAZZA C GOLDONI

VIA DELLA

Palazzo Corsini

VIA L BARTOLINI

PIAZZA DI VERZAIA

V BORGO

PIAZZA DEL TIRATOIO

VIA DEL LEONE

PIAZZA DI CESTELLO

SODERINI

PONTE A CARRAIA

LUNG CO

202

A
B
C

San Frediano

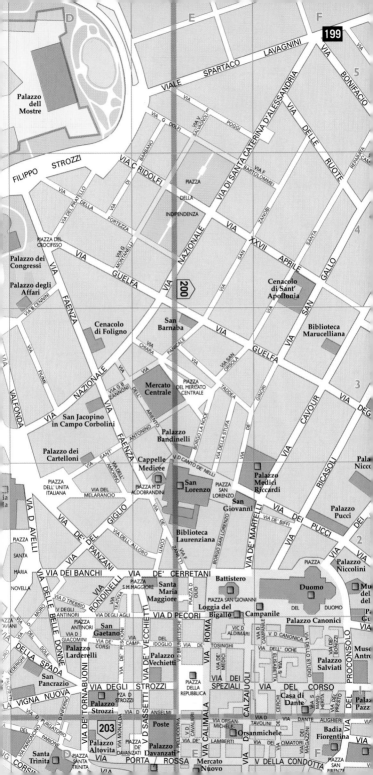

Palazzo dell Mostre

FILIPPO STROZZI

Palazzo dei Congressi

Palazzo degli Affari

PIAZZA DEL CROCIFISSO

VIA C RIDOLFI

VIA DI SANTA CATERINA D'ALESSANDRIA

VIALE SPARTACO LAVAGNINI

VIA

VIA G. DOLFI

VIA V. GIUSTI

VIA GIORDANO F.

POGGI

PIAZZA DELLA INDIPENDENZA

VIA F. BARTOLOMMEI

BARBANO

VIA DEL PRATELLO DELLA

VIA DELLA FORTEZZA

VIA G. MONTANELLI

VIA NAZIONALE

VIA XXVII APRILE

VIA SAN ZANOBI

SANTA

VIA DELLE RUOTE

REPARATA

VIA GALLO

VIA BONIFACIO

Cenacolo di Sant' Apollonia

Biblioteca Marucelliana

VIA GUELFA

Cenacolo di Foligno

San Barnaba

PIAZZA DEL MERCATO CENTRALE

VIA CHIARA

PANICALE

VIA SAN ORSOLA

VIA GUELFA

VIA SAN

VIA GINORI

VIA CAVOUR

VIA DEG

VIA B. CENNINI

VALFONDA

VIA NAZIONALE

VIA FAENZA

San Jacopino in Campo Corbolini

Palazzo dei Cartelloni

VIA FLUME

VIA G B ZANNONI

VIA DELL' ARIENTO

Mercato Centrale

Palazzo Bandinelli

ANTONINO

BORGO LA NOCE

VIA DELLA STUFA

VIA DE'

Palazzo Nicco

Cappelle Medicee

VIA SANT'

VIA PELL' ANCORINO

N D CANTO DE' NELLI

Palazzo Medici Riccardi

VIA RICASOLI

PIAZZA DELL'UNITÀ ITALIANA

VIA DEL MELARANCIO

PIAZZA M D ALDOBRANDINI

San Lorenzo

PIAZZA SAN LORENZO

San Giovanni

VIA DE' BIFFI

Palazzo Pucci

Pala Nicco

VIA D. AVELLI

VIA DE' PANZANI

VIA GIGLIO

VIA DELL'ALLORO

LINOTI

VIA F. ZANETTI

Biblioteca Laurenziana

BORGO SAN LORENZO

VIA DE' MARTELLI

VIA DEI PUCCI

DEI

PIAZZA

Palazzo Niccolini

PIAZZA SANTA MARIA NOVELLA

VIA DELLE BELLE

VIA DEI BANCHI

VIA DE' CERRETANI

Santa Maria Maggiore

PIAZZA D OLIO

Battistero

PIAZZA SAN GIOVANNI

Duomo

DEL DUOMO

Mu del del

VIA D TREBBIO

VIA DEGLI ANTINORI

VIA DI RONDINELLI

VIA S.M. MAGGIORE

PIAZZA TEATINA

VIA DEGLI AGLI

Loggia del Bigallo

Campanile

VIA D CANONICA

Palazzo Canonici

VIA DELLO STUDIO

VIC D ALDIMARI

VIA D CAMPANILE

Pa Gi

Pa

VIA DEGLI ANTINORI

Palazzo Antinori

San Gaetano

VIA D GIACOMINI

PIAZZA ANTINORI

VIA D CORSI

VIA DE' PESCIONI

DEL IDOGLIO

VIA D PECORI

VIA DE' BRUNELLESCHI

VIA D TOSINGHI

VIA ROMA

VIA DE' MEDICI

VIA DE' OCHE

VIA D ELISABETTA

VIA D STUDIO

Palazzo Salviati

Muse Antro

Palazzo Larderelli

VIA DE' VECCHIETTI

Palazzo Vecchietti

VIA DE' CERCHI

VIA DEI SPEZIALI

VIA DEL CORSO

VIA DANTE ALIGHIERI

VIA S M S MARG HERITA

VIA DEI MAGAZZINI

VIA DE' PRESTO

Casa di Dante

Palaz Pazz

San Pancrazio

DELLA SPADA

VIA DEL SOLE

REDI

VIA DELLE DONNE

VIA DEL PURGATORIO

VIA DEL PARIONE

VIGNA NUOVA

VIA DE' TORNABUONI

Palazzo Strozzi

PZA D STROZZI

VIA DEGLI STROZZI

VIA D SASSETTI

VIA ANSELMI

PIAZZA DELLA REPUBBLICA

VIA CALZAIUOLI

Orsanmichele

VIA DEI TAVOLINI

VIA DANTE

VIA D CIMATORI

Badia Fiorentina

PIAZZA SAN FIRENZE

VIA

VIA DEL FOSSO

VIA DEL PROCONSOLO

VIA DELL' INFERNO

VIA DEL PARIONCINO

VIA DEL PURGATORIO

Santa Trinita

PIAZZA SANTA TRINITA

Poste

Palazzo Altovita

PIAZZA DE' DAVANZATI

Palazzo Davanzati

VIA PORTA ROSSA

VIA MONALDA

VIA D CAVALIERI

VIA D ANSELMI

VIA DE' PELLICCERIA

VIA D CAVALIERI

VIA LAMBERTI

VIA ORSAN MICHELE

VIA DE'

Mercato Nuovo

V DELLA CONDOTTA

VIA CORSO

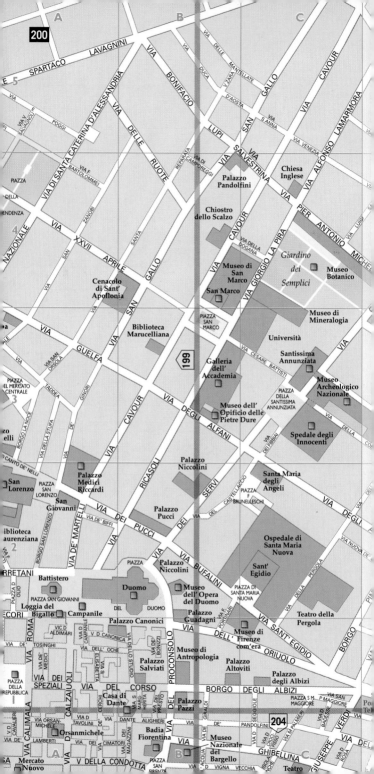

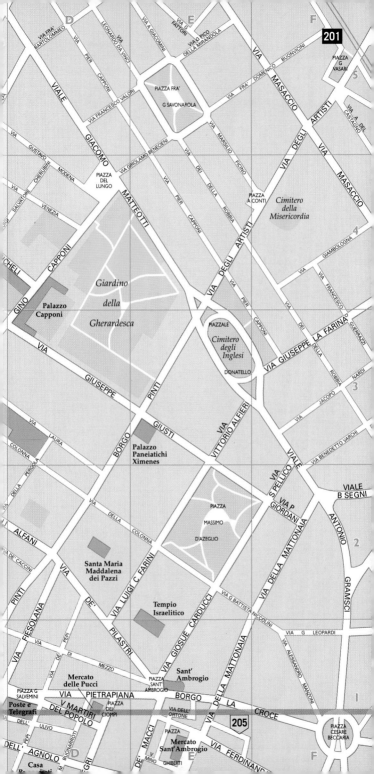

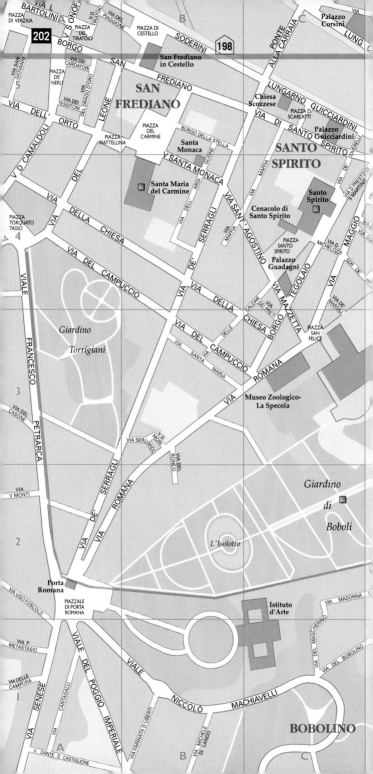

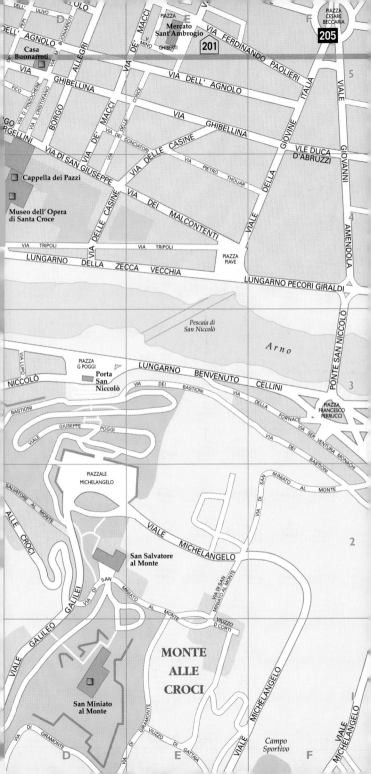

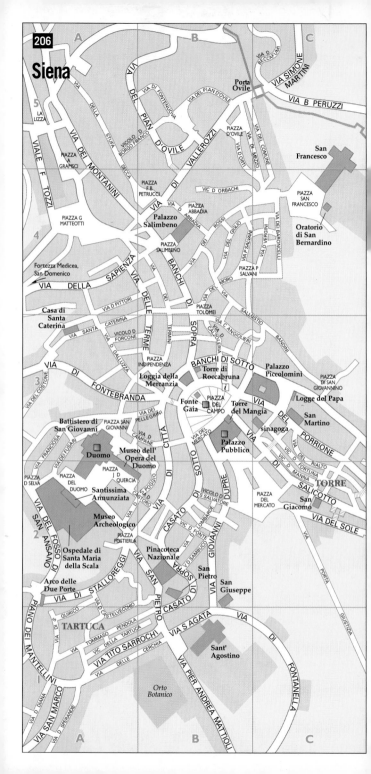

Questionnaire

Dear Traveler

Your comments, opinions and recommendations are very important to us. So please help us to improve our travel guides by taking a few minutes to complete this simple questionnaire.

Send to: Spiral Guides, MailStop 66, 1000 AAA Drive, Heathrow, FL 32746–5063

Your recommendations...

We always encourage readers' recommendations for restaurants, nightlife or shopping – if your recommendation is added to the next edition of the guide, we will send you a FREE AAA Spiral Guide of your choice. Please state below the establishment name, location and your reasons for recommending it.

_____

_____

_____

_____

_____

Please send me AAA Spiral_____

(see list of titles inside the back cover)

About this guide...

Which title did you buy?

_____ **AAA Spiral**

Where did you buy it?_____

When? m m / y y

Why did you choose a AAA Spiral Guide?_____

_____

_____

_____

Did this guide meet your expectations?

Exceeded ☐   Met all ☐   Met most ☐   Fell below ☐

Please give your reasons_____

_____

_____

_____

continued on next page...

Were there any aspects of this guide that you particularly liked?

_____

_____

_____

_____

Is there anything we could have done better?

_____

_____

_____

_____

_____

About you...

Name (Mr/Mrs/Ms)_____

Address_____

_____

_____ Zip_____

Daytime tel nos. _____

Which age group are you in?

Under 25 ☐   25–34 ☐   35–44 ☐   45–54 ☐   55–64 ☐   65+ ☐

How many trips do you make a year?

Less than one ☐   One ☐   Two ☐   Three or more ☐

Are you a AAA member? Yes ☐   No ☐

Name of AAA club _____

About your trip...

When did you book? m m / y y   When did you travel? m m / y y

How long did you stay?_____

Was it for business or leisure?_____

Did you buy any other travel guides for your trip?   ☐ Yes   ☐ No

If yes, which ones?_____

_____

Thank you for taking the time to complete this questionnaire.